Investigating
YOUR CAREER

3e

Ann K. Jordan

Tena B. Crews

SOUTH-WESTERN
CENGAGE Learning·

Australia · Brazil · Japan · Korea · Mexico · Singapore · Spain · United Kingdom · United States

SOUTH-WESTERN
CENGAGE Learning·

Investigating Your Career, Third Edition
Ann Jordan and Tena Crews

Vice President of Editorial, Business:
Jack W. Calhoun

Vice President/Editor-in-Chief: Karen Schmohe

Associate Acquisitions Editor: Michael
Guendelsberger

Senior Developmental Editor: Penny Shank

Editorial Assistant: Anne Merrill

Marketing Program Manager: Linda Kuper

Marketing Coordinator: Julia Tucker

Media Editor: Lysa Kosins

Manufacturing Planner: Kevin Kluck

Design Direction, Production Management,
and Composition: PreMediaGlobal

Senior Art Director: Michelle Kunkler

Cover Designer: Grannan Graphic Design, Ltd.

Cover Images (clockwise, from top):
©Catherine Yeulet, ©David Jones,
©Neustockimages, ©kali9, iStock;
©TetraImages, ©Corbis Super RF, ©Blend
Images, Alamy; ©Jim Barber, Shutterstock

Rights Acquisition Director: Audrey Pettingill

Rights Acquisition Specialist, Text and Image:
Amber Hosea

All model documents: ©Cengage Learning

For product information and technology assistance, contact us at
Cengage Learning Customer & Sales Support, 1-800-354-9706
For permission to use material from this text or product,
submit all requests online at **www.cengage.com/permissions**
Further permissions questions can be emailed to
permissionrequest@cengage.com

The Career Clusters icons are being used with permission of the:

States' Career Clusters Initiative, 2012, www.careerclusters.org

ISBN-13: 978-1-111-57550-2

ISBN-10: 1-111-57550-9

South-Western
5191 Natorp Boulevard
Mason, OH 45040
USA

Cengage Learning products are represented in Canada by
Nelson Education, Ltd.

For your course and learning solutions, visit **www.cengage.com**
Visit our company website at **www.cengage.com**

Printed in the United States of America
1 2 3 4 5 6 7 16 15 14 13 12

Brief Contents

Contents

Your *P*A*T*H* to Success

*Passions *Attitude *Talents *Heart

Determines Your Career Success!

It's Never Too Early to Start . . . Investigating Your Career!

Let's Get Started!

Each CHAPTER opens with a scenario to introduce the content and describe an individual career interest, helping you understand why the topics are important for career success.

CHAPTER 2

Discovering Ca
Choice Influenc

Lesson 2.1 People
Lesson 2.2 Values
Lesson 2.3 Web Influences

Marek and technology grew up together. As a toddler, Marek sat on his father's lap as his dad worked on the computer. Later, Marek learned sounds, numbers, and letters through simple computer games. As a teenager, he explored web sites and chatted online with friends.

As Marek advanced from toy computers to the family computer to his personal laptop, his parents encouraged him to learn more about technology. For example, they allowed him to use their smartphone to search web sites and try out different applications or apps.

Marek's exploration with the smartphone eventually bored him. He decided to create an app of his own. His parents helped him find a family friend who developed the software for the app to be used on a smartphone. During that creation, Marek suggested the design and sounds. Marek was the creator, but all while learning the software development.

Today Marek has two fully operational apps that can be purchased for a brand of smartphone. Though he is not rich by any means, the work that Marek did added to his resume and college application. As a result, Marek will att...
software deve...
Marek's curios...

What Do You Know

1. Whose opinions are important influences on your future? Family? Teachers or other school personnel? Peers?

2. How could the Internet influence your career search and your future?

24

What Do You Know

questions encourage classroom discussion on how the chapter topics relate to your future.

Planning a Career In . . .

correlates to The 16 Career Clusters and presents the employment outlook, possible job titles, and needed skills and education for a career in that cluster.

Planning a Career in . . . Information Technology

Technology is the heart of this career cluster. Information Technology (IT) involves a dynamic and an ever-changing work environment.

Because technology is always evolving, IT has a revolutionary impact on society and the economy. IT careers are not only in Information Technology; they are needed in every industry—from Medical Services to Finance, from Environmental Engineering to Business. The rigorous pace of this career requires a love of change.

Employment Outlook
- Strong demand in organizations of all sizes.
- High demand for a variety of positions, especially in Financial Services and Business.

Career Possibilities
- PC Support Specialist
- Software Applications
- Telecommunications Engineer
- Technical Writer
- Game Programmer

Needed Skills
- Education needs vary by position, ranging from career and technical education to a bachelor's degree.
- Problem solving with an attention to detail.
- Strong background in math and science.
- Certifications necessary for many skills and levels of expertise.

What's It Like to Work in Information Technology?
No matter what area of Information Technology you choose, it will involve change. Newer and better technology emerges constantly. You will never be bored.

Positions are available in every industry, in companies large and small. IT positions exist around the world. You can assist with communication in Paris—or you could work there!

Technology disasters demand immediate attention. Until you find the source of the problem and fix it, you cannot leave the project. Holidays and weekends do not matter when there are technology problems. You and your team may work long hours, but you will finish your day with a sense of satisfaction. Your customers will be happy that you have fixed their technology problems.

The satisfaction you will receive from troubleshooting problems and making sure every step of the way is completed makes Information Technology a great choice for a career.

What about You?
Are you a problem solver? Do you like to work on puzzles and do detail work? Are you willing to change as technology upgrades? Information Technology is the Future's career.

Each LESSON begins with a list of goals and terms to help you focus your reading.

Goals
outline the main objectives of the lesson.

Terms
list the new vocabulary defined in the lesson.

LESSON
4.1   Futurecasting

Goals
* Examine the demographics of the U.S. labor force.
* Identify how technology is most important for careers of the future.
* Describe how trends can affect future careers.

Terms
* trend, p. 76
* futurecasting, p. 76
* workforce trends, p. 77
* workplace trends, p. 77
* labor force, p. 77
* demographics, p. 77
* electives, p. 80
* STEM, p. 80

Real Life Focus

Each generation of the workforce has things in common. Of course, everyone in each generation was born within a certain time period. But each generation shares other things also.
Write down what you believe best describes your generation:
* movie
* music—type of music or artist
* event

Now, share the results as a class. Are there similarities? Why did people choose what they chose?

Information is everywhere. How do you know what information is important for you and your future?

One way is to study trends that show how the world may be changing. A **trend** is a general direction or change over a period of time, a prediction based on data. Fashion is a trend, though it lasts only a short time.

Making predictions based on trends is **futurecasting**. The key to successful futurecasting is identifying trends that may be important to your career. Recognizing career trends may help you in the following very important areas:

* Whether your career will exist when you begin working
* Whether there will be a need for your career throughout your employment future
* How your career field might change in the next 10 or 20 years

Of course, no one can foresee the future with perfect accuracy. Unusual twists in national or global politics, unanticipated economic or social changes, and unexpected weather conditions can affect current predictions.

Real Life Focus

introduces and reinforces concepts covered in each lesson for better comprehension.

Real Life Focus

Before they were famous, many celebrities had jobs that were not at all glamorous.
* Queen Latifah worked at Burger King.
* Jennifer Aniston waited tables.
* Sean "Diddy" Combs delivered newspapers.
* Gwen Stefani scrubbed floors at Dairy Queen.
* Michael Dell of Dell Computers washed dishes.

Maybe not all your jobs will be exciting, but that work experience can help you decide what career you do *not* want to choose.

icon identifies specific documents that you can put into your career portfolio.

Consider questions help you determine how a topic relates to you and your career.

Consider

What are some activities you enjoy that match your personality? How could these personality traits help you in a career?

Focus on
Features . . .

Real People / Real Careers

tells engaging, true stories that spotlight interesting careers and career paths.

Real People / Real Careers

Adam Jordan / *Chef*

At a young age, Adam Jordan learned to cook—more for self-defense His mother did not like cooking; in fact, she was better at burning. But his father grilled well. Also, his grandmother cooked delicious, well-balanced meals and baked excellent pies.

When Adam was 15, he got a part-time job working as a cook in an upscale hamburger franchise. He soon learned that he had a higher paying job than his friends—and he liked the work too! During college Adam was a chef at a gourmet pizza restaurant, where the owner allowed him to use his imagination to create exotic pizza combinations.

Adam loves cooking because it allows him to be creative, to be a food artist. His art college education has helped him in his career. His culinary education has been mostly on-the-job training.

Currently, Adam is a sauté chef in an elite country club. The variety of his day is tremendous. He sautés primarily, but also preps, plates, and fills in when needed at parties. Adam remarked, "I'm glad the opportunities to cook presented themselves. I really enjoy what I do—and so do my customers."

For more information about:

* culinary careers
* culinary schools and credentialing

Access **www.cengage.com/school/iyc** and click on the appropriate links in Chapter 1.

Source: *Personal Interview*, April 2011

Career FACT

In 1971, an accounting professor at Portland State University in Oregon saw Carolyn Davidson, a graphic design student, drawing. He was interested in her work and commissioned her to create a logo for the company he co-founded, Blue Ribbon Sports.

Carolyn created a "swoosh" logo and sold it to the professor, Phil Knight, for $35.

Why is this important? Blue Ribbon Sports was soon renamed Nike. When Carolyn Davidson left Nike in 1983, Phil Knight presented her with a ring with the swoosh in diamonds – and an envelope full of Nike stock certificates.

—Interview with Phil Knight
The Oprah Winfrey Show, April 2011

Career FACT

presents interesting facts, findings, and trends in the real world of work.

Web Connections

Web sites offer information to create your career path. You can explore career stories, information and statistics, and planning information.

Access the Web Connection link for Chapter 1. Search at two areas in one of the sites listed. As you are navigating the site, write down ideas that may help you learn more about yourself and your career plan. Share your ideas with the class.

www.cengage.com/school/iyc

Web Connections

provides Internet Activities that allow you to expand your knowledge of career topics and to hone your research skills.

To keep pace with the way 21st century workers and students communicate, a lesson on Social Media is included, with the topic also infused throughout the chapters.

What are wikis? How can they help your future?

A wiki is a web site that users can edit. A person or a group will create a wiki and invite others to join. For example, many teachers will have a wiki for a class, student organization, or subject. The members of the class are the users; other users need invitations to join. Wikis generally have excellent user management and security. Whether you write or post a comment on a wiki or blog, remember that all users can read what you write. Once you submit a post, you usually cannot delete it.

Social Media

Social media uses web-based technology for communication. A social media web site offers interaction through electronic comments and discussions. Types of social media include collaboration as with a wiki, multimedia as with YouTube and Picasa, review sites as with Yelp, and entertainment as with Second Life.

Social Networking

Social networking sites allow users to build a profile and connect with others. Depending on the type of the site, you can share pictures, videos, thoughts, and plans with friends or others who share your interests. However, when you communicate on a social networking web site, you are also sharing with the world. Even with the privacy settings on, your page may have a wider audience than you think. Watch the language you use online. Think before you post photos. Coaches, teachers, relatives, employers, college admissions, and even police officers may view your page. The recommendation is that you should not post anything that you are not comfortable with others seeing.

How does social networking influence your career choice? Employees often search social networking pages of potential employees. Many college admissions officers do also. Students, who have posted inappropriate photos and information such as underage drinking, too much partying,

42   Part 1 • Preparation

Blogging: Financial Goals

As you continue to blog or journal about your career plan process, refle[ct] upon your financial goals and what you have learned in this chapter. Blo[g] about how your financial goals have changed or how they have remaine[d] the same. Explain why you believe your financial goals have changed or remained the same. Access www.cengage.com/school/iyc and click on the appropriate links in Chapter 7.

Blogging:
activities at the end of each chapter allow you to write about a topic related to the chapter's content and your own career journey.

Capstone Project: Part I

A **capstone project** is an in-depth exploration of a subject. Throughout this course, you will be working towards the completion of your Capstone Project. Your project should use your skills and knowledge, especially the contents of your Career Portfolio and your blog.

Your first Capstone Project assignment is to gather a list of resources that you may use to explore the career-related topic you will be choosing in the next chapter.

Explore the following types of resources. They are options for you to research your project. Explore the options for each type of resource. Make notes on each resource's usefulness for your research. Discuss the results as a class.

- Search engines. A list of these is available at www.cengage.com/school/iyc, Chapter 4.
- *Career Transitions*
- School media center resources:
  Online databases
  Online catalogs
  Online collections
- Types of people and groups to interview

Capstone Project:
assignments at the end of each part use the skills and knowledge learned and the content of your Career Portfolio to culminate in a final, comprehensive Capstone project.

Workplace Connection

In small groups of career cluster teams, research several careers within the cluster that interests the group. Each team member should research one career.

23. Survey three to five people employed in the career cluster, asking the following information.

- Type of work involved in the career
- Working conditions
- Educational background, personal qualities, and skills needed for the career
- Employment outlook
- Earnings
- Related careers, including advancement

24. Share your survey results with the class. Discuss the careers each group researched.

Workplace Connection

activities at the end of each chapter link chapter content with the workplace and relate school success to career success.

FOCUS ON FEATURES

Focus on Assessment . . . *End of Lesson*

Activities help you identify your strengths, interests, and goals and build the skills needed to be successful in the career that is right for you.

Learning from Others

activities require you to interview various people, providing first-hand knowledge about the requirements for career success.

Team activites refer to the lesson and help develop leadership skills.

Focus on Assessment . . . *End of Chapter*

End of Chapter Assessment provides a summary of the main points. Questions and activities test your knowledge.

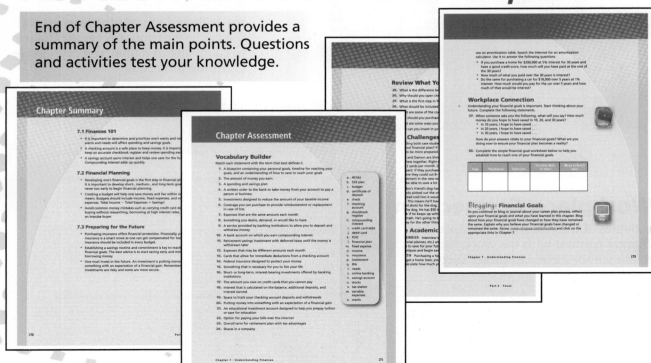

CareerTransitions

Explore Your Career Interests!

You now have instant access to the most valuable, complete career exploration and job-seeking resources available online with this one-of-a-kind application. *Career Transitions* guides you through the entire career process—from individualized assessment of personal strengths and corresponding career opportunities to focused, effective activities that will help you discover a career of your choice.

Effective Career Exploration:

- **You define and determine ideal career paths** using intuitive, engaging activities.

- **Individualized assessments** help you candidly evaluate personal abilities, test skill sets, and determine career opportunities that most closely align with your *P*A*T*H to Success*: your *Passions, Attitudes, Talents,* and *Heart.*

- **Clear, reliable information** highlights green, new economy, and high-growth occupations.

- **Candid videos** provide realistic glimpses into daily job and career choices.

Practical Job-Seeking Expertise:

- **Unmatched, practical job-seeking tools** provide the broadest expanse of job postings online and draw from reliable sources such as indeed®.com, monster®, CareerBuilder®, and thousands of company websites.

- **Interactive interview simulation** provides you with strategies and real practice for excelling in interview situations.

- **Professional resources help perfect presentations**, from resumes and cover letters to interview techniques for employment success.

Visit www.gale.cengage.com/careertransitions to learn more!

Reviewers

Ronalyn Arseneua
Business Teacher
Westwood High School
Ishpeming, Michigan

Crystal Bolamperti
Business Teacher and Curriculum Leader
Westside Middle School
Omaha, Nebraska

Nicole Critchfield
Business Teacher
Marshalltown High School
Marshalltown, Iowa

Cheryl English
Teacher
Peabody Vocational High School
Peabody, Massachusetts

Mary Flesberg
Business Education Teacher and
 Department Chair
Moorhead High School
Moorhead, Minnesota

Mike Fritz
Dean of Satellites
Great Oaks Institute of Technology and
 Career Development
Cincinnati, Ohio

Tennille Gifford
Business Teacher
Kearney High School
Kearney, Nebraska

Anthony Harper
Business Teacher
Borden High School
Borden, Indiana

Douglas Haskell
Associate Professor and Director of
 Professional Development
Economics Center at the University of Cincinnati
Cincinnati, Ohio

Patricia L. Jolliff
Business Teacher
Copenhagen Central School
Copenhagen, New York

Kellee Kanith
Business Teacher
North Hills School District
Pittsburgh, Pennsylvania

Deborah P. Lydic
Career Development and Business
 Education Instructor
Crisp County Middle School
Cordele, Georgia

Jennifer Feiler Shay
English Instructor
Great Oaks Institute of Technology and
 Career Development
Cincinnati, Ohio

Felicia M. Short
Business Teacher
Bedford High School
Bedford, Ohio

Kim Slaton
Certified Professional Resume Writer and
 Career Consultant
Jewish Vocational Service
Cincinnati, Ohio

Vicki J. Sursa
Teacher
Western Heights Middle School
Oklahoma City, Oklahoma

Diane Beall Watts
Teacher and Guidance Counselor
North College Hill High School
Cincinnati, Ohio

Darlene Whitlock
Business Teacher
Ford Madison Community School District
Fort Madison, Iowa

Angela N. Williams
Business Department Head
Hilton Head Island High School
Hilton Head Island, South Carolina

About the Authors

Ann Jordan has served as the Career Development Manager for the Great Oaks Institute of Technology & Career Development in Cincinnati, OH, where she supervised the K-12 Career Development program. In this capacity, she oversaw career development programs for over 115,000 K-12 students across 36 school districts. Currently, Ann works as a career development consultant for various organizations and school districts in Southwest Ohio. Ann is the co-author of *Communicating for Success* and *Discovering Your Career*.

Tena B. Crews is a Professor of Integrated Information Technology (IIT) at the University of South Carolina, Columbia, SC. She is also the Director of Online Learning and Development for the College of Hospitality, Retail and Sport Management at the University of South Carolina (USC). She previously served as the Director of Business Education at USC and as an Associate Director of Technology Pedagogy at the Center for Teaching Excellence (CTE). She is the author of *Fundamentals of Insurance,* which has been adopted by many secondary and post-secondary schools. She has served on numerous executive boards for state, regional, national, and international professional organizations. Tena has won several awards for her teaching and research and continues to teach in both the face-to-face classroom and online.

To the Student

Take Charge of Your Career!

You will be spending more hours of your life working than any other activity. A wise career choice allows you to wake up every day wanting to go to work. Look for a career that makes you feel fulfilled and allows you to have the type of lifestyle you want.

Investigating Your Career helps you:

- Identify your passions, talents, values, and goals.
- Investigate career clusters while keeping your future in mind.
- Plan realistically, using decision-making tools to develop your personal career plan.
- Practice the education and job search skills you need to implement your career path.

The results are exciting! Make discoveries about what is important to you. Explore interesting career possibilities. Investigate education and training opportunities. Learn practical skills you can use your entire life. You will consult with your family, teachers, classmates, counselors, and members of the community. Using what you discover, you will make informed decisions about your future. **You** will decide the **P*A*T*H to Success** that you want your life to take.

This book relates to the real world. You will read about real people and their real careers. You will find interesting stories of how students just like you use the career journey process. Throughout the book, you will keep documents from your own career journey in your Career Portfolio.

What This Book Does

Investigating Your Career has five parts that will help you in your career planning.

Part 1: Preparation
Discover the importance of choosing a career that matches your interests, personality, skills, and values. You learn about yourself through activities and assessments. You will also find out how career events, job shadowing, internships, and service learning can help you make career decisions. As you explore current and future workforce and workplace trends, you will learn how technology, workforce diversity, and global markets influence career options.

Part 2: Focus
In Part 2, begin a decision-making process to make education and training choices. You will identify goals to help you accomplish your education, career, and lifestyle dreams. You will learn skills critical to success — how to manage your time and understand finances.

Part 3: Decisions
You will plan the process of your career preparation path in Part 3. Using the tools provided, you will evaluate and select career preparation options.

Part 4: Career Readiness
Part 4 explains the tools and skills you need to continue your career journey outside the classroom as an employee or entrepreneur.

Part 5: Tools for the Future
The last part explains the skills and knowledge you will need to be successful in the workplace. You will learn which behaviors and skills employers require. You also learn how employment laws, types of employment, and employer expectations affect careers.

Preparation

PART 1

Monkey Business Images / Shutterstock.com

Photodisc/Jupiter Images

Sid loved to work with food. As a little boy, he helped his grandmother in the kitchen to learn her secrets for baking delicious pies. Growing up, Sid hoped to have a career that included creating menus and trying new dishes for beautiful dinner tables.

Some people tried to convince Sid that working in the food industry would not earn a good income unless he was a celebrity chef. However, when he investigated several culinary arts careers, Sid found that some careers did not always involve cooking. One was restaurant management.

Working with his teachers, counselor, and family, Sid set goals for his future and developed an education plan. He chose to attend a career and technical center for his last two years of high school. During those years, he also had jobs bussing tables and serving customers. His education and work experience gave him a jumpstart on the courses he took at the Culinary Institute.

Today Sid's education and skills support his passion. His love of food and his management skills were the reasons that a local firm hired him to help them start a new restaurant near downtown. After it opens, Sid will be working in the front of the house managing the wait staff, bussers, and runners. That position can lead to future responsibilities in marketing and management. By developing a career plan and making adjustments as he progressed, Sid achieved his dream of earning his living in the food industry.

Planning a Career in . . . Culinary Arts

Take your passion for cooking and build it into a profession, and you have the recipe for a career in Culinary Arts, one of Hospitality and Tourism's pathways.

Chefs perform many tasks—from using different knife skills to cooking with various techniques. They prepare plates with consistency and within time limits. But chefs do more than just cook. They must also clean, plan menus, order supplies, and supervise kitchen staff. The rigorous pace of this career requires much stamina.

Employment Outlook

- Strong demand and some growth. Large number of employees. Higher turnover rate for entry-level positions.
- Good advancement for culinary and hospitality graduates.

Career Possibilities

- Chef
- Caterer
- Dietician
- Food/Beverage Distributor
- Restaurant Owner

Needed Skills

- Excellent communication skills.
- Work with all types of people.
- Problem solving.
- Career and technical education and/or on-the-job training is a must.

What's It Like to Work in . . . Culinary Arts?

No matter where you work, being a chef is important work. If you love to cook, you will not want to do anything else.

You will never be bored. Trying new spice combinations, new recipes, and new techniques will stretch your creativity. If you have any time between orders, you will be prepping for later dishes and cleaning up after the previous dish.

Long hours await you, but the rewards are worth it. Every day is different. The variety of your food is challenging and creative. Customers beam, though they may be fussy. On the other hand, shifts either begin early morning or end late at night. Of course, you will be working weekends and holidays.

The work is physically demanding. You will stand long hours. Often you will lift heavy bags and pots. Mixing large containers and rolling out pounds of dough requires fitness. And yes, you are likely to be burned and cut by knives and other kitchen tools.

However, the satisfaction you realize during your hours at work and at the end of every day makes Culinary Arts a great career choice.

What about You?

Do you like variety in the workplace? Can you solve problems and work with all types of people? Do you have stamina? Culinary Arts has many choices, all ending with the customer's needs in mind.

Career Expectations

Goals

- Recognize personal career expectations.
- Describe U.S. teens' career expectations.
- Identify career expectations: choices vs. reality.

Terms

- professional career, p. 5
- blue-collar career, p. 6
- Bureau of Labor Statistics (BLS), p. 7

Real Life Focus

How many careers are there? Think about it. Think of something you use often, like your MP3 player. For every product, people:

- created the idea.
- discovered how to make the product.
- anticipated and solved problems.
- produced it.
- marketed it.
- sold it.
- delivered it.
- concluded the business by collecting payment and customer feedback.
- repaired it.

Every step of product development, from beginning to end, requires one or more careers to make that product an effective reality. When you say, "I want to work with web sites," do you mean you will design it, do the technology, create the artwork, take the photographs, or compose the music? In other words, you have many choices ahead of you.

Your Personal Career Expectations

Even if you do not know what you want as your career, you probably have thought about it often. Everyone has ideas of what work is and what a career means. You watch and listen to your relatives and family friends talk about their careers. You also observe people working—from your teacher in the classroom to your doctor to the clerk in the convenience store.

Pasang loved to write. He was part of the team that wrote and edited the school e-zine. Researching and organizing the information was something he enjoyed. At home, Pasang wrote an entry at least once a week on the blog he created about teenagers in Minneapolis. The blog was popular; the increasing readership drew many comments. Six months ago, a digital company contacted Pasang and offered to host his blog.

After his parents and his school advisor investigated the company, Pasang got his parents' permission to be part of the national digital hosting company. His blog readership grew tremendously with the national coverage. As a result, several journalism schools have contacted him about attending their school, with the real possibility of financial aid. Pasang's passion is not just a hobby. That hobby led him to a career.

Your interests and skills should greatly influence your career decisions. Even if you do not know what you want for a career, you probably have some ideas about what you expect to do. For example, you may assume that you will make a lot of money or travel the world. You may also have general expectations about the type of work you will be doing. Perhaps you think about working outdoors or in a laboratory. Perhaps you see yourself using technology. Should you work alone or with people? These factors—and more—make up the many pieces you will consider in making a career decision.

U.S. Teens' Expectations

What do teens think about the future? What do they anticipate for the future?

An Arizona State University study discovered that teenagers have the following expectations about their futures:

- The majority said "doing work that you enjoy" and "having a happy family" were necessary for a good life.

- Nearly 90 percent said that having a college degree is essential for a good future.

- The majority said they would graduate from college.

- Over half intend to have a **professional career**. A professional career is usually classified as work that requires a college degree and special training.

- Nearly 70 percent of teens said they do volunteer work, though more do it as a school requirement than as career exploration.

- Nearly 80 percent of teens say they look forward to the future.

- Only one-fourth of teens agreed that "adults will leave the world in good shape for people my age."

Why do many teens do volunteer work?

Jaren Jai Wicklund/Shutterstock.com

Career FACT

You might be surprised to learn which careers make people the happiest. According to a recent survey, these are the "happiest careers" in the U.S.

- Biotechnology
- Administrative-Clerical
- Customer Service
- Purchasing
- Education

Does money buy happiness? No. What makes people happiest in a career is their relationships with co-workers and personal control.

—CareerBliss.com

According to the study, teens realize that work is important for the future, but they do not necessarily expect to enjoy their future. Many of them have not yet discovered that the secret to enjoying work is to choose work that uses their strengths. When teens know their strengths and learn about career possibilities, they set higher career goals and better understand how to choose a fulfilling career.

For most students, their parents and family members, teachers, and friends—in that order—have the greatest influence on their career decisions. When family members and other adults understand and explain the rewards of choosing a career that fits each individual, teens will have a clearer understanding of how to choose a career path that will be satisfying in the future.

The influence of friends also is important to students when they choose and prepare for their careers. Students are more likely to be involved in school activities when their friends are involved in school activities. Also, students tend to be more interested in careers when their friends are interested in career decisions.

Consider

Are the teenagers' expectations realistic? Why or why not?

Choices versus Reality

An annual Gallup Poll Youth Survey asked teens ages 13 to 17 their top career choices. The results were:

1. Teacher (top female choice)
2. Doctor
3. Lawyer
4. Sports field (top male choice)
5. Science/biology

All of these choices are professional careers. Not one **blue-collar career**—whose workers typically perform manual labor and earn an hourly wage—made the top choices for either males or females.

sjlocke/iStockphoto.com

Why do Health Science careers dominate the list of fastest-growing careers for the future?

The reality, however, is a contrast. The **Bureau of Labor Statistics (BLS)**, a research agency of the U.S. Department of Labor that compiles statistics on career information, has predicted the careers that are the fastest-growing for the next ten years. Of the top 30:

- 25 are Health-related (Previously, computers/information technology [IT] and health split the list.)

- 2 are IT careers (networking; apps & software specialist or engineer)

- 1—Financial Management

- 1—Compliance Officer (Ensures that an organization follows regulations.)

- 1—Adult Education Instructor.

Eight of the careers are blue-collar occupations and require career and technical training and/or on-the-job training. Twelve need associate degrees or higher. Only ten would be defined as professional careers.

When you are exploring careers, be aware that the career demands of the future are not the same as career demands of today. Battelle Institute predicts that of the top ten careers for 2018, none currently exists in the same form today. The BLS states that when today's kindergarten students reach the job market, nearly 100 percent of their careers will either be in fields that do not exist today or will require skills different from those used in the same careers today.

Labor market trends are important for you to understand as you plan your career. What if you prepared for a career in the DVD industry, only to find out that downloading and more advanced forms of technology were making DVDs obsolete? You want to make sure you prepare for a career that will be available when you finish your education or skill training. Chapter 4 will give you more help in choosing a career that has long-term prospects.

Career-Planning Quiz

Do you have realistic career expectations? How much do you know about planning a career? Some of the answers may surprise you.

Decide whether the following statements are *true* or *false*. After you answer the questions, your teacher will distribute the answers to you.

1. For the average adult in the United States, work activities take more time than any other type of activity.

2. Without actually working in a career, you cannot tell if the career is the one for you.

3. Anyone can do any job as long as he or she decides to do it.

4. Most careers in the future will require more than a high school education.

5. If you just wait, the right job opportunity will come your way.

6. The majority of people spend their adult lives in the same career.

7. Anyone who plans to work right out of high school needs the same basic academic skills as someone who plans to go to college.

8. Choose math, science, and technology electives to fill in your schedule. They will provide the most skills for careers of the future.

9. The top ten fastest-growing careers have not changed in over twenty years.

10. Most career fields that use technology, such as web design, require a bachelor's degree.

11. The No. 1 reason people are fired from jobs is that they are lazy.

Your P*A*T*H to Success

Goals

- Explain the difference between a job and a career.
- Describe the steps in the P*A*T*H to Success.

Terms

- job, p. 9
- career, p. 10
- occupation, p. 10
- career cluster, p. 10
- passion, p. 12
- attitude, p. 12
- talents, p. 12
- heart, p. 13

Real Life Focus

Before they were famous, many celebrities had jobs that were not at all glamorous.

- Queen Latifah worked at Burger King.
- Jennifer Aniston waited tables.
- Sean "Diddy" Combs delivered newspapers.
- Gwen Stefani scrubbed floors at Dairy Queen.
- Michael Dell of Dell Computers washed dishes.

Maybe not all your jobs will be exciting, but that work experience can help you decide what career you do *not* want to choose.

Job versus Career

Job and *career*—people use these terms often. Do they have the same meaning, or are they different?

Job

By now, you may already have had a job. If not, you will certainly have one soon. Your job may be assisting in an office, cleaning house, babysitting, or doing yard work. A **job** is a paid position involving a specific place, time, and tasks set by an employer. A job allows you to save for something, to pay bills, or to put money in your bank account.

You probably can easily define a job. Many students get a job to earn money to meet their needs. Sometimes you may like what you are doing, but you may choose a job simply because of the benefits you will receive from the money you earn. Another reason you may take a job is to gain experience in a career field you are considering.

A job is often temporary. In fact, between the ages of 18 and 42, a person changes jobs an average of nearly 11 times. A job may become a way of trying out different career fields.

Career

When asked to explain the difference between a job and a career, people often say that a career is something for life and a job is temporary. A job satisfies a short-term need. But a career is much more than that. In fact, many students say that a career is for a lifetime.

A **career** describes employment in a particular field for the long-term, maybe even for a lifetime. When choosing a career, many people base their choice on what they are interested in doing. What makes you happy is often a great choice for what you choose for your working life. Instead of picking a career as just a means of earning a living, you will have a career as an important, positive part of your life.

You may see the term *occupation* used in place of the words, *job* and *career*. An **occupation** is a type of work that has a specific set of skills. Those skills may require special training, education, or experience. That type of work may be part of a number of different work settings. Occupations allow a person to move from one industry to another as needed.

Sales is an example of an occupation that easily fits into different industries. Effective salespeople possess strong communication skills and have extensive knowledge of the product or service they sell. Whether selling shoes at a local store or supporting the use of government policies, a skilled salesperson is a necessity in any career field.

A **career cluster** is all the possible careers grouped in an entire subject area. For example, dental assistants, registered nurses, radiology technicians, personal trainers, and doctors all have careers in the Health Science cluster. Most people begin their career in an entry-level position, no matter the career cluster. Then they improve their skills and progress to more complex careers. While people do change careers, they do not switch as often as they change jobs. The average person changes careers eight times between ages 18 and 42.

Web Connections

Web sites offer information to create your career path. You can explore career stories, information and statistics, and planning information.

Access the Web Connection link for Chapter 1. Search at least two areas in one of the sites listed. As you are investigating the site, write down ideas that may help you learn more about yourself and your career plan. Share your ideas with the class.

www.cengage.com/school/iyc

A Career or a Job?

Many times, you will choose a job because of its pay or its location. You may think, "I know why I need the job. It does not matter if I like the job because it meets my needs I have right now."

When you choose a career, however, it is important that you like your choice. The career path you choose will affect every part of your life—your frame of mind, your life outside your work, and even the work itself. Research shows that people who enjoy their careers are more satisfied with their lives. They see a career as an important, positive part of their lives. The closer your career matches your talents and passions, the more satisfied you will be.

How will the courses you take in school today relate to your future career?

Chad worked after school in the garden center owned by his neighbor, Sara. He hauled plants into place, put them in customers' cars, and cleaned the floors. Though he enjoyed talking to Sara about the plants, he also wondered why she worked such long days.

Sara explained that she began work in a similar business when she was in school. Her love of plants led her to take more biology classes in high school and college. Sara experimented with scientific formulas for increasing plant growth organically. She practiced on plants in what eventually became her own garden center. As a result, customers bought both her plants and her fertilizers.

While he was working, Chad observed the business procedures. He enjoyed thinking of changes he would make as an owner. Talking over some of those ideas with Sara, Chad decided to take business courses, as well as those in agriculture, his future career.

Now Sara's business partner, Chad has two careers: a soil and water specialist and a greenhouse manager. His working life also includes the occupation of retail agriculture sales. Chad's career includes both of his passions—plants and business.

Consider

Why would people change jobs more than careers during their working lives? Why change careers at all?

The *P*A*T*H to Success*

Finding your path to a satisfying career requires careful planning. You will need to make thoughtful decisions. It is not easy, but challenging and exciting. When you explore careers, do you realize that you are making decisions that will help you discover your career? The key to success is knowing yourself. Deciding your career path begins with you.

Your journey to a successful career starts with your setting goals. Although your goals may change over time, what you enjoy doing and the talents that you have will grow, but not change.

Your career choice depends on *you*. The journey to your career will be rewarding, and you will achieve career satisfaction. However, before you can follow your passions and talents to a career, you must investigate your interests, your values, and your skills. You need to realize who you are before you can discover what career path you will take.

Investigating Your Career offers you ways to find the path that will lead to a satisfying career, one that fits your passions and talents. The *P*A*T*H to Success* is one tool. It will help you begin your self-discovery process.

What did you enjoy playing with as a child? Would that be a possibility for your career?

bikerlondon/Shutterstock.com

Passion

Uncovering your passions is the first step on your *P*A*T*H to Success*. **Passion** is the strong, positive feeling you experience while enjoying something. Begin to identify your career-related passions by thinking about what makes you happy. What were your favorite play activities as a child? What do you choose to do in your spare time when you are not in school? Remember, though, that doing something very well does not always mean you enjoy doing it.

Attitude

Attitude involves your feelings. Think about one of the activities that you chose as a passion of yours. Does doing that activity excite you? Do you excel at it? Your enthusiasm and your belief that you will do the activity well give you a positive attitude. A positive attitude will help you believe that you can achieve anything you want to do. Deciding to have a positive attitude is the second step on your *P*A*T*H to Success*.

Talents

Talents are your natural abilities and strengths. Everyone has talents. The third step of the *P*A*T*H to Success* is to realize and develop your talents. By choosing a career that matches your talents, you can expand them through your career path. Consider your talents when looking at career clusters.

Heart

Heart refers to what you believe is important to your choices in life. The fourth step on your *P*A*T*H to Success* is finding your heart. Answer these questions: "What are my values? Who and what are the important influences in my life?" Your answers to these and other questions will help you believe in yourself, choose a lifestyle and career you enjoy, and develop the determination and flexibility you need to reach your career goals.

ACTIVITY 1.2

Learning from Others

In this activity, you will discover how successful people planned and chose their careers.

1. Interview at least one adult in a career area that interests you. Ask the person questions to learn about his or her career. Some questions you may ask are:

   - How did you choose your career?

   - Did you start with a career plan? If so, how did you create your plan? If not, why not?

   - What was your education/training path?

   - Were there events in the region or the world that helped your career decision? How?

   - What are some of the best experiences you have had in your career? Why?

   - What were some difficulties you encountered? How did you overcome them?

   - What were you doing at my age to prepare you for your career?

   - What could you have done differently before high school graduation to help you prepare for your career?

   - What advice would you give to someone beginning a career similar to yours?

2. Summarize your findings for a class discussion or written report. Explain what you learned from the person you interviewed that will help you plan your career.

3. Prepare a timeline to show the career path of the person you interviewed.

4. Write a thank-you note to the person you interviewed within three days of the interview.

Planning for Career Success

Goals
- Explain why your career planning should begin now.
- Discuss how career planning supports career success.

Terms
- transferable skills, p. 15
- skill sets, p. 15
- career plan, p. 16
- Career Portfolio, p. 17

Real Life Focus

How many times have you been asked, "What are you going to do when you grow up?" "What are you going to do after high school?" "Are you going to college? Where?"

These questions are hard to answer right now. After all, don't you have to decide on your career first? But then you may have heard:

Choosing a career is simple

And that is one of the biggest myths of career planning. This is your life. Spending time exploring careers is the starting point to a great career.

Why Have a Career Plan?

Imagine that you live in Washington, DC. You want to drive from DC across the United States to Portland, Oregon, after graduation. Would you leave without a map? Or luggage? Of course not. You would plan for a successful trip.

Career planning is very similar, except that the results affect your entire life, not just a few weeks of it. When your grandparents and probably your parents were teenagers, schools did not help students plan their career path much before high school graduation. At that point, students often accepted either the best job they could find—which was maybe not a job suited for them—or they started college, hoping to find a career while taking classes. Career research and assessments were simply tools that students sometimes used to fit themselves into careers.

In college, career planning was usually as uncommon as it was as in high school. The emphasis was on completing a degree instead of preparing students for available jobs in the labor market. Some students earned a degree first and *then* started thinking about job possibilities. However, going to college is *not* a career plan; it is *part* of the career plan.

Until the mid-1980s, people often stayed in one career all of their working lives. Employers usually began an employee's career change through transfers, promotions, or even terminations. In 1980, adults changed careers only an average of three times in their lifetime. Today the average is seven times between the ages of 18 to 42.

Advances in global competition and technology are responsible for many changes in the workplace. In today's labor market, people need to be independent. Often employers expect employees to be in charge of their own career path.

To be successful in today's competitive job market, people need to be aware of two types of skills:

1. **Transferable skills** are work tasks used in various types of careers. According to Quintcareers.com, there are five basic transferable skills:
    - Communication—Expressing, reporting, and interpreting
    - Research and Planning—Current and future planning
    - Human Relations—Interpersonal skills, including resolving conflict
    - Organization, Management, and Leadership—Being part of a team and coaching the team
    - Work Survival—Creating day-to-day skills for a productive and satisfying workplace

2. **Skill sets** are the unique knowledge and abilities needed for specific occupations. For example, the ability to install intranet data systems and the ability to operate a backhoe are skill sets.

Skill sets follow occupations and cross into various career clusters. Having a broad skill base gives people more career choices and more flexibility in their working lives. That flexibility will help people adapt to the changing labor market.

The fastest-growing career fields in the labor market continue to change rapidly. New technologies and global economic competition mean greater opportunities and challenges. You can succeed by taking responsibility for your own career planning, including a commitment to lifelong learning.

Planning for Career Success

Using the *P*A*T*H to Success*, your passions, your attitude, your talents, and your heart will be the guide for using this book to plan for your career.

How do your interests relate to your future career?

Comstock/Jupiter Images

"Life is 10 percent what happens to you—and 90 percent how you respond to it," said Lou Holtz, the famous football coach. His words are very true.

Kathleen loved to organize her younger brothers and sisters' activities at home. She created a family library, planned summer events, wrote plays, and created shows to entertain her siblings. In school, Kathleen either acted or worked backstage in every play. She also took part in speech competitions. Her part-time job was working in the local library.

When Kathleen began planning her career, she had so many choices. She listened to the ideas of her family, teachers, and friends. Then she thought, "Why would I want to do something that other people think I should do? Why not do what I enjoy doing?" So Kathleen planned a career as a drama, speech, and English teacher. Her early teaching skills and talent for organizing became her working life. What she liked to do—and did well—became her career choice.

What Is a Career Plan?

Throughout your life, you will constantly discover more about yourself through your activities and accomplishments. Your career will be part of that lifelong journey. A **career plan** is the schedule for your career journey, similar to a proposed plan for traveling.

Real People / Real Careers

Adam Jordan / *Chef*

At a young age, Adam Jordan learned to cook—more for self-defense His mother did not like cooking; in fact, she was better at burning. But his father grilled well. Also, his grandmother cooked delicious, well-balanced meals and baked excellent pies.

When Adam was 15, he got a part-time job working as a cook in an upscale hamburger franchise. He soon learned that he had a higher paying job than his friends—and he liked the work too! During college Adam was a chef at a gourmet pizza restaurant, where the owner allowed him to use his imagination to create exotic pizza combinations.

Adam loves cooking because it allows him to be creative, to be a food artist. His art college education has helped him in his career. His culinary education has been mostly on-the-job training.

Currently, Adam is a sauté chef in an elite country club. The variety of his day is tremendous. He sautés primarily, but also preps, plates, and fills in when needed at parties. Adam remarked, "I'm glad the opportunities to cook presented themselves. I really enjoy what I do—and so do my customers."

For more information about:

* culinary careers
* culinary schools and credentialing

Access **www.cengage.com/school/iyc** and click on the appropriate links in Chapter 1.

Source: *Personal Interview*, April 2011

Photo courtesy of Matthew C. Jordan

To develop your career plan, you will:

- Travel the *P*A*T*H to Success*.

- Research career clusters to find career fields that work with your passions, inspire a positive attitude, allow you to use your talents, and fill your heart.

- Identify the skills needed for your career choices.

- Set goals for your education, training, and experience.

Finally, you will design your career plan by listing the steps you need to take to reach your goals.

As you begin the steps on your career path, you will find that you need to be flexible. Life does not always go according to plan. However, if you start planning now, you can use your career plan to help you make decisions that will lead toward the goals you set.

Some people say, "I'll do this when I win the lottery." Or, "If I could run the company, I would…." Those statements show that those people are not in control—of their own lives! A career plan allows you to be in charge. Rather than going through life waiting for a big break, you can make your own luck. Now is the time to design a winning game plan for achieving your dream career.

Throughout this book, you will see the portfolio icon. This icon suggests that you put a specific document into your Career Portfolio. Your **Career Portfolio** is a collection place for activities that help you make career decisions. Some documents may be samples that illustrate your passions and talents, assessment results, career interviews, personal notes, and much more. You may keep items on your computer, online, or in a folder. When you look through the folder, you can review the results of your career planning efforts. Summaries of your personal *P*A*T*H to Success*, results of your career research, and samples of your imagination will help you in the process of discovering your career.

Planning for Career Success

Creating your career plan is a process. That process will change over time. You may have starts and stops, but the process of developing your career plan will help you organize your thoughts toward your future in a career that will satisfy you. You will be able to set and accomplish goals that help you build career success.

What Happens Without a Career Plan?

Not having a career plan is a direct cause for many students' problems, according to the U.S. Departments of Education and Labor. The reality:

- One out of four teens does not graduate from high school. These students attended school for 10 to 12 years. Now, because of dropping out, they will have trouble being hired as an entry-level employee.

■ Three out of 10 high school graduates finish high school with no plans for further education and training. The majority of those students have no specialized skills. In reality, until they develop a career plan, they will have a difficult time building a satisfying career.

■ One out of four students who start college will not graduate. A career plan would give these students an advantage.

■ Approximately half of all college graduates will take a position that is not in their major. Developing a career plan and setting goals would help those students.

Some students and some families believe that they should postpone career planning until after high school. Others believe that career planning should happen during college. However, college is not a career plan. The costs of going to college make it an expensive way to experiment with career choices.

Consider

What might happen if you decided not to plan for your career before high school graduation? Why not wait until college to plan your career?

Career Planning Checklist

At the end of *Investigating Your Career*, you will be able to picture your future. Why? Because you started planning now. You will have a good idea of where your career path is going and a design of how to get there. You will be saying *yes* to the following statements:

✔ School is the starting point for my career path. As I develop my career plan, I will take advantage of what school has to offer.

✔ My family, my teachers, my counselor, and my friends—as well as other factors—may influence my career choices. I used the input to decide my career area.

✔ I took career assessments to help me identify my passions and talents for potential career cluster choices.

✔ I researched career clusters and career possibilities that use my talents and passions.

✔ I want to train and educate myself for a career that will be in demand in the future. I will research to understand career trends and the demands of a global economy.

✔ I discussed careers with people in career areas that interest me. I listened to their advice.

✔ I investigated the education and training needed after high school for careers in my career cluster.

✔ I am aware of the cost of education and training for my career area. I know how to create a financial plan and how to research financial aid.

What are some of the activities outside school that will help you explore careers?

AISPIX/Shutterstock.com

- ✔ I have my education plan in writing, including the courses I am taking now and plan to take in the future. My courses match my *P*A*T*H to Success*.
- ✔ I will work part-time and participate in service learning whenever possible. These activities will help me gain experience for my career decision.
- ✔ I know the job search process.
- ✔ I have a Career Portfolio. I will update it regularly and use it as a guide to make my career decisions.

This checklist may seem long. However, a successful future depends on preparation, research, and planning—the more the better.

With planning brings reality. Reality will help you set and achieve your goals more clearly. According to a Charles Schwab survey, nearly 75 percent of teens believe they will be earning "plenty of money" when they are independent. Over half of them believe that they will be better off financially than their families. The truth is that without a career plan, the predictions are that today's teens will earn *less* money than their families.

ACTIVITY 1.3

Leadership

What Is a Team?

Understanding teams and teamwork is important to the success of sports teams, classroom learning, and the workplace. In this activity, you and your teammates will discover what makes a successful team.

1. In small groups, discuss what is a team. As a group, pick three to five words that describe what a *team* is to the group. One person will start the discussion; that person is the *leader*. One person will record the group's words; that person is the *recorder*. One person will share the answers with the class; that person is the *reporter*. Groups will report to the class.

2. Your group will now define *teamwork*. You may use some of the words that you and the groups

used in Step 1. Each group's reporters will share the group's results with the class.

3. Use the results from Steps 1 and 2 to create three guidelines or rules to help a team succeed. Share the rules with the class.

4. Create a team pennant with your group. Use some of the ideas from Steps 1-3.

5. When all the groups are finished working, reporters will share their group's pennants with the class. Explain some of the reasons behind your group's choices.

Chapter Summary

1.1 Career Expectations

- A person's personal interests influence his or her career choices. The advice and experience of others and education and skills training will also influence career choices.

- U.S. teens have high expectations for their career future. However, the influence of others—especially parents and other family members, teachers, and friends—will have the greatest influence on their career decisions.

- U.S. teens' career preferences often do not match the reality of the career demands of the future.

1.2 Your *P*A*T*H to Success*

- The difference between a job and career is important. A *job* is a paid position that involves a specific place, time, and tasks set by an employer. A *career* describes employment in a particular field for a long period.

- The *P*A*T*H to Success* has four steps: uncovering career-related *passions*, choosing a positive *attitude*, identifying *talents*, and discovering what is important to your *heart*.

1.3 Planning for Career Success

- Developing a career plan now allows a person to focus on education and skill training in the direction of specific career clusters. Choosing classes and activities that help in preparation for a future career will help in the decision-making process.

- A career plan is necessary to guide a person through a career journey. The many steps help with a thorough preparation for the future.

Chapter Assessment

Vocabulary Builder

Match each statement with the term that best defines it.

1. A long-term work history in a particular field
2. Strong, positive feelings you experience while enjoying something
3. A type of career that usually has manual labor and an hourly wage
4. Type of work with specific skills
5. Natural strengths and abilities
6. Collection place for activities that help with career decisions
7. A group of all of the possible careers in an entire subject area
8. A specific set of skills for unique occupations
9. The schedule for the career journey
10. Work tasks that are used in various types of careers
11. Refers to the way you feel about something
12. A type of career that usually requires a college degree and specialized training
13. The U.S. Department of Labor agency that creates career information statistics
14. A paid position involving a specific time and specific tasks set by an employer

15. what you believe is important to your choices in life

a. attitude
b. blue-collar career
c. Bureau of Labor Statistics
d. career
e. career cluster
f. career plan
g. Career Portfolio
h. heart
i. job
j. occupation
k. passion
l. professional career
m. talents
n. skill sets
o. transferable skills

Review What You Have Learned

15. What do you expect from your future careers?
16. What factors influence most students' career decisions?
17. What do students choose as their top five career fields?
18. What do the fastest-growing careers of the future have in common?
19. What is the difference between a job and a career?
20. What are the four components of the *P*A*T*H to Success*?
21. Why should you develop a career plan before high school graduation?
22. What is the difference between transferable skills and skill sets?
23. What are some of the specific steps in creating a career plan?
24. What are some of the benefits of creating a career plan?

Case Challenges

After reading both case studies on the next page, analyze each career planning situation. Have the students successfully prepared for the future? If so, explain why. If not, suggest activities they can do to make clearer career decisions.

25. Julio plans on going to college after he graduates from high school. He has not thought about what courses he will take, because colleges have advisors to help students, right? Besides, he has his college fund, and his grades are good enough for a scholarship towards his first-year tuition. Since his family is pushing him into college, he figures they will pay his expenses. He will have at least four years to make his career decision. Why decide a college major now?

26. School does not really interest Dakota. She is only scheduling the classes she needs to graduate. Any other classes would be "fun" classes to fill her schedule. So what if her grades are not terrific? She just wants to have fun with her friends and pass her classes. After all, what does school have to do with the real world anyway? Dakota works at a fast-food restaurant, and she believes she can cover her expenses on her own. If she needs more money, she can use a credit card. After all, she will be sharing an apartment with Sabrina and Petra after graduation.

Make Academic Connections

27. LANGUAGE ARTS   Volunteering is an excellent way to "try out" a career field. Research volunteer opportunities in your school and your community. Choose at least one organization that interests you. Write a letter to the head of the group or organization asking for information on volunteer opportunities. After you receive the information, follow up with a thank-you note. You may even schedule an interview to pursue the opportunities.

28. MATH   Below is a list of three careers, the number of people currently employed in that career, and the percent of projected increase by 2018. Use the projected increase to calculate the approximate number of people employed in that career in 2018.

Career	Number currently employed	Projected increase by 2018	Number employed in 2018
Physician assistant	66,000	27 percent	
Physical therapist assistant	21,200	33 percent	
Dental assistant	280,000	29.2 percent	

Workplace Connection

Learning about yourself is one of the first steps to discovering your career. Survey your strengths by exploring your past and yourself today.

29. Complete the following statements.
- As a child, I liked to …..
- Today I like to …..
- Others describe me as …..
- I am best at ….

Portfolio

30. The more transferable skills you have, the greater your career opportunities.
- List three activities you like to do after school.
- List the transferable skills you are developing through these activities.
- Identify some careers that use these skills.

Portfolio

	Activity	Transferable Skills	Career Area
Examples	Playing Video Games	using technology	digital design
		problem solving	Help Desk
		multi-tasking	Home technology designer

Blogging: An Introduction

Throughout your career journey, you will be blogging or journaling your career plan process. Before you write your first blog entry or post, you will deconstruct or analyze a blog post. Access www.cengage.com/school/iyc and click on the appropriate links in Chapter 1.

1. What is the blog headline? Does it fit the post? Why? If there is not a headline, write one.

2. Summarize the post in one sentence.

3. Who is the blogger? What are his or her qualifications?

4. List the pluses and minuses about the post. Did the blogger succeed or not?

Blog

Discovering Career Choice Influences

sd619/iStockphoto.com

Marek and technology grew up together. As a toddler, Marek sat on his father's lap as his dad worked on the computer. Later, Marek learned sounds, numbers, and letters through simple computer games. As a teenager, he explored web sites and chatted online with friends.

As Marek advanced from toy computers to the family computer to his personal laptop, his parents encouraged him to learn more about technology. For example, they allowed him to use their smartphone to search web sites and try out different applications or apps.

Marek's exploration with the smartphone eventually bored him. He decided to create an app of his own. His parents helped him find a family friend who developed the software for the app to be used on a smartphone. During that creation, Marek suggested the design and sounds. Marek was the creator, but all while learning the software development.

Today Marek has two fully operational apps that can be purchased for a brand of smartphone. Though he is not rich by any means, the work that Marek did added to his resume and college application. As a result, Marek will attend a university that has majors in programming and software development. His future is a result of his family's encouraging Marek's curiosity and creativity.

Planning a Career in . . . Information Technology

Technology is the heart of this career cluster. Information Technology (IT) involves a dynamic and an ever-changing work environment.

Because technology is always evolving, IT has a revolutionary impact on society and the economy. IT careers are not only in Information Technology; they are needed in every industry—from Medical Services to Finance, from Environmental Engineering to Business. The rigorous pace of this career requires a love of change.

Employment Outlook

- Strong demand in organizations of all sizes.
- High demand for a variety of positions, especially in Financial Services and Business.

Career Possibilities

- PC Support Specialist
- Software Applications
- Telecommunications Engineer
- Technical Writer
- Game Programmer

Needed Skills

- Education needs vary by position, ranging from career and technical education to a bachelor's degree.
- Problem solving with an attention to detail.
- Strong background in math and science.
- Certifications necessary for many skills and levels of expertise.

What's It Like to Work in Information Technology?

No matter what area of Information Technology you choose, it will involve change. Newer and better technology emerges constantly. You will never be bored.

Positions are available in every industry, in companies large and small. IT positions exist around the world. You can assist with communication in Paris—or you could work there!

Technology disasters demand immediate attention. Until you find the source of the problem and fix it, you cannot leave the project. Holidays and weekends do not matter when there are technology problems. You and your team may work long hours, but you will finish your day with a sense of satisfaction. Your customers will be happy that you have fixed their technology problems.

The satisfaction you will receive from troubleshooting problems and making sure every step of the way is completed makes Information Technology a great choice for a career.

What about You?

Are you a problem solver? Do you like to work on puzzles and do detail work? Are you willing to change as technology upgrades? Information Technology is the Future's career.

darrenwise/iStockphoto.com

Goals

- Recognize how influence affects career decisions.
- Explain how people influence you and your decisions.
- Identify how groups in the community influence your values.

Terms

- influence, p. 26
- motivation, p. 26
- mentor, p. 32

Real Life Focus

What do you like to do? Write down 20 things that make you happy when you do them. The list should include your interests relating to your future, not just what you like to do for entertainment. Code each item with the following symbols.

$ Things that cost money to do

R Anything that involves risk (physical, intellectual, or emotional risk)

F Things someone in your family may have had on a list at your age

P Best done with other people

A Best done alone

5 Items probably not on the list in 5 years

Which of the categories influences you most? Why do you think that category has the most effect?

Portfolio

Influence

Everything and everyone around you influences you every day. **Influence** is the power of someone or something that affects you directly or indirectly. Sometimes you may realize that people, places, ideas, experiences, or things have an effect on you. However, often you do not notice the effects directly.

Influences may be positive or negative. For example, if you are allergic to cats and you work as a veterinary technician in an animal clinic, your environment will have a negative influence on you. Persuasion and manipulation are ways to influence someone, often negatively.

Not all influences affect your behavior and decisions in the same way. For example, when you respect and admire someone, the advice and opinions of that person are likely to motivate you. **Motivation** is why you set goals and make certain decisions. When you are motivated to act, your behavior has more purpose and control.

Influence affects you and your decisions. In this chapter, you will determine who or what may influence you and your career decisions. As you plan your career journey, you can decide what additional advice or experiences you want to influence your career decisions.

People Who May Influence Your Career Decision

Since you were a toddler, you have heard people ask you if you wanted to be a firefighter or a nurse or a ballerina. You learned about these careers—and the workplace in general—from many sources. However, people—especially the people you know—have the most influence on your career decision. Family members, teachers, peers, community members, and many others will give advice and share work experiences with you. Listening to and observing how people discuss their careers and their workplaces may give you a positive or negative impression of work. Sometimes when you talk with people about their careers, you can tell that they enjoy waking up every day and going to work. On the other hand, people who come home from work exhausted and grumpy and griping most days may not enjoy their careers.

Learn why people chose their career. Find what makes them happy or unhappy with their workplace. The results can help you in your career discovery. Listen to people talk about their workday. Watch their interactions on the job if you can. These are some of the ways you can research careers to help you with your career decision-making.

Parents And Other Family Members

Your family is the greatest influence on your career decision making, according to the Ohio Career Development survey of middle and high school students. The result of that survey seems natural since you are generally with your family more than any other group of people. As expected, parents and/or other family members would be the starting place for your ideas about various careers. Not only have you heard them talk about different types of careers, but you also observe them. For example, the way they react to their own work situations can affect how you view working life.

> Consuelo really enjoys her career as a cosmetologist. When she puts the final touches on customers' hair, she delights in seeing people's faces light up with pleasure. She has a knack for enhancing her customers' inner beauty by skillfully flattering a client's appearance. Consuelo's knowledge and skill in using color helps her to create new hair designs. In fact, Consuelo is one of the most popular cosmetologists in town.
>
> Working with people and beauty is Consuelo's passion. However, she comes home every day exhausted and complaining about her work. Consuelo never reveals her love of her career at home. Instead, she grumbles about her customers, her aching feet, and the long hours.
>
> Because of her mother's behavior, Donna has mixed feelings about training for a cosmetology career. Does her mother really hate her work? If not, why does she complain every day? How can Donna get a clearer understanding of the profession?

You may get conflicting messages about a certain career as Donna did about cosmetology. The way your parents and family members react to work may affect your own feelings about work—either positively or negatively. Have a conversation with them about work and how they feel about their career and their workday.

Whatever their feelings about work and careers, you should not ignore your family's advice. They know you well. They may encourage you and help you make decisions. However, if a family member discourages you from a certain career, ask him or her why. Hearing their reasons can help you form your career decision.

Expectations Your family may have expectations for your career choice. They not only have hopes and dreams for your future, but they also might expect you to choose the career they pick for you.

If there is a family business, your family may expect you to join it. Occasionally, a family may be against certain careers because of mistaken beliefs.

Michael's dad, Lou, has a successful family dental practice. Since he was 12 years old, Michael helped his dad in the office. He learned to sterilize instruments, clean equipment, help the receptionist, and run errands. Lou always thought that Michael would become a dentist and work with him in the practice. Eventually, Lou wanted to give the practice to Michael.

Michael closely watched his father's work as he helped out in the office. However, his observations and experiences helped Michael decide that

Real People / Real Careers

Huy Sam / *Electronics Repair*

As a boy in Vietnam, Huy Sam liked to tinker with any technology—whatever he could find. Spending hours with wires and light bulbs and batteries, his goal was to find out how something worked.

Huy Sam's thirst for technology paid off with rewards in his elementary and high schools for technology research. His love of technology resulted in several inventions, including a diaper sensor to let the family know the baby's diaper needed changing. Robotic toys and irrigation sensors were two more inventions.

Huy Sam came to the United States at the age of 20. Despite the language barrier, he earned a bachelor's degree in computer science. However, the most valuable skill Huy Sam learned was to repair a computer's motherboard. Saving customers hundreds of dollars with this type of repair led him to open his store, LaptopOnCall Inc.

Only 10 percent of LaptopOnCall's business is local. Personal computer repair shops from all over the U.S. send Huy Sam their most difficult repairs. Increasing his business is Sam's goal now, but eventually he would like to return to inventing timesaving technology devices.

For more information about:

* information technology careers
* electronic repair

Access **www.cengage.com/school/iyc** and click on the appropriate links in Chapter 2.

Source: *Cincinnati Enquirer* and *Personal Interview*, May 2011

Photo courtesy of Huy Sam

he did not want to become a dentist. He loves working with people, but not in a medical profession.

When Michael told his father his decision, Lou had a difficult time accepting it. He wondered what would happen to the dental practice that he worked so hard to build. Michael explained how he wanted to follow his father's example and build a career of his own. Instead of dentistry, Michael was more interested in working as a stockbroker. He hoped eventually to become a financial adviser.

Lou listened carefully. He realized that he and Michael were alike because they loved to work with people. However, just as Lou's interests were different from his own father's, Michael's interests were different from Lou's.

If your family expects you to follow a career path that does not really suit you, show them the successes you have had in your courses, extracurricular activities, and part-time jobs as a starting point for your chosen career path. Starting this conversation may be difficult, but if you begin by discussing the reasons for the career path you like, the discussion will become easier. After all, you are setting the stage for your family to listen to and support your dreams.

Encouragement Parents and family members can help you develop your career focus in so many ways. They can encourage you to take courses to explore your career interests. Developing your talents and supporting your passions will require your family's assistance. Your family can help you to create your plans and goals for the future to find your *P*A*T*H to Success*.

Talk about your dreams with your family. Discuss what you enjoy now and how you hope those passions will become your future. Who knows— they may be able to introduce you to someone in your career. Your family's encouragement will give you confidence to guide your future education and training, leading to your career path.

School Influences

The second most influential group on students' career decisions are people you interact with at school. After all, teachers, coaches, counselors, and other people who work in your school have expertise and knowledge in their career area. If you do well in Spanish and are considering a career using the language, who better to talk to than your Spanish teacher?

Teachers and Coaches If English interests you, think about all the careers that involve using English and the tools of writing and research every day. Discuss this with your English teacher. Journalists and editors are not the only ones who need good English skills. Actually, communication skills are important for any career, as is writing in an organized style with correct spelling and grammar.

Do you realize that math plays an important part for careers in music? For example, standards, frequencies, and ratios are the basis for a music scale. Without musical "math," few people would enjoy listening to a melody. Math teachers have a direct influence on your career success. Some careers use math every day, such as engineers, designers, and x-ray technicians. However, math also plays an important part in the careers of funeral directors, electricians, broadcast technicians, and musicians.

Coaches are the experts if you are interested in sports or sports-related careers. They can also give you insight into your own behavior. How you act in a team situation, for example, is often how you will act in a work situation.

In fact, many courses and activities in school require the same type of behaviors used in the workforce. Observing you in action shows teachers whether you can cooperate in team situations and whether you have leadership skills. Teachers know if you are organized, punctual, and dependable. They can be impartial and truthful with you when discussing your work qualities. The comments that teachers make can help you improve behaviors that you may need to change. Teachers often are the best references for you to choose for college and job applications.

For the most help, first talk to teachers whose classes you enjoy, including those teachers who have been pleased with your work. Ask for suggestions about how they can help you develop your career focus using the skills you have learned in class. These discussions can provide you with a wealth of information and can give you confidence to take charge of your future.

Counselors School guidance counselors can help you with the process of developing your career. They have several responsibilities.

- *Provide information to guide you as you make decisions for your future.* They can suggest courses that relate to your activities, talents, interests, and grades. Counselors can offer you ways to research educational options and may also provide business contacts for career experiences.

- *Help you discover your options.* For example, suppose you go to the counselor's office to find out about a career in medicine. Your counselor may ask what particular career—for example, doctor, nurse, dental hygienist, or pharmacist. The two of you might talk about the courses you should take before you graduate to prepare for your career.

Video - Study + Work habits

You and your counselor might also talk about other careers in medicine you had not considered—perhaps music therapy or nutrition.

■ ***Assist you with choosing and starting your education and training pathway towards your career goal.*** The counselor will provide planning checklists, information on courses, suggestions for career experiences, and tips for taking control of your homework. The counselor can help you set goals for your education, training, and experience.

Consider

What types of classes are your favorites? What careers relate to those classes?

Peers

Peer advice and peer pressure may seem to have the most influence in your life. In fact, you and your friends and classmates influence one another every day in many ways. The expectations of what clothes to wear, what games to play, what classes to take, and what music to download are everyday influences. However, how much influence should your friends have on your future life and career? You may continue hanging out with your friends after you graduate, but do you want to build your future around their choices?

Caitlin's friends believe that she has the most fashion sense of anyone in their class. Her combinations of accessories are creative. She can put on an ordinary belt and turn it into a fashion statement. With her eye for color and design, Caitlin seems to be a perfect match for a career as a stylist or fashion designer.

Tsuki, Caitlin's best friend, wants Caitlin to move with her to Chicago after graduation, where Tsuki has a job as a receptionist. After all, Chicago has a history of fashion and furniture design.

Thinking about her decision, Caitlin realized that by staying with Tsuki, she would be postponing her plans for fashion design school. But is delaying her career dream what she wanted to do? No, fashion design is Caitlin's passion. She is eager to begin her education. Instead, Caitlin decided to share an apartment with Tsuki during the summer and attend fashion design school in another state in the fall. Caitlin promised to help Tsuki find a roommate before she leaves for school.

Use your judgment in deciding whether to consider your friends' advice when you make your career decisions. Your friends have good intentions. However, they may not truly understand what is best for your future. They may be thinking more of themselves and your friendship rather than your future. While your friends' opinions are important to you, you must analyze their advice in terms of your interests. Remember, these are your goals and passions. This is *your* future.

Community Influences

Parents, other family members, teachers, and peers are not the only people who can influence your career choice. People in the community can also influence your decisions.

Having a mentor, doing job shadowing, and conducting information interviews are ways business people and others in your community can help you gather career information. In Chapter 3, you will learn more about ways you can find out about careers. The more information you have about the reality of a career you are considering, the better.

An employer can help you make career decisions in several ways. A part-time job provides you with work experience. You can also observe employees at the workplace to see if you like a certain type of career. On a break or after work, you can interview someone who works in a career field that interests you.

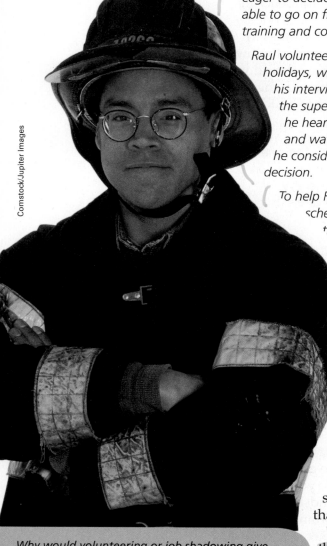

Comstock/Jupiter Images

Joining an Explorer Firefighting post was a wise choice for Raul. He was eager to decide if firefighting was the career for him. Although he is not able to go on fire calls until he is 18, Raul can participate in Explorer fire training and competitions.

Raul volunteers at the Anderson Fire Department on weekends and holidays, where he can watch the daily work of a firefighter. During his interview with the fire department, Raul spoke with Ms. House, the supervisor. He told her that ever since he was little, whenever he heard a fire truck, he would stop whatever he was doing and watch the truck pass. Raul wanted Ms. House to know that he considered the volunteer position to be research for his career decision.

To help Raul with his career focus, Ms. House taught him scheduling and other routine station work. His Explorer training suggests different aspects of a career in firefighting. Raul likes working with the equipment and teaching children fire safety. He finds firefighting to be challenging. However, Raul is weighing his decision based on the hazards of the career.

Ms. House hopes Raul is a good employee who will continue to work while he is in school. Raul hopes to work full-time for the Anderson Fire Department after he receives his training and Emergency Medical certification through career and technical school training.

Ms. House is a mentor for Raul. A **mentor** supports you through listening and advising. The guidance of a mentor is invaluable to helping you on your career journey. The mentor can be part of a career experience, such as Ms. House is to Raul, or a listener, a counselor that you can trust to offer you sound advice.

Working as a volunteer can help you understand the skills that are necessary for a successful career. Also, part-time employment is a great way to help you with your career decision. Chapter 3 discusses those options in more detail.

Why would volunteering or job shadowing give you insight into a career choice?

Family Expectations

When your family thinks of your future, how do they feel? Do they have certain career expectations for you?

1. From the following list, choose the expectations that you believe your family has for you. Feel free to add other expectations to your list.

   - doctor
   - minister
   - incredibly successful
   - President of the United States
   - independent
   - just like the rest of your family
   - perfect
   - able to support a family
   - star athlete
   - the next Bill Gates
   - do better than they have done
   - college graduate
   - millionaire
   - whatever makes you happy

2. In small groups, discuss the results of your family's expectations. Explain some of the reasons for your choices. Why is family so important in shaping who you are? Each team should choose one person to lead the team, one to record the discussion points, and one to report the team's results.

3. When all the groups are finished working, each group's reporters will share the group's results with the class. Include some explanations for your group members' choices.

Andy Dean Photography/Shutterstock.com

Portfolio

Real Life Focus

Where do you expect to live 10 or 15 years from now? What do you expect your life to be like?

■ What climate do you prefer? Dry or humid? Do you want changing seasons or consistent weather? Cold weather or warm weather the majority of the time?

■ Location is important. Small town or big city? Downtown, rural, or suburban living? Near mountains or hills or flat land? Near water?

■ You need to consider conveniences and services. A few are: close to transportation, cost of living, neighborhood safety, family-oriented community, available health care, and education.

Environmental influences affect your career satisfaction. What would be your preferences in the future? What are the benefits of your choices?

Values

People give many different reasons for why they chose their career. "My work helps people, and I really love that." "Someone has to do it." "It pays the bills." "Creating something makes me feel very good." "The hours I work are great."

What would mean career success for you? Being famous? Being a leader? Earning lots of money? Providing service to others? Your values influence your answers. Your **values** are the principles or qualities that are important to you. Your values are the motivation behind your goals and decisions.

You are the only one who knows your values. Only *you* can determine what motivates you to achieve success. If you make your career decision with your values in mind, you will be happier with your life and career. However, your view of success depends on not only your personal values, but also the values of your family and culture, your economic values, and your lifestyle choices. In the end, only you can define what career success means to you.

Personal and Family Values

As soon as you were born, your family began instilling its values in you. Those values are the beliefs your family considers the most important. Each family in your neighborhood has a different set of values that are meaningful to them. However, just as you and your siblings are different, the way each family member interprets those values may vary.

Elizabeth's family believes that each family member should give back to the community. Ever since she was a child, her parents' church activities included helping the community. Elizabeth worked in a kitchen serving the homeless. She collected hotel soaps and shampoos for the women's shelter.

In addition, Elizabeth's mother always volunteers at the polling place on Election Day. One of Elizabeth's earliest memories is helping her mother pass out the "I Voted Today" stickers.

Because of the values her family taught her, Elizabeth believes that helping others should be part of her life. She is exploring careers in teaching, social work, and health care.

Your family's values will help to guide you until you set your individual values. They may not be exactly the same as your family's. Gradually, you will establish your own unique values.

While creating your own values, you may use only some of your family's values, while adding new ones that are especially important to you. You may begin with your father's independence and your mother's trust in people. Add your grandmother's thriftiness, your grandfather's love of land, and your cousin's passion for justice. You may finish with the addition of new beliefs. The result? You have formed your personal value system.

Zoltan believes in his work. He prides himself on being the person whose work is unique. His creativity results in his award-winning science experiments. Zoltan's theories may seem unusual, but his use of exacting research techniques makes his science theories trustworthy.

Zoltan knows that he has his family to thank for his values. Zoltan's grandparents taught him honesty, so his research does not attempt to deceive others. His mother's dedication to perfection is part of Zoltan's character. His father's exactness guides Zoltan's scientific studies. In his work, Zoltan will not sacrifice what is right and true. He preserves the values of his family.

You are an original—a mixture of your relatives' values as well as the ones you develop for yourself.

admkaz/iStockphoto.com

Cultural Expectations—and Values

Your culture may have expectations for you. Those expectations and the culture's values may affect your work values. Your **culture** is your social, ethnic, or religious background. It may also include the community where you live. Your culture often has certain beliefs and expects certain behaviors. Answering the following questions will help you begin to identify your culture's expectations and values. As you answer the questions, think about whether or not the expectations and values can have an effect on your work values.

- Is helping others important in your culture?

- Is religion an important part of your traditions? Does your culture consider religion the most important part of your life?

- Is caring for the environment something that is important to you and your culture and community?

- Does money play an important role in your culture?

- Does your culture want its members to work and live inside your community, as the Amish culture believes?

- Will your business interactions with other cultures affect your choice of careers? The answer to this question is harder to predict, but needs consideration.

In the Navajo tribe, the elders have expectations for their youth. Nizhoni's Native American upbringing will help form her values. Regardless of whether she starts her career while living on the reservation or moves to another city, Nizhoni will have the core values that come from her tribe and family. One of those values is respect for her elders.

Cultural traditions also affect Nizhoni's career choice. Having one's photograph taken or being videotaped is discouraged in her culture. Her heritage is important to Nizhoni. Therefore, Nizhoni will avoid careers that involve working in front of a television or still camera. Nizhoni will always respect the Navajo customs and will never abandon her beliefs.

Since your culture has been part of your life since birth, you may be unaware of some of the cultural expectations that can influence your career decisions. Their influence may not be obvious. Consider issues that are important in your culture. How could those issues influence your career decision?

What are some aspects of your family's cultural heritage that might influence your career and lifestyle decisions?

Lifestyle Influences

The lifestyle you want impacts your career decisions in many ways. The following questions relate to lifestyle. The answers relate to your environment—either your social environment or your work environment. Your **social environment** includes the community where you live and work and your lifestyle choices. **Work environment** is the surroundings and conditions of your workplace.

- Do you want to work with other people or work more by yourself?

- Do you want to live in the same area as you do now? Which do you prefer: a rural, urban, or suburban environment?

- Do you want to continue your education nearby?

- Is climate important to you? Do you prefer a change of seasons? Or a climate that is consistent year round?

- How important is the outdoors in influencing your choice of career? For example, is mountain biking an important activity for you? Or are you an avid surfer or snowboarder?

- Is there a future for people in your career field in the community where you want to live?

Social Environment

Why should a climate that has a change of seasons influence a career path? To some people, climate may be an important factor in making a career choice. They seem to focus on work better when they are in the type of climate they prefer.

Climate is a vital factor for some careers because those careers require you to be near certain resources. To study marine biology, you may need to live near a coastal community, a large body of water, or an aquarium or a zoo. If you are in certain types of construction, you may want a warm climate so you can work year-round instead of just three seasons.

Other career situations allow you to choose your social environment because the work environment does not depend on location. Some careers require frequent travel, such as conference planner or network systems troubleshooter. For those careers, you may be able to live wherever you want, but you may not be home much of the time. An editor, an e-marketer, and some digital developers may work from home.

Work Environment

You may consider choosing a career because of its pay or its location. You may think, "I know why I need the job. It does not matter if I like the job because it meets the needs I have right now." But your career success depends partly on knowing the type of workplace you prefer. The atmosphere of your workplace and your interaction with other people are important work environmental factors to consider.

When you choose a career, however, you must like your choice. The career path you choose will affect every part of your life: your attitude, your life outside your work—and even the work itself. Research shows that people who enjoy their careers are more satisfied with their lives. They see a career as an important, positive part of their everyday living and their future.

Economic Importance

What kind of financial lifestyle do you want in the future? Do you want to have the latest technology, a fantastic car, and the most up-to-date fashions? Maybe you want to buy a home, marry, and raise a family. No matter what your answers, whatever lifestyle you choose involves money. To have money means you need to earn an income.

In making career decisions, you need to determine how important money is to you. In what order would you rank the following statements about your future? Which is the most important to you?

- A career that uses your passions and talents
- A career that provides you with a large income
- A career that provides you with status
- A career that allows you to pay the bills, plus have money for savings and extras

In considering economic expectations, a career will either give you intrinsic or extrinsic rewards. The careers that offer you **intrinsic rewards** have the incentives built-in. The feelings that intrinsic careers give you will be more important to you than your pay. Other careers offer **extrinsic**, or external, **rewards**. In extrinsic careers, the money and benefits mean more to you than the work you do.

For example, you may choose to work at an assisted living facility for the elderly after school and on weekends. You may chose to work there for the extrinsic rewards, thinking that with the paycheck you receive, you can buy concert tickets, music downloads, clothes, food—and maybe even save a little. On the other hand, you may choose to work at an assisted living facility for the intrinsic rewards. You receive pay for your efforts, but more importantly, you enjoy making elderly people's lives less lonely.

Web Connections

Personal values can influence your career journey. Using online quizzes, or self-assessments, helps you discover more about yourself. Access the Web Connections link for Chapter 2, and complete the activity.

Review the assessment results. Add to them any additional values that are important to you. List the five that are most essential to you. Write down the reasons for your choices.

www.cengage.com/school/iyc

Another factor influencing income is education. The Bureau of Labor Statistics (BLS) reports that the more you learn, the more you earn—and the less likely you are to be unemployed. That fact does not mean that you need to have a bachelor's degree to earn a high wage. However, you must continue to improve your education over your lifetime to earn a high wage.

In reality, the more years in education may pay off. Some employers believe that educated workers learn tasks more easily. That quality may not be true, but the perception is there. If a candidate for a job has the same skills, but has more education, that person will often be hired over one with less education. Also, a person with a college degree can enter a career that requires less education if he or she meets the other job requirements. The reverse is generally not true. If the job requires a degree plus additional skills, a person without a degree and with the additional skills will most likely not be hired.

Few people choose a career based solely on income. Remember that income is only one factor in your choice of a satisfying career.

ACTIVITY 2.2

Portfolio

Learning from Others

How much do you know about the careers of some people who influence you?

1. Interview a family member or other relative about his or her current career. Use the following questions as the guideline for your interview.

   • What do you consider to be the core values of our family? What cultural expectations does our family have?

   • How important were those values in choosing your career?

   • Describe your current career. Why did you choose it?

   • What products or services does your workplace provide? Who are the customers?

   • What are your work values? Are they similar to your personal values? Why or why not?

   • Did the economic lifestyle you hoped for have an influence on your career choice?

   • How has this career changed over the years? Does it still have the same influence on your values? What is the best part of your career? Are your personal values the reason for your answer? Why?

   • What things don't you like about your career? Do the things you mentioned go against your personal values? Why?

   • What is your advice for preparing for success in your career field—while maintaining your beliefs?

2. How did the results of the interview influence your thinking about the importance of values and career decision-making? In a class discussion, explain what you learned from the person you interviewed that will help you plan your career.

Goals

- Recognize the ways web sites can help with career information.
- List the types of social media and their uses.
- Identify different types of technology devices and how they could influence your future.

Terms

- search engine, p. 41
- URL, p. 41
- Wikipedia, p. 41
- blog, p. 41
- wiki, p. 42
- social media, p. 42
- social networking, p. 42
- microblogs, p. 43
- smartphones, p. 44
- apps, p. 44
- QR or quick response code, p. 44

Real Life Focus

The Internet is huge. In fact, 70% of people surveyed believe that the Internet has too much information. How big is it?

- North America makes up 76.2% of the world's Internet population but is only 5% of the world's population.
- The Internet currently holds 15 million terabytes of data. The human brain holds 1 to 10 terabytes. Approximately one million human brains would hold the entire Internet's information.
- Teens spend an average of 31 hours per week online. The majority of the time is spent IM'ing, on YouTube, or in chat rooms.
- World users send 247 billion emails daily. (81% are spam.)
- 20 hours of video are uploaded to YouTube every minute. (To keep that pace, Hollywood would have to release 86,000 films weekly.)

—makeuseof.com

To see second-by-second statistics on Internet use, access www.cengage.com/school/iyc and click on the appropriate link in Chapter 2.

Web Sites

The Internet is really a recent creation. In 1991, the first web page was launched. The estimate is that by the late 1990s, Internet use was growing by 100 percent per year. With all this information available, of course the Internet will influence your career information and expectations.

Research

Career exploration often begins with a recommended web site or a search. With enough information on the Internet that it would take one billion DVDs to hold, how can you tell if the information is accurate?

A **search engine**, such as Google or Bing, is a web site that gathers and lists information available on the Internet. For example, in .06 seconds, you could produce a list of 120,000,000 web sites that will give you information on *architect*. These web sites include schools, architect firms, definitions, types of architects, works by architects, and much more. How do you decide what to use?

When a search engine suggests a web site, look at the end of the **URL** (Uniform Resource Locator), the web site address, after the final dot. The end of the URL is often *.com* or *.org*. A *.com* ending means that the web site is a commercial site; the term *com* stands for *company*. Though there are no requirements for registration, nonprofit organizations usually end with *.org*.

If you are doing career research online, sites ending with *.org* will often be organizations that give information. Advertisers will not influence the site's content generally. If the site asks for donations, it is usually to purchase materials for the group. The information on this type of web site is generally more unbiased.

Wikipedia is a web site that usually is near the top of the suggested web sites when you research through a search engine. It is a free encyclopedia created by its users. Though much of Wikipedia's information is reliable, the accuracy of the entries depends on their sources. Always double-check the information with other sources.

Finding Careers

Another great source of career information is to search through online employment sites. The information on the job postings will often give you a glimpse into the education requirements, job skills, personality traits, pay, and other aspects of the career. You can find this information at a variety of sites:

- Education and training sites may post job openings for recent and past graduates. Often created by universities or nonprofit agencies, these lists will be accurate, reliable, and current.

- Commercial sites advertise not only local and regional job openings, but also national and international. The largest commercial sites are CareerBuilder and Monster.

- Government employment sites list state, national, and local job openings. The U. S. government site is America's Career InfoNet.

- Social networking sites, such as LinkedIn, offer work-related information and employment leads.

Blogs

A **blog** is an online journal written for others to read and is regularly updated. Bloggers encourage readers to discuss or comment on the blog subject matter. Though some blogs are more like the writer's diary, some bloggers write about specific topics. You can find blogs on a particular career through a search engine. However, remember that the blog is just one person's opinion. Always check the truthfulness of the information in a blog.

What are wikis? How can they help your future?

A **wiki** is a web site that users can edit. A person or a group will create a wiki and invite others to join. For example, many teachers will have a wiki for a class, student organization, or subject. The members of the class are the users; other users need invitations to join. Wikis generally have excellent user management and security. Whether you write or post a comment on a wiki or blog, remember that all users can read what you write. Once you submit a post, you usually cannot delete it.

Social Media

Social media uses web-based technology for communication. A social media web site offers interaction through electronic comments and discussions. Types of social media include collaboration as with a wiki, multimedia as with YouTube and Picasa, review sites as with Yelp, and entertainment as with Second Life.

Social Networking

Social networking sites allow users to build a profile and connect with others. Depending on the type of the site, you can share pictures, videos, thoughts, and plans with friends or others who share your interests. However, when you communicate on a social networking web site, you are also sharing with the world. Even with the privacy settings on, your page may have a wider audience than you think. Watch the language you use online. Think before you post photos. Coaches, teachers, relatives, employers, college admissions, and even police officers may view your page. The recommendation is that you should not post anything that you are not comfortable with others seeing.

How does social networking influence your career choice? Employees often search social networking pages of potential employees. Many college admissions officers do also. Students, who have posted inappropriate photos and information such as underage drinking, too much partying, or swearing, have been denied a job or admission because of such postings. Even if you delete the photos, most search engines can still retrieve them.

Some of the more popular social networking sites are:

- **Facebook.** There are over a half billion Facebook users worldwide. Limit your Facebook friends to your close friends and family. Make sure you know someone before you accept his or her friend request. Facebook also has "fan" pages for different businesses, events, causes, and celebrities. Those pages can give you excellent career-related information, though it may not all be accurate or unbiased.

- **Multimedia sites.** YouTube is the primary site to upload video. MySpace is the most used music-sharing site. Musicians can promote themselves on both sites. Artists and animators also use YouTube to share their work. Users can comment on and discuss reactions to posts on multimedia sites.

- **LinkedIn.** As mentioned previously, LinkedIn is a business-oriented social networking site. Your LinkedIn page can include work-related discussions, employment information, recommendations, and your business profile, which is similar to a brief resume. You can invite others to "link" to your page. LinkedIn is a great resource to build your career network, allowing you to build a network of people in a career that interests you, including possible mentors.

Even though you may think that only your friends can see your page and postings, never give out personal information on a social networking site. Information like addresses, phone numbers, and financial and personal information and numbers are private. Social networking sites can be great resources for you as you investigate careers. Be sure to project a professional image wherever you go online.

Communication

Some sites on the Internet are purely for communicating. These sites may stand alone or be a feature of a social networking site.

- A chat room is a web site where people discuss a specific topic and comment on others' messages. You may be part of a chat room that discusses a video game, a type of career, a celebrity, and so forth. The site posts the comments in real time; however, generally all comments stay on the site until the discussion is closed.

- **Microblogs** are blogs limited to a certain number of characters, including spaces. Twitter is the most popular microblog. The site limits users to 140 characters per message, so they must be brief and to the point. Twitter accounts can be open; that is, any user may "follow" a Twitter account. Open accounts tend to be celebrities and companies. The average Twitter user has a private account.

Because the communication is over the Internet, you cannot be sure that the person you are talking with electronically is really the person he or she claims to be. Trust your instincts. If someone makes you uncomfortable, inform an adult. Suspicions have a way of being right.

Technology Devices

The ways that you access information online varies greatly. To add to the confusion, technology devices upgrade regularly—almost monthly it seems. These devices give you access to many online applications, including research, news, the Internet, music, photos, and email.

The influence of technology can be very positive. Remembering the Golden Rule helps. Treat others the way you want to be treated. The manners and respect your families taught you since you were a child need to be applied as you use the latest technology. Never use technology to bully or harass others. It could be embarrassing, unsafe, or even illegal.

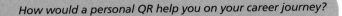

How would a personal QR help you on your career journey?

OBJECT 3 – CODE 0904983475

franckreporter/iStockphoto.com

Smartphones

Mobile phones that have capabilities beyond communication, photos, and video are **smartphones**. Application programs, also known as **apps**, are smartphone software shortcuts to assist with business or entertainment. One app that is very helpful in research is the **QR or quick response code**. It is a square bar code that automatically gives you information and/or links you to a web site's URL. You can even create your own QR codes for linking your resume or college application, as well as for other uses.

Smartphones allow you to be creative. You can take photos and videos and instantly share them on the Web. However, you must think about your privacy and of others' confidentiality before you post. The best solution is to capture the media and then check with an adult before posting. It is much easier to think about it first rather than do damage control later.

Technology's Influence

Think about how you use technology. You are responsible for your actions whether in person or using technology. Privacy is important—not only yours, but also your friends'.

Future employers and colleges can find information about you online the same way you research information. If someone asks you for information or a photo, remember that with technology, that information—even text messages and IMs—never goes away. It remains online, in the computer, or with the Internet or phone provider forever.

Consider

How do you feel about technology? Are you an early user, someone who tries new technology as soon as you can? Or do you wait until many of your friends have new technology before you try it? Maybe you are not a fan of technology at all and use it only when you absolutely need it?

Career Media

You can use social networking sites for more than communicating with family and friends. Companies, organizations, and causes have fan pages. Why not careers?

1. In small groups, choose a career page that you would like to feature on a site like Facebook or YouTube. Use these questions to get you started.

   - What content would you include on the wall or in the video?

   - What photo albums or video would you include?

   - What groups would the career link to or sponsor?

2. If you are choosing a site such as Facebook, create a plan for your site.

3. If you are creating a video, plan a storyboard or plot outline to organize your project.

4. Your teacher will give you specific information as to the format for either project.

5. When all the groups are finished working, share the projects with the class.

Chapter Summary

2.1 People

- After determining who or what influences will affect career decision making, a person can explore the advice and experiences that will make an impact.

- Family members have the strongest influence on career decisions. School staff, such as teachers, coaches, and counselors, are also important. Friends' advice influences career decisions as well.

- Community groups such as businesses and other organizations may have an influence on career decisions. Especially important are volunteer and work experiences.

2.2 Values

- Values are the qualities that are important to a person. They are the motivation behind goals set and decisions made for the future.

- The values from one's family will influence career choice and will affect a person's personal value system. One's cultural heritage may also create expectations that influence work and career.

- The lifestyle one chooses for the future will influence career decisions. Economic values and work and social environment are important to consider.

2.3 Web Influences

- A wealth of career information is available online. One can research careers and even communicate with people working in fields of interest.

- Social media can influence not only one's career decision but also education and job search.

- The amount of technology is increasing rapidly, as are the number and upgrades of devices used for communication and research. Above all, one should remember that whatever one communicates through technology is permanent.

Chapter Assessment

Vocabulary Builder

Match each statement with the term that best defines it.

1. Sites that allow users to build a profile and connect with others
2. External rewards
3. Rewards with incentives built in
4. An online journal written for others to read and is regularly updated
5. The power of someone or something that affects you directly or indirectly
6. A web site that is a free encyclopedia created by its users
7. Web site that created by a person or group that users can edit
8. The community where you live and work, along with your lifestyle choices
9. The surroundings and conditions of your workplace
10. A web site that gathers and lists information available on the Internet
11. A blog limited to a certain number of characters
12. Software shortcuts to assist with business or entertainment
13. A type of mobile phone that has capabilities beyond communication, photos, and video
14. The web site address
15. A type of web site that offers interaction through electronic comments and discussions
16. A person who supports you through listening and advising
17. Your social, ethnic, and religious background influences that have certain beliefs and behaviors
18. Influences that may have a greater effect on your behavior and decisions
19. A square bar code that automatically gives you information and/or links you to a web site's URL
20. Principles and qualities important to you

a. apps
b. blog
c. culture
d. extrinsic rewards
e. influence
f. intrinsic rewards
g. mentor
h. microblog
i. motivation
j. QR/quick response code
k. search engine
l. smartphone
m. social environment
n. social media
o. social networking
p. URL
q. values
r. wiki
s. Wikipedia
t. work environment

Review What You Have Learned

21. Why does influence have so much effect on your *P*A*T*H to Success?*
22. How do your parents and family members have an influence on your career success?
23. What effect do school personnel, such as teachers, coaches, and counselors, have on your career decision?
24. What do your classes have to do with your career choice?
25. How can the community help with your career decisions?

26. How do your values, including those of your family, influence your future career?

27. Cultural expectations can affect career decisions. Give an example.

28. Why would your lifestyle expectations for the future affect your career choice?

29. What are some of ways that web sites can assist in career decision making?

30. Social networking and communicating online can have positive and negative effects on your future. Give an example of each type of effect.

31. What impact do technology devices have on your future?

Case Challenges

After reading each situation below, analyze each situation. What advice would you give to the person involved?

- What is the person's motivation in the situation?
- What personal values might motivate the career choice?
- What is the work environment choice?
- What other influences play a role in the case?

32. Crisanto received his associate degree as a registered nurse (RN) from the local community college. He enjoys many outdoor activities, including biking and running, so he prefers working the flexible hours of a homecare nurse. Although Crisanto enjoys nursing, the hours for home-based nursing care are not always steady. Sometimes the pay does not cover his expenses.

    Crisanto's friend told him about job openings at the post office. So Crisanto took the test, passed it, and became a letter carrier. He now works regular hours. However, he wonders if he made the right decision. He misses medicine and his contact with patients.

    a. Should Crisanto go back to school to become a surgical nurse, a skilled position with regular hours?
    b. Should he take a job at a hospital with regular, but less flexible hours?
    c. Should he continue his job as a letter carrier?

33. Charles teaches social studies and enjoys working with students. His school and his students know that Charles is a first-rate teacher. Violet, Charles's wife, is a principal in a neighboring high school. She works long hours, including many evenings and Saturdays.

    Charles and Violet's first baby is due in two months. Both parents believe that one of them should stay home with the new baby while the other parent works. Both Charles and Violet can take three months off from their jobs when the baby is born.

    a. Who in this family should stay home, and who should work?
    b. Should Violet return to her job as a principal?
    c. Should they find a child care provider for their baby?

Make Academic Connections

34. SOCIAL STUDIES Most organizations have a technology policy. It gives the policies or rules that employees must follow when using the organization's technology, including the Internet. Visit or write a letter to a business in your local community, asking for a copy of its employee technology policy. You will use the policy in a class discussion to compare organizations' technology policy with your school's policy provided by your teacher.

35. TECHNOLOGY Respectful, ethical behavior is very important when you interact with people—in person and on the Internet. Begin to build a web site using the tools your instructor provides. On the web site, list five values or character traits that are important for a good employee in any career. To find suggestions for character traits and their definitions, access www.cengage.com/school/iyc and click on the appropriate link in Chapter 2.

Portfolio

Workplace Connection

Discovering a career that includes the positive influences of people and surroundings is important. Create an image of the influences of your family and culture.

36. Write a list of the ways your family and your culture influence your future career.

Portfolio

37. Find images and words that represent the influences you listed. Using the materials your teacher provides, create a collage. Choosing the images and words are important. However, do not worry about being artistic.

38. Display your collage in your classroom. Answer the following questions about the class's collages. Discuss the results as a class.
- What are the similar influences in others' collages?
- What made your collage unique?

Blogging: Setting the Boundaries

Beginning with Chapter 3, you will write blog entries about your career planning process. Before starting the writing, your class must create a Blog Policy Guide (BlogPG).

Blog

   In small groups, consider the following while you create suggestions for the BlogPG.

1. What responsibilities do you have as the blog's author?

2. What is the goal of the blog?

3. Who might cause problems if or when the blog entry is made public?

4. What are the rules of grammar, spelling, and plagiarism?

5. You are writing about your career plans. What is the policy concerning personal information?

Share your group's list with the class. As a class, vote on which policies will become the BlogPG.

ACTIVITY 3.1

Learning from Others

Knowing more in-depth about a career will help you make a more informed career decision.

Contact the person you interviewed for Activity 1.2—the person in a career that interests you. If possible, observe that person at work for at least two hours. In addition, interview the person by asking the following questions:

- What does your department do for the organization?
- What are your duties and responsibilities?
- What type of training do you have? What will I need to work in this career?
- What were your favorite courses in school? Did they help you choose your career?

- What extracurricular and/or organized activities outside of school did you enjoy the most? Did they help you choose your career? Explain.
- How does your career make you feel satisfied? Why?
- What are some misunderstandings about your career?
- Describe a typical day in your career.

Do you see yourself working in this particular career? Explain why or why not. Then discuss the results in small groups. Share the groups' experiences with the class.

Photodisc/Jupiter Images

Learning about Yourself

Goals

- Recognize how assessments can help your career journey focus.
- Describe what is a self-assessment.
- Identify types of formal assessments, and explain how to use the results.

Terms

- assessments, p. 55
- self-assessments, p. 56
- formal assessments, p. 56
- interest inventories, p. 57
- skills assessments, p. 57
- personality assessment, p. 58
- work values, p. 59

Real Life Focus

Remember the *P*A*T*H to Success* in Chapter 1?

Passion, Attitude, Talents, and Heart

Draw an outline of your outstretched hand on a piece of paper. Next, write on each finger:

- Your gifts on the thumb
- Your fascinations on the index finger
- Your personality on the middle finger
- Your values on the ring finger
- Your experience (activities, jobs) on the little finger

How did what you wrote match your *P*A*T*H to Success?* Keep the drawing in your portfolio. Whenever you think of something else, add it to your drawing.

Portfolio

Assessments

Assessments—aren't those types of tests? You may be thinking, "Why should I take a test to find what kind of person I am? I want just to think about it. I can just write down facts about myself. That would be my assessment. Wouldn't thinking answer all of my questions?"

However, if *thinking* alone could tell who you are and identify your career path, everyone would be happy in his or her career. But finding a career path requires more than just thinking. By using your own qualities to guide you on your *P*A*T*H to Success*, you can find a satisfying career field.

Assessments are a way of collecting and evaluating information for measurement purposes. When you take an assessment or test in social studies, your teacher is measuring how much you have learned. When you complete a career assessment, the results provide information that will help you choose a career based on your unique talents and passions. If you use the results in your career choice, hopefully you will not look back and dream about what you could have done in your life. You will already be doing it.

Magazines, web sites, and counselors' offices are full of quizzes, which are assessments. You can take an assessment to find out if you are color-blind. You can answer questions to see if you are a bad driver. You can even take a test to find out what your dreams mean. What do you think the basis is for informal assessments?

Career assessments focus on what makes you a unique person. The questions center on the activities you like, your natural talents and abilities, the features of your personality, and the qualities you value in a workplace. Career assessments help you investigate, identify, and recognize your interests, personality traits, abilities, values, attitudes, and individual preferences. Analyzing the results can help you set your career and life goals. Once you have set goals, you can identify the steps needed to take action for your career journey. Then you use the results to discover your *Internal Career Design*.

Postponing these decisions will only delay your *P*A*T*H to Success*. You want your career to be a part of you. You want your career to allow you to follow your passions. The challenge is how to use the results. Learning about yourself is one of the first steps toward finding your ideal career.

Taking assessments will help you discover your career path. The pieces of your *Internal Career Design* will eventually fall into place, and you will understand why your career journey makes sense for you.

Portfolio

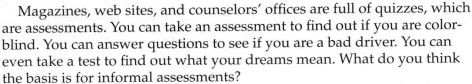

Web Connections

Exploring your personality traits and work values is part of the career planning process. Evaluating yourself will help you understand yourself better.

Access the Web Connections link for Chapter 3. Complete at least one of the Personality Assessments.

Write or draw the major personality-type results on the upper right section of the Coat of Arms diagram in Activity 3.2.

Next, take one of the Work Values quizzes. In the lower right section of the Coat of Arms, write or draw the top one or two work types or values. Share your ideas with the class.

www.cengage.com/school/iyc

Self-Assessments

The questions you answer in a self-assessment can help you begin to learn more about yourself. **Self-assessments** base the results on what you think of yourself. You generally complete this type of assessment in more of an informal setting with no time limits. A self-assessment may be a list of questions or a checklist. The knowledge you gain from a career self-assessment can be a good foundation for your career plan.

If you searched the Internet for career assessments, you would find millions of them. The best career self-assessments are often on government or college web sites. But even college self-assessments may be biased, leading you to career majors that particular school wants to market. Before you take the time to complete a self-assessment, check with your teacher about the assessment's reliability.

Formal Assessments

Psychologists and career counselors research careers and career skills to create **formal assessments**. The companies often charge a fee for the assessment and/or the scoring if your school does not have a site license. The results are usually more in-depth than self-assessment results.

You can use formal assessments for several purposes. For example, they can help you with career planning decisions. Colleges and universities may use them for admissions to assist in matching you with suitable majors. Employers may use them to make hiring decisions. Interests, skills, personality, and work values are four categories of formal assessments that will help you discover your *Internal Career Design*.

Interest Inventories

What do you like to do? Which activity would you pick? **Interest inventories** are designed to help you relate your interests to career clusters.

How can your passion, such as sports, become a realistic career choice?

> *All Bob ever wanted to do was to play sports. Basketball was his favorite. Whenever possible, he was playing basketball at the school down the street or at a neighborhood basketball court. He read every sports magazine he could find.*
>
> *To no one's surprise, Bob's interest inventory revealed his love for sports. It also showed an interest for speaking in public. However, Bob did not know how to tie those two interests to a career. In thinking about college, he decided to major in education until his counselor saw the university had a new major—sports information. Bob realized that a career in that area would enable him to satisfy both of his interests.*
>
> *Today Bob heads the television production studio for his city's community college and broadcasts sports and other events. He has found a career that continues his childhood love of sports, his life's passion.*

In an interest inventory, you are selecting what you prefer to do. The results often provide some career cluster suggestions or career choices that match your interests. In Chapter 5, you will use interest inventory information to discover your *Internal Career Design*. However, interests cannot be the only way to choose a career.

Skills Assessments

Do you have the necessary talents to succeed in a career? That should be the next question. Yes, when you begin your education and training for your chosen career field, you will master specific skills. But do you have the foundation, the ability to master the future skills? **Skills assessments** measure how well you perform specific tasks now and whether you can achieve certain skills in the future.

Ranu had been thinking about a career as a civil engineer. To help him in his decision, he decided to take a skills assessment to learn if he had the natural talents for that career.

However, Ranu's test results showed that his math ability was not high enough for a career in engineering. In fact, his results showed that Ranu had higher art and verbal skills than math skills. He decided to investigate careers in graphic design. That career would use his interest in building and creating, but not depend so much on his math ability.

By using skills assessment results, you can avoid making a career decision that would not be a good fit.

Personality Assessments

Do you like planning every step of a solution to a problem? Knowing the solution before it happens? Or do you like to start doing a task, working each step of the problem on the way to the solution? Do you like to be around people—does their energy make you enthusiastic? Or do you like to make decisions alone? Your answers to those questions are part of your personality. A **personality assessment** reveals the behavior style that makes you unique.

The results of a personality assessment reveal the personal qualities that best describe you. The results often suggest your preferences for various social and private situations. In addition, you may find out the type of work environment that fits your personality traits.

Knowing your character or personality can help you to choose a specific career within a career cluster. For example, if you want to work in a health-related field, you can become a nurse practitioner, where you interact with many people, or a biotechnologist, where you will work alone in a laboratory much of the time.

Originally, counselors created personality assessments to discover potential problem employees. Today, these assessments can help match a person's personality traits to those of top employers in certain career areas. Employers may use the results before hiring to assess an applicant's likely behavior. The results can help determine how a potential employee will interact with other team members in the workplace.

A personality assessment can help you understand whether you will be successful in a particular career. The qualities measured include how practical you are, how achievement-oriented you are, how much variety you need, how decisive you are, how orderly you are, and so on.

Consider

What are some activities you enjoy that match your personality? How could these personality traits help you in a career?

Work Values

What are the reasons a person wants to work? Why does someone choose a certain career? Is it for a certain income, status, respect from others, independence, service to others, or some other reason? **Work values** are the aspects about a career and the workplace that are important to you. The reasons how and why a person works depend on the individual. Those traits represent a person's work values. Assessing work values helps you discover why you want to work. They also help you find characteristics of careers that appeal to you.

Jeri loved books. With the encouragement of her primary school teachers, she became passionate about reading. She knew she had to be part of a career that involved books.

When Jeri took an interest assessment, the results supported her love of books. She spent even more time with books when she began her part-time job at the branch library. Should she get a degree in library science? That degree involved at least six years of college.

To help direct her career path, Jeri took a work values assessment. The assessment showed that a position in a library would not be a good fit for Jeri. She needed independence in her career. Jeri also needed creativity and interaction with people.

Jeri knew that because of her need for independence and her love of books, her ultimate career goal was to own a bookstore some day. She decided to work for a local bookstore on weekends to gain experience and to explore the retail book business. Through her work at the bookstore, Jeri realized that she needed to take courses in display design, accounting, marketing, and business management, especially in small business ownership.

How can you discover which work values are important to you?

Digital Vision/Jupiter Images

Jeri's assessment results and her education plan helped her develop her career plan. As part of a college course, she wrote a business plan to secure financial backing for her bookstore. In the future, Jeri may open a bookstore in town or start one online. Whatever she chooses, Jeri is in charge of her career. She is looking forward to being surrounded by books, her passion.

Formal Assessment Results

Formal assessments are useful. They measure skills and interests and give you insight into yourself. However, formal assessments *are only the beginning* of your search for the career for you. What you do with the assessment results is most important.

Keep the following ideas in mind when using formal assessment results:

■ ***Different ways of assessing appeal to different types of people.*** Assessments ask similar questions in different ways and request different types of answers. One assessment may force your choice, such as deciding between managing a sports team, collecting coins, and wiring a lamp. None of the choices may appeal to you, but your answer will reveal qualities about you. Another way of questioning may ask you how you would react in a particular situation. You may find that you like one way of asking questions over another.

■ ***Use the results of assessments as suggestions for new ideas.*** No single assessment is completely accurate. Assessments reflect your responses. The assessment results may change as you add to your experiences. Do not think of the results as the only truth. Instead, use them as a step in analyzing your career choice.

■ ***Different assessments give different results.*** Some people may like a certain skills assessment. Just because an assessment is right for your best friend does not mean it is the best one for you. If you do not like one assessment, try another one. You may get strange results depending on your attitude about a certain assessment.

■ ***You are unique.*** Because assessments tend to categorize people into types, you may believe you are only one of a group. Although others may have similar traits, you are unique in your combination of talents and passions. Just because an assessment says nursing is a career for you, that does not mean that all nursing positions are the same. A pediatric nurse's career is far different from an emergency room nurse's career.

■ ***Taking more than one assessment will give you a more complete picture of yourself.*** Personality, interest, ability, and work value assessments are all different. Taking all types of the formal assessments, and adding informal assessment results, will help you discover your *Internal Career Design* more accurately.

■ ***Remember that you know more about yourself than any assessment can tell you.*** If assessment results point you toward being a landscape architect but you have grass allergies, then you should avoid that career path. Exploring a career as an outdoorscape designer might be an alternative. Perhaps your love of solving complex problems leads you to the career area of chemical engineering. However, you would much rather work outdoors. In that case, consider another type of engineering, such as civil engineering, that would regularly take you to work sites.

Career FACT

When teens were surveyed about what they wanted most from a career, the results were

- Doing work they enjoy
- Having a happy family
- Earning a college degree

Above all, they were looking forward to the future. However, they are not sure that adults will leave the future in "good shape."

—Morrison Institute for Public Policy, Arizona State University

■ *The assessment does not tell you everything.* Assessment results give you much to think about, but they do not determine your career path by themselves. You should use the results along with other activities to help you discover your *Internal Career Design*.

Assessments cannot make your decisions for you. They are only tools that will help you identify your talents and interests. They can confirm what you believe to be your strengths and your passions. They can reassure you that the career plan you have started on is the right track. Assessment results are resources for your *P*A*T*H to Success*. Include them in your Career Portfolio. You will use them to help you create your *Internal Career Design*.

Portfolio

Coat of Arms

A Coat of Arms tells the story of a person's individuality. In this activity, you will make the base of your Coat of Arms as you fill in your interests and abilities. You will finish the Coat of Arms in the Web Connection on page 56. Access the Coat of Arms diagram at www.cengage.com/school/iyc, Chapter 3.

1. In the bottom left section of the Coat of Arms, write or draw your passions—the interests most important to you. Think not only of your school interests, but also what makes you happy outside of school, including your family and friends.

2. In the upper left section, write or draw your talents, the skills you believe you do well.

Granite/Shutterstock.com

Informal Assessments

Goals

- Describe how career events can help you with your career planning.
- Explain exploring careers through discussions and conversation.
- Discuss how extended experiences are ways to "try out" careers.

Terms

- informal assessment, p. 62
- career fair, p. 63
- career days, p. 63
- informational interview, p. 64
- job shadowing, p. 66
- service learning, p. 67

Portfolio

Real Life Focus

Knowing your interests and abilities will help you create your *P*A*T*H to Success*. However, realizing the importance of your interests and abilities will help you understand what careers within a career cluster you should explore.

In the following list of skills, decide which are:

> *Very Important to Me*
> *Somewhat Important to Me*
> *Not Important to Me*

- Working with ideas
- Working with numbers
- Doing creative work
- Making decisions
- Evaluating information

The self-assessment's results are work values. You can use them to help you determine which informal assessment types are best for your further career exploration.

With formal assessments, you answer questions on a computer or sometimes with paper and pencil. **Informal assessment** experiences are activities in which you talk to someone in a career or observe or assist someone working in a career. The informal experience may be an event or a long-term experience.

Shiva always wanted to become a veterinarian. She loved puppies and kittens, especially her dog, Pookie. When Shiva had the opportunity to spend a day observing her vet, Dr. Sternos, she was excited.

What Shiva did not realize in her vision of a veterinarian career was that animals are not always puppies and kittens—or even always healthy. After seeing surgeries, skin rashes, and euthanasia procedures performed on both small and large animals, Shiva changed her mind about her career choice. She decided she would explore the world of animal training or grooming rather than work with sick animals.

Informal assessment activities give you insight into specific career areas. Informal assessments such as career events, informational interviews, job shadowing, internships, and service learning can help you:

- Learn firsthand about types of jobs in a career field and the job requirements.

- Eliminate possible careers. You will learn early on that a career is not a match for you. Eliminating a possibly poor career choice is valuable.

- Become familiar with the positive and negative aspects of the workplace.

- Create your *Internal Career Design*.

Career Events

Using your assessment results, try attending a career event. Career events will help you with your career decision-making.

Career Fair

A **career fair** is an opportunity to talk with many businesses about many careers at one time. Occasionally, career fairs are open only to one career cluster, such as a health careers fair. Often your school will host the career fair in a large room with tables set up for representatives from various businesses and careers. Community organizations also sometimes host career or job fairs.

The advantage of a career fair is that you can learn about many careers at one time and make contacts for job shadowing or a part-time job. A major disadvantage is that some students simply pick up printed materials and do not interact with the businesspeople attending . Often your teacher will give you interview questions to ask several of the career fair participants.

Career Day

You can listen to, interact with, and ask questions of people in careers that interest you at organized **career days.** In one type of career day, you move from room to room to hear several speakers. Your interest assessment results usually determine your schedule for this type of career day. You may hear speakers talk about careers that may not be your top choices, but generally, you are scheduled to hear at least one speaker that interests you.

Professional groups, such as construction or nursing associations, organize another other type of career day. Again, you go to this type of career day because that career area interests you. One example is Construction Career Days held in Cincinnati and Houston. In each city, approximately 3,000 students attend these annual half-day events.

An advantage of either type of career day is that you can hear about the career in-depth, ask questions, and have more time to make connections with the career speakers. Some students set up job shadowing or informational interviews with speakers they meet.

iodrakon/Shutterstock.com

What can I learn about careers at an event such as a career fair?

Discussions and Conversations

Meeting and talking to people who are in career fields you are considering can help confirm your career decisions.

Informational Interviews

How better to learn about a career than by talking to a person who is working in it? You will have a *human moment*, getting honest information from face-to-face contact. The conversation is an **informational interview**. The goal of an informational interview is to get facts and an understanding about a career area you are considering.

Ameera is 16. Because she is under 18, she cannot ride in a patrol car with a deputy to learn about a career in law enforcement. After all, Ameera knows that a real police career cannot be the same as on television shows. So she arranges an informational interview with Deputy Mooney to explore the career.

Real People / Real Careers

Emily Madden / *Fashion Merchandising*

Barbies, Barbies, and more Barbies! That is all Emily Madden wanted to play with as a little girl. She loved dressing them up and playing with them in her Dream House for hours. If she wasn't playing with her Barbies, she was coloring and playing with cutout dolls.

During high school, Emily got a job at an upscale consignment store. She learned about merchandising and how to run a business from the store manager. Her experience at the store helped Emily choose a career focus. Fashion Merchandising was Emily's choice because the fashion world changes constantly. According to Emily, "I chose fashion for my merchandising focus, because it is amazing how good a great outfit can make someone feel!"

In her sophomore year in college, Emily was faced with a project designed to have students create their own businesses. Emily's project idea came from her dream of one day opening her own jewelry business. She did her research by talking with women who owned and worked in jewelry stores. From this, she constructed a business plan with the realization that what began as a class project could be the opportunity to achieve her dream.

Emily Madden has been the owner of Miss Em's Fine Jewelry and Accessories for several years now. She sells at conferences and shows, online, and at-home parties. Why jewelry? As Emily enthusiastically says, "Anyone of any size and age can have FABULOUS jewelry. It's amazing how jewelry can impact an outfit!"

For more information about:

* fashion merchandising
* merchandising and retail careers

Access **www.cengage.com/school/iyc** and click on the appropriate links in Chapter 3.

Source: *Personal Interview,* May 2011

Photo courtesy of Emily Madden

You are in charge of the informational interview. You get to direct the questions. Interviewing an average employee, rather than upper-level management, will give you more insight into the actual workday.

In preparation for the interview, send some of your questions to the person you are interviewing. The advance notice might help him or her prepare answers for questions that may be unfamiliar or that require research.

Other Conversations

Exploring through conversations is also done in other ways. Lunch with the Pros is an excellent example. This is a series of career cluster events where a panel of employees representing a variety of careers in one cluster talk and answer questions while the students eat lunch. Students attend the lunch based on their interest inventory results. For example, a Lunch with the Pros for health careers might include an emergency room nurse, a licensed massage therapist, a chiropractor, an x-ray technician, and a personal trainer.

Social networking online also provides opportunities to discuss details of a career with organizations or individuals. Before interacting on a social media site or commenting on a blog, however, have your family or your teacher check to see if the site will provide accurate knowledge and if the site is appropriate for students.

Extended Experiences

Experiences that are longer than a class period or an interview are valuable. They give you a more in-depth perspective than a brief conversation can provide.

How do you find people who can offer extended experiences in specific career areas that interest you? First, consider relatives and family friends. They are probably the easiest people for you to arrange an appointment with. If that option does not fit your career needs, talk to your counselor or a teacher of classes related to the career you want to learn more about. They may not be able to provide specific names of people, but they can probably give you the names of companies you can contact to arrange a visit.

Ask your teacher for tips on manners or business etiquette in the workplace. Also, learn some of the details of the workplace surroundings ahead of time. Both will help you be more comfortable and make a good impression during your extended experience.

Some extended experiences may require additional preparation or equipment. For example, being in a doctor's office may require you to complete an orientation on patient confidentiality and working around disease-causing germs. You may also need to wear special clothing, especially at a construction site, an office, or manufacturing plant.

Job Shadowing

Observing a worker and asking questions will help you learn much more about a career area. Sometimes an informational interview is not enough. **Job shadowing** is an informal assessment activity where you spend several hours observing a worker at the job location. The experience may take from two to six hours. Seeing someone actually working in a career often helps you confirm or remove a career field as a choice for your future.

Three-year-old Isaiah found several tools from the family toolbox on the kitchen table. He started playing with real tools, instead of the plastic ones he had in his play box. Under his father's supervision, Isaiah copied what he had seen his father do.

Isaiah's love of tools grew into a love of electricity. He began rewiring small appliances and lamps for his family and neighbors. Recently he started a part-time job putting together stereo systems for the local appliance store. Isaiah knew that being an electrician was the career for him. Plus, his good grades in science and math confirmed his decision.

For Isaiah, the best way to become an electrician was to take career and technical courses at the regional career center while in high school. Then he would continue classes, as well as work with local electrical workers to become a journeyman. With at least four years of training ahead of him, Isaiah realized he must be sure that his career choice was the right one.

Isaiah talked about his situation with his counselor and his physics teacher. He took their advice and made appointments to job shadow both a residential electrician and a commercial electrician each for one day. The job shadowing experiences confirmed Isaiah's career decision of becoming a residential electrician.

Sometimes job shadowing is part of your class curriculum or part of a special event such as "Take Our Daughters and Sons to Work Day" on the fourth Thursday in April or "Groundhog Shadowing Day" on February 2. These events provide good opportunities for career exploration.

Share the results of job shadowing in small groups or with your class. Hearing others' experiences will teach you about several career fields and the working world in general. Some career opportunities are available in several types of workplaces. For example, hospitals, insurance companies, government offices, and schools all need accountants, web site designers, and public relations personnel. By listening to others' experiences, you will understand that though the career is the same, the workplace is very different. You will become more aware of which type of work environment is right for you. This information can become a vital part of your career planning.

How can job shadowing help you confirm a career choice?

auremar/Shutterstock.com

Service Learning

Service learning is a program for you to volunteer your time to help the community. Though service learning is often a graduation and/or course requirement or part of a club activity, it is also a way to learn more about career fields that interest you.

When choosing a service learning project, focus using your volunteering experience to build skills you will need in the workplace, to help determine the focus of your career path, and to help discover your work values.

Habitat for Humanity is an organization that helps low-income families build their own homes. During spring break, Tomas's church group helped with a Habitat for Humanity project in a neighboring state. Before leaving on the trip, Tomas learned that, through his construction work, he could earn credit for the service learning hours required by his school.

As Tomas worked on a team with Habitat, he learned to communicate more directly with different types of people. He experienced the rewards of working for others. What he learned about himself and others helped him gain a greater understanding of some of his work values. His service learning experience did not just benefit the family whose new home he built. It benefitted Tomas as well.

While you give of your time and talents in a service learning experience, you also learn from the people you serve. The experiences often involve a mutual give-and-take. Blog your service learning projects. They can easily become part of your Career Portfolio, helping you create your *Internal Career Design*.

Jill's Literary Club advisor assigned her to work with residents at Beecher's Assisted Living facility. Reluctantly, Jill went on her assignment, though she knew she did not want to work with senior citizens. She was sure that writing their stories would be so boring.

Jill's task was to interview and transcribe oral histories of the residents. Through her interviews, she learned much about the history of the eras the seniors described, plus much local history. More importantly, she learned about the residents' rich experiences—and actually liked talking with them.

Jill had always known writing would be part of her career. Because of her service learning experience, she now knows that she also wants to work with senior citizens in the future.

"Service is the rent we pay for living," said Marian Wright-Edelman, founder of the Children's Defense Fund.

Why would a part-time job help in choosing my career?

Other Long-term Experiences

Internships, co-op experiences, and part-time jobs are other types of long-term career exploration experiences. These types of extended experiences offer practical knowledge about specific careers. They are ways to test careers before making a decision.

Internships, co-ops, and jobs offer you a longer time to experience a career. Many interns are volunteers; some are paid. Co-op positions and jobs are paid positions. They all provide work experience that may lead to a job or even entry into a career.

> As part of Ruby's school's job-shadowing day, her counselor assigned her to work in the Water Works office. The activities of the office and its work around the community fascinated her. Because Ruby showed such an interest with her questions, the Water Works office offered Ruby an internship. Though the internship was a nonpaid position, it allowed Ruby to explore careers in civil service.
>
> Ruby now has a strong interest in pursuing a government career, because of her study of city government and planning. Ruby told her class, "You need to experience the work for yourself. If you don't, how do you know you should train for that career? You might not even like it."

After an extended career experience, you may decide not to pursue the career. Not choosing a career area is as important as having the experience support your career choice. Your career decisions will affect much of your future. Learn early whether a specific career is right—or wrong—for you.

Leadership

Be a Community Leader

As a team member, you have the power to increase your information by including ideas from other team members.

1. In small groups, each group member will contribute the name of an organization for a service learning experience and why he or she chose it. The groups may be community organizations, including religious groups, schools, or nonprofit organizations. For each idea, write the reason for using the organization.

2. Answer the following questions about each team member's suggestion.

   - What project will you do with the organization? Describe it.

   - How will your activity benefit the organization?

   - How will the activity help you with your career exploration?

Portfolio

3. When all the groups are finished working, reporters will share their group's results with the class. Also, include an explanation of some of the reasons behind your group's choices.

4. As a class, vote on the organizations named by the teams as the top service learning possibilities.

JBryson/iStockphoto.com

Chapter Summary

3.1 Career Development

- Career development is a process that a person follows over a period of time. Knowing the steps is important as one follows the career journey.

- In following the career development process and creating a *P*A*T*H to Success*, the *Internal Career Design* will evolve.

3.2 Learning about Yourself

- Career assessments help a person analyze the results and make lifetime decisions.

- The results of self-assessments will help one understand more through self-discovery.

- Interest inventories, skills assessments, personality assessments, and work values surveys are the types of formal assessments. They can help a person match interests, talents, personality, and values to discover his or her *Internal Career Design*.

3.3 Informal Assessments

- A career event, such as a career fair or career day, allows people to interact with individuals whose careers match their own interests.

- More in-depth discussions with those in career fields a person is considering can help confirm his/her career decisions.

- Job shadowing, service learning, and other extended informal assessments can give one knowledge and possibly experience in a specific career.

Chapter Assessment

Vocabulary Builder

Match each statement with the term that best defines it. Some terms may not be used.

1. Aspects about a career and the workplace that are important to you ○
2. An informal assessment activity where you spend several hours observing a worker at his or her workplace I
3. Measures how well you perform specific tasks now and whether you can master certain skills in the future n
4. Surveys designed to help you relate your interests to career clusters g
5. Talking to people about careers to gather facts and gain an understanding about a career area you are considering f
6. Written by psychologists and career counselors who research careers and career skills to create the tests d
7. Volunteering your time to help an organization or the community m
8. Way of collecting and evaluating data for measurement purposes a
9. The results of these tests are based on what you think of yourself k
10. An organized time that allows you to listen to and interact with people in careers that interest you b
11. The results reveal the behavior style that makes you unique j
12. Unique to you, matching your interests, abilities, personality, and work values to an ideal career field for you H
13. Activities in which you talk to someone working in a career, work in a specific career, or observe someone working in a career e
14. An event that allows you to talk with many businesses at one time c

15. Knowing yourself at the present time L

- a. assessment
- b. career day
- c. career fair
- d. formal assessment
- e. informal assessment
- f. informational interview
- g. interest inventories
- h. *Internal Career Design*
- i. job shadowing
- j. personality assessment
- k. self-assessment
- l. self-awareness
- m. service learning
- n. skills assessment
- o. work values

Review What You Have Learned

15. What are the steps in the career development process?
16. Why is creating your *Internal Career Design* important to you?
17. Name the four types of formal assessments. What is the purpose of each?
18. What should you understand when interpreting formal assessment results?
19. What is the difference between a self-assessment and a formal assessment?
20. Describe the three categories of informal assessments. How is each of them important in creating your career path?
21. What are some of the ways assessment results can help you create your *Internal Career Design*?

Case Challenges

After reading each case study, decide which type or types of assessment would help the person featured. Explain your answers.

22. Jing scheduled an informational interview with an EMS (Emergency Medical Services) technician at Sherman Hospital. After the interview, Jing sent a thank-you note to the EMS technician. As a result, the technician offered Jing a day of job shadowing with him in the ER.

    During his job shadowing, Jing was able to observe how the team members interacted with patients. He saw how teams worked with optimal speed and efficiency. But at the end of the day, Jing had mixed feelings. He had found working in the emergency room exciting, but he also was worried. Was he meant to work in a hospital? How would he know?

23. Bella wants a career where she interacts with people most of the day. Her counselor arranged two job-shadowing appointments—one with a group sales representative at a large hotel nearby and one with the front-end manager of the large local grocery. Bella found both experiences exciting, especially because she enjoyed interacting with customers. The grocery offered Bella a part-time job, but she is not sure she wants to work there. The hotel work seemed more exciting. Bella wonders which position is the type of career she would like.

24. Though he has definite goals, Lucas is torn. He loves working with wood. Both his father and uncle are carpenters, and he likes working with them on the weekends. His grades are excellent, but he does not believe he needs education after graduation, or even additional training. On the other hand, Lucas's counselor is encouraging him to take more academic courses. She is urging him to get a bachelor's degree. With his grades, she says Lucas "would be wasting his brain."

Make Academic Connections

25. **LANGUAGE ARTS** After completing Activity 3.1, write a Trip Report memo of your visit. Use an accurate memo heading. This includes:

    TO: memo recipient (your teacher)
    FROM: author of memo (you)
    DATE: date you wrote the memo
    RE: subject of the memo

Paragraph 1—Write a short introductory paragraph that states the purpose of your trip and describes the reasons for the trip.

Paragraph 2—Summarize your trip. Focus on the main points of your trip. If it was a fact-finding trip, describe your findings.

Paragraph 3—Describe the results of your trip. Make sure your results focus on the purpose you gave for your visit in paragraph 1.

26. MATH Ask permission of a restaurant or retail store manager to observe one worker for an hour. If you choose a restaurant, observe during mealtime. Record each task the employee does and the amount of time for each task on a table similar to the one below. Also include time the employee spends not working. Then calculate the percentage of time for each type of task. What conclusions can you make?

Task	Minutes on Task	Percentage of Hour Spent on Task
Wiping tables	5	8%

Workplace Connection

Your personal qualities and skills will make you a good worker. However, what are the qualities needed for careers that interest you? Use the Web Connection results on page 56 to complete the activity.

Portfolio

27. Write the work values from the Web Connection.

- Choose your strongest three qualities.
- For each quality, give an example that shows you have this quality. Be specific.

28. Write the personality results from the Web Connection. List three activities you like to do after school.

- Choose your three strongest personality traits.
- For each trait, give an example that shows you have this trait.

29. List two careers that you are interested in investigating.

- List at least three work values and three personality traits required for each career.
- List the work values and personality traits that you will need to improve for these careers.

Save the results of this activity for Chapter 5.

Blogging: My Dreams

You will be starting your blog with the topic, *My Dreams*. To get you started, use the results from:

Blog

- Real Life Focus 2.1
- Real Life Focus 2.2
- Activity, Lesson 3.2
- This chapter's Web Connection

Each blog entry will have a topic. Your writing is similar to a journal entry.

The length of each entry should be an average of two or three paragraphs. The minimum number of blog entries is one per chapter, beginning with this chapter. However, your teacher may assign additional entries.

Refer to the BlogPG your class created for Chapter 2.

Looking into the Future

Lesson 4.1 Futurecasting
Lesson 4.2 Workplace Trends
Lesson 4.3 Working Differently

Creatas/Jupiter Images

When he was three years old, Erik learned to ride a bike. He has not stopped riding since then. In high school, Erik helped start a cycling club that held bike events such as races and clinics. The club promoted health and wellness in his bike-friendly city.

Erik was then faced with making a career decision, one that he hoped would include biking. In doing his career research, Erik discovered that bike manufacturing is a growth industry, especially for custom-made bikes tailored to fit individual riders.

But what could Erik do with a career in bike manufacturing? Should he research manufacturing facilities? Should he study how he could create his own firm? What if there is no need for the career in ten or twenty years?

Erik decided to get his associate degree in manufacturing, earning the national certifications needed to get a highly skilled job in the industry. He had an apprentice position waiting for him at a national bike manufacturing company near Chicago when he finished his degree.

Today Erik has completed his apprenticeship and works at the bike company. His high-skills, high-wage position allows him to save the start-up money he needs to create his own custom bike manufacturing business. He has started the business in his garage in his free time. Within three years, he hopes to have a small manufacturing company. Erik's dream of owning his own business and manufacturing bikes is on the way to becoming a reality.

Planning a Career in . . . Manufacturing

From producing airplane parts to movie-theater popcorn machines, caskets, or building blocks, manufacturing is essential to the economy.

This diverse career cluster includes careers in planning, managing, and processing materials into products. You may work on the shop floor making parts or assembling them. You may work with machines, design products, or plan for the manufacturing process. Manufacturing offers variety with its many components.

Employment Outlook

- Strong demand with many retiring and a shift to high skills.

- High demand for skilled workers for the more efficient, highly technical manufacturing world.

- Though a third fewer workers are needed, they must be highly skilled.

Career Possibilities

- Computer Operator
- Welder
- Bioscience Technician
- Team Assembler
- Electro-Mechanical Technician

Needed Skills

- Critical thinking skills.
- High-level math and science courses.
- Problem solving and communications.
- Certifications in manufacturing specialties.
- Associate degree a plus for advancement.

What's It Like to Work in Manufacturing?

Manufacturing has an image problem. The perception of a manufacturing career is that the workplace is dirty, dark, and dangerous. Nothing could be further from the truth.

In fact, manufacturing is a very high-tech, precise, clean industry. Manufacturing firms spend over $200 million annually to research and develop new products and systems to keep the United State competitive globally.

In fact, 80 percent of manufacturing employers have serious problems finding highly skilled, qualified workers. The reality is an exciting, high-paying career with many opportunities for advancement. Manufacturing careers pay more than 20 percent higher wages and benefits than construction, service, and retail occupations.

Keep the economy strong. Consider manufacturing for a career.

What about You?

When you think of manufacturing, what image comes to mind? Do you love technology? Are math and science your strengths? Manufacturing firms are investments needed to keep the United States competitive.

Futurecasting

Goals

- Examine the demographics of the U.S. labor force.
- Identify how technology is most important for careers of the future.
- Describe how trends can affect future careers.

Terms

- trend, p. 76
- futurecasting, p. 76
- workforce trends, p. 77
- workplace trends, p. 77
- labor force, p. 77
- demographics, p. 77
- electives, p. 80
- STEM, p. 80

Real Life Focus

Each generation of the workforce has things in common. Of course, everyone in each generation was born within a certain time period. But each generation shares other things also.

Write down what you believe best describes your generation:

- movie
- music—type of music or artist
- event

Now, share the results as a class. Are there similarities? Why did people choose what they chose?

Information is everywhere. How do you know what information is important for you and your future?

One way is to study trends that show how the world may be changing. A **trend** is a general direction or change over a period of time, a prediction based on data. Fashion is a trend, though it lasts only a short time.

Making predictions based on trends is **futurecasting**. The key to successful futurecasting is identifying trends that may be important to your career. Recognizing career trends may help you in the following very important areas:

- Whether your career will exist when you begin working
- Whether there will be a need for your career throughout your employment future
- How your career field might change in the next 10 or 20 years

Of course, no one can foresee the future with perfect accuracy. Unusual twists in national or global politics, unanticipated economic or social changes, and unexpected weather conditions can affect current predictions.

Peshkova/Shutterstock.com

Workforce Trends

The key to futurecasting is for you to be aware of trends that will influence your career. Two types of trends important for your career are workplace trends and workforce trends. **Workforce trends** are changes *employees* make to allow them to meet their personal and professional goals and responsibilities. **Workplace trends** are changes *employers* make to be more competitive. Researching the two types of trends can help you predict future changes in career fields.

Workforce trends change rapidly. Change in the **labor force**, which includes all people aged 16 and older who are working or actively seeking employment, makes trend watching very important for futurecasting. In addition, change occurs not only in the United States, but in all parts of the world as well.

Some trends may affect your life in the near future; others may not have an effect for 10 or 20 years. You need to recognize long-term trends and how they might influence your future career. As you learned in Chapter 1, the Bureau of Labor Statistics (BLS) predicts future trends. Using past and current information helps the BLS revise the trends every two years.

In particular, changes in **demographics**, the information about population such as age and ethnic background, will continue to influence career fields. Among the demographic changes that may affect your career are the generations in the labor force, family structure, and the increase in ethnic diversity.

Age-Related Changes

Diversity of age makes this period the first one in the history of the United States' labor force that four generations work side-by-side. Each age group has unique characteristics. The generations are:

- Gen Z, born in 1999 or later. This is the first generation predicted to live beyond 100 years, but their income will average less than their parents.

- Digital or Millennial Generation, also known as Gen Y, born between 1982–1998, is currently the largest population group in the U.S.

- Generation X, born between 1961–1981, is the smallest population group in the U.S. They change careers more than any other generation.

- Baby Boomers, born between 1943–1960, make up the second largest population group, but the largest *workforce* group—currently, and for the next 10 to 15 years.

- Silent Generation, born between 1925–1942. Though they may change careers, many continue to work far beyond retirement age.

Currently, adults age 65 and older outnumber teenagers. When older and younger employees work together, problems may result. For example, adapting to change may be difficult for some older workers. Also, younger workers may supervise older workers, which may cause communication problems.

Ethnicity

The American population has changed in the last decade. It includes more people of diverse ethnic groups and cultures. This change has carried over to the workplace, creating a different workforce. With workforce diversity, the workplace includes a variety of workers with different backgrounds, viewpoints, experiences, and ideas.

A change occurring in both the U.S. population and its workforce is the increase in minorities. Caucasians are the largest group of the population, but the U.S. Census Bureau predicts that minorities will become the majority of the U.S. population by 2042.

Hispanics are the largest minority in the United States. Over half are of Mexican descent.

How does this change in population affect your career? In many professions, knowing a second language can lead to career success. Many large companies have customers and offices around the world, so learning the customs of other cultures would help you communicate effectively. In addition, the ability to communicate with coworkers from different backgrounds would increase your career success.

Why is a diverse workplace important?

Comstock/Jupiter Images

Families

Two demographic changes that affect the labor force are the increase in two-career families and the increase in single-parent households. The Bureau of Labor Statistics (BLS) reports that in 47 percent of couples with children, both parents have careers. The numbers have decreased 15 percent in ten years. More stay-at-home fathers and more mothers staying home after having children are the reasons for the decrease. How can those changes affect your career?

With the changes in families' demographics, the needs of the labor force have changed. For example, if you can provide a service that allows people more leisure time, you increase your chance of having a successful career. In addition, the childcare industry is growing because many women join or return to the workforce soon after their children are born.

Technology's Domination

During the past sixty years, the employment world has been evolving from the Industrial Age to the Digital Age. The start of the Digital Age began with computer technology. Technology now affects everyone's life and nearly all careers.

Lawrence received his bachelor's degree in agricultural and mechanical engineering in the 1970s. He began his career designing machinery parts for a major farm equipment company. To create his designs, Lawrence used paper and pencil on a drawing board. He did his calculations with a slide rule. After Lawrence completed his drawings, a drafter redrew them on special paper. The drafter then put the paper through a blueprint machine, where it underwent a chemical transformation. The paper became a permanent blueprint, or copy, of the drawing.

Today Lawrence is amazed at the transformation of mechanical engineering. He now uses a drafting computer program for the majority of his drawings. The program does the necessary calculations. A drafter may assist him, but Lawrence prefers using the computer to make his revisions and final drawings himself. (In fact, a drafting career is becoming extinct, replaced by engineering technicians.) The computer stores Lawrence's drawings and produces any required number of perfect copies, not blueprints. In addition, he is able to e-mail his drawings to customers for approval.

The technological changes Lawrence experienced during the years are amazing, but not unusual. Although no one predicted the technological revolution, everyone has experienced it. The trend toward increased breakthroughs in technology continues at an incredible rate.

Technological Changes

Since IBM first introduced its desktop personal computer (PC) to the public in 1981, PCs have become smaller and more powerful. Tablets and laptops are replacing the desktop computer. Smartphones do multiple tasks. Cell phones, introduced to the public in 1983, are now in nearly every household—and pocket or purse. Many people carry two cell or smartphones—one for home and one for work. In an extremely short span of time, digital technology has reshaped the way society works, communicates, and even thinks.

Why does technology dominate our lives? Not long ago, economic growth depended mostly on increasing the supply of workers. Today and in the future, economic growth comes from companies investing in technology. Companies will invest in employees who have the skills to use the technology to produce goods and services. New technologies help businesses increase productivity and keep costs down for both companies and consumers.

How will technology affect you and your career? Employers struggle to keep up with the need for an increasing number of new high-tech positions. Companies continue to pursue workers who have technology skills. Workers with those skills will allow the companies to compete for their share of the market.

Technology and You

Future careers will involve technology. That is a fact. What can you do about preparing yourself for technology in the future? According to the BLS, technology is the most important factor in the fastest-growing jobs. After you fill your schedule with the required courses, choose **electives** or optional courses that are **STEM**, courses related to Science, Technology, Engineering, or Math. Some STEM careers are on the list of the best careers of the future–those that are increasing in demand and involve technology. The BLS predicts that 85 percent of tomorrow's workers will need training beyond high school. By having the necessary education, you have a better chance of being successful at your career.

Also, beware of declining careers. Automation is replacing these careers. For example, there are fewer order clerks and more web site orders. Photo sharing and design sites are replacing the photo machinist. More and more, robotics is doing the work of some manufacturing employees and assisting surgeons. There are fewer lower-level banking and accounting positions because of ATMs and complex banking software.

Web Connections

To keep current with employment trends, business news, and career trends, you should read some web sites on a regular basis.

Access the Web Connections link for Chapter 4 and research at least one web site in two of the four categories. What can each site tell you about employment trends, business news, or career trends? How can you use this web site in futurecasting your career field? Share your results with the class.

www.cengage.com/school/iyc

Trends Affect Careers

For the next decade, the BLS has made the following predictions:

- The U.S. economy will stay ahead of the world's economy, but with less and less domination.

- The female workforce will continue to be the larger percentage of the workforce. The male workforce is decreasing in all age groups.

- The workforce will be more ethnically diverse as minority groups grow faster than the Caucasian population. However, Caucasians will still be the majority of the population in most states.

- Service occupations will have the most job openings. These careers include contact with people, such as nursing, teaching, and retail sales.

- The fastest-growing industries are health-related careers. Of the top 30 fastest-growing careers, 25 are in health services.

- Careers requiring education beyond a high school diploma will grow the fastest. However, of the 30 fastest-growing careers, 20 need an associate degree or career and technical education.

What is the best way to prepare for tomorrow's careers? Education is the answer, and lifelong learning is the key. However, education can take place on the job, in an Internet course, and in various types of classrooms and facilities. Technology and the workplace are continually changing.

Overall, the greatest danger to career success is not keeping up with change. The modern world is creative and productive. Therefore, the workplace of the future needs a flexible, educated workforce. You can be part of that workforce. You need to plan for a career that will grow.

Consider

Which predictions may affect your career planning directly?

Your Planning

How can you learn about ongoing and future trends? How can you investigate what trends mean for your career?

When you have access to the Internet, cost is not a factor. You can read many articles and publications online. Make sure that your resource is a quality source—one that is reliable and truthful. Check with your teacher if you are unsure. Some basic resources include the following.

- The BLS offers employment projections through news releases, data, and publications such as the *Occupational Outlook Handbook* and the *Occupational Outlook Quarterly*.

- America's Career InfoNet provides both occupational and economic information.

- The U.S. Census Bureau site includes tools such as maps; employment statistics; and data and trends in many areas, including population, education, and immigration.

- *The Wall Street Journal* and many other business publications have information on careers and education.

Robnoll/Shutterstock.com

Trends in Employment

The traditional workplace certainly has changed. Today, employers want workers who have a wide range of skills and who can contribute to many areas of a business. Today, and in the future, employers value employees who can make effective day-to-day decisions and communicate those decisions to customers. The success of a company often depends on its relationships with customers and the community.

Adaptability and change are key ingredients for workers in today's businesses. Change means more than adjusting job titles. Companies and their workforces need to be self-directed and self-motivated.

What should you do to make yourself more adaptable to change? Employers are interested in what you can do. Attitude also is key. Being positive about yourself, being passionate about what you do, and having confidence in your ability will help you advance in your career. In addition, because change occurs rapidly, you need to be willing to learn about new products and procedures.

Trends Quiz

Are you good at futurecasting? Let's test your knowledge about changes and trends in career fields predicted for the next ten years. You may not be an expert, but previous chapters will provide some of the answers.

1. What year were you born? List at least three inventions that have had an impact on society since you were born.

2. What is the average number of jobs a person has between the ages of 18 and 42?

3. What is the average number of careers a person has between the ages of 18 and 42?

4. Which career areas will have the most job openings?

5. Which will be the fastest-growing career areas?

6. Which elective courses should you take in high school to prepare for careers in the future?

7. What percentage of careers in the future will require a bachelor's degree?

8. What is the average length of time that it takes to complete a bachelor's degree (wrongly called a four-year degree)?

9. What percentage of careers in the future will generally need little or no training or education beyond a high school diploma?

10. Which of the following age groups includes the largest number of people?
    - Gen Z, born in 1999 or later
    - Digital or Millennial Generation, born between 1982–1998
    - Generation X, born between 1961–1981
    - Baby Boomers, born between 1943–1960
    - Silent Generation, born between 1925–1942

    Why is knowing the answer to this question important to your career future?

11. In the next ten years, which ethnic group will be the largest percentage of the labor force?

12. In what year was the cellular phone available to the public?

13. In what year was the Internet accessible to the public?

14. Who makes more computers, Dell or Ford?

15. What invention has made the most impact on your generation?

Workplace Trends

Goals

- Examine characteristics of several types of demographics.
- Describe the various types of workforce diversity and their effects on the workplace.
- Explain how workplace and workforce trends are changing the way people work.

Terms

- workplace diversity, p. 83
- equity, p. 83
- discrimination, p. 84
- communication style, p. 84
- disability, p. 85
- reasonable accommodations, p. 86
- nontraditional career, p. 87
- lifelong learning, p. 91
- virtual learning, p. 91

Real Life Focus

Below are several statements. Decide if each one shows *equity* or *inequity*. In other words, are they fair or unfair?

■ When faced with two qualified candidates, a man and a woman, the employer should consider the gender of the job candidate.

■ Men are better matched to more careers than women.

■ Women are more emotional than men and would not make good supervisors.

■ Women should have the same career options as men.

■ Employers should consider that men need to support their families.

■ Men and women who have the same skill sets can do the same job.

■ A woman's first responsibility is to her family.

Why did you choose your answers? Discuss the results as a class.

Diversity

Workplace diversity occurs when a workplace includes a variety of workers with different backgrounds, viewpoints, experiences, and ideas. The face of the future workforce is changing to include more ethnic groups, more people with disabilities, and equal numbers of men and women. The United States workforce is increasingly diverse.

Equity includes equal pay and freedom from employment discrimination on the basis of race, color, religion, sex, national origin, age, disability, or genetic information.

The workplace should be a place that encourages respect. It also should celebrate the individuality of all employees. Companies succeed when a positive attitude comes from the head of the organization. Employers who believe in the benefits of a diverse workforce realize that diversity promotes creativity. It also helps them understand their customers. Employers can learn from their employees how to develop products and services for their increasingly diverse customers.

Expectations of a Diverse Workplace

Instead of someone assuming that a person of a particular ethnic group or sex performs a certain career, workforce diversity brings new ways of thinking about careers. These changes in the workforce require changes in the behavior expectations of workers and employers.

As a member of the future workforce, you need to respect others' differences and not show prejudice or discrimination. **Discrimination** occurs when people act on their prejudices negatively. In a diverse workplace, you are free to pursue a career based on your passion instead of your ethnic group, gender, or culture.

Spoken, written, and nonverbal communication varies among people with different backgrounds and viewpoints. Your **communication style** consists of three components: how you say or write something, when you say or write it, and why you say or write it. Miscommunication generally results because one person's style of communication is different from another's. In your career, you will work with coworkers whose communication styles differ from yours. Communicating effectively with your coworkers and supervisors is necessary no matter what your career field is.

Use these guidelines to improve your communication with others:

- Remember that people of different age groups, economic classes, education levels, work experiences, and personalities often have different communication styles.

- Take time to learn about other communication styles. Different ethnic groups, as well as different sexes, may express messages differently. Every person is an individual. The time spent concentrating on communication will benefit you and your workplace.

- Make an extra effort to communicate effectively yourself. Concentrate on creating messages that are clear, accurate, and courteous.

- Use language that promotes trust and agreement in what you say or write, especially e-mails. Avoid jokes, words, or expressions that may reflect prejudice, such as those based on ethnicity, gender, disability, religion, or age.

- Analyze what might be causing misunderstanding. Be aware of your assumptions and your audience's expectations. What message you are trying to express?

- Think in terms of a workplace where people are free to be different. Do not judge people because of the way they speak, act, or dress.

Promoting understanding in a diverse workplace is an important goal of employers. Good communication can unify a workplace. However, lack of communication can divide coworkers. The challenge for today's employer is to ensure that workforce diversity is a source of strength rather than a source of tension. However, employers are not solely responsible. *You* and all other employees share in the responsibility.

Cultural Differences in the Workplace

One of the results of workforce diversity is that the workplace includes a wide variety of cultures. Your workplace has a culture that you share with your coworkers, although your personal culture may be different from theirs.

Your culture connects you to people who share the same background as you. On the other hand, your culture also can separate you from individuals from different cultures. Does this mean that you should hide your culture to avoid problems in your workplace? No. Use your cultural differences to help your coworkers, your workplace, and your customers. For example, if you speak a second language, offer to serve as an interpreter for customers who share that language. Healthcare facilities always have a particular need for interpreters in areas that have a large ethnic population.

Diverse cultures can make your workplace more interesting. Explaining your culture's traditions and sharing food customs can improve the atmosphere. You can offer to teach coworkers basic words and key phrases. You may become more comfortable talking about your culture when you learn more about other cultures.

Consider

When has a difference in culture been an advantage for you? When has it been a disadvantage? Think about times when you met people of different cultures at school, work, or community events.

Persons with Disabilities

In the past, businesses often separated people with disabilities from other workers or developed separate jobs for them. Today, however, persons with disabilities are part of the workplace. Companies are hiring more individuals with disabilities as part of the mainstream workplace. More people with disabilities succeed in their careers because of equal employment opportunities.

A person has a **disability** when he or she has a physical or mental impairment that greatly limits a major life activity. Some examples are hearing, seeing, speaking, thinking, walking, breathing, and performing manual tasks. Also, a qualified individual must have the skills to perform the desired job.

Ever since she started training at Children's Hospital, Erica knew she should be an employee there. She enters data on new patients and delivers documents from her department.

Erica is legally blind. Neither her coworkers nor any other members of the hospital staff show discrimination against her because of her lack of sight. Occasionally, she visits some of the patients, who also accept her blindness.

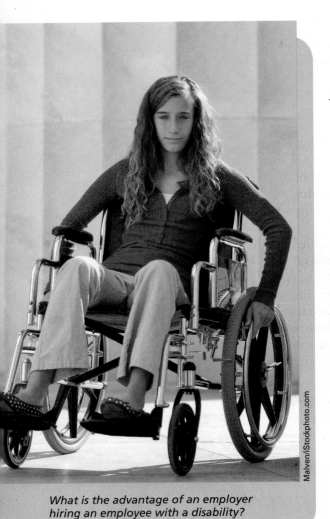

What is the advantage of an employer hiring an employee with a disability?

When Erica started her training, the hospital made a few accommodations for her disability. Some of the devices were a computer with voice recognition software and a magnifier for reading. Those accommodations allow Erica to perform her job as well as any person with sight.

The Americans with Disabilities Act (ADA) provides protections for an individual with a disability. Accommodations increase employment opportunities for people with disabilities. Qualified people have a right to request a reasonable accommodation during the hiring process or on the job. **Reasonable accommodations** change the job or the work environment to provide assistance to do the job properly.

The ADA also protects individuals with disabilities from harassment, including making rude remarks and name-calling about a disability. Just as harassment at school, often called bullying, is against school policy, harassment in the workplace is against workplace policy.

The Age-friendly Workplace

As mentioned earlier in this chapter, today's workplace is filled with people from four generations—all working together. Soon, as Gen Zers become employees, there will be five generations side-by-side.

Understanding the spirit of each generation will help your behavior as an employee. You can show employees of different ages that someone young and full of new ideas is not someone to be feared. Looking at issues through the eyes of another generation will help you understand them better and make progress in the workplace. Collaboration is key—meshing, rather than pulling apart.

Gender Equity in the Workplace

For hundreds of years, men and women have been treated differently in school, in the workplace, and in everyday life. Fortunately, changes in society has moved the workplace toward more gender equity—equal opportunity regardless of sex. The Equal Employment Opportunity Commission (EEOC) enforces legislation that ensures equity in the workplace. It regulates federal legislation that ensures gender equity. Such laws include equal pay for men and women who perform equal work. The laws also ensure freedom from discrimination in all aspects of employment.

Gender equity means working toward breaking down barriers between the sexes. Those barriers maintain a workforce divided into male and female careers. For example, today employers say that childcare, work, and family balance are *family* issues, not women's issues.

Women have career and lifestyle choices. As men become more involved in parenting, they too become more outspoken about having flexibility in their work roles. They want to have time for their responsibilities as parents. The home, work, and family balance change.

Nontraditional Employment

If you are male, would you consider being a kindergarten teacher or a dental hygienist? If you are female, would you consider becoming an auto mechanic or an airline pilot?

Many students do not have much knowledge about careers that do not fit the traditional work models for men and women. According to the U.S. Department of Labor, a **nontraditional career** has one gender with 25 percent or fewer workers. Women are a larger percentage of the workers in medical, legal, and media positions. Men lead the career fields in business and technology. Women tend to work in careers in which they can help or nurture. Men want more challenge, status, and money in their careers.

Women are slowly becoming more interested in nontraditional mechanical and technical careers. The reason for the increased interest is the shortage of skilled workers, especially in blue-collar careers.

In high school, Rhonda did whatever her friends did. When her friends took business office courses, Rhonda took them too. After graduation, Rhonda got a position as an accounting clerk. However, after two years, Rhonda understood that her future at the company would never change. She would be working behind a desk day after day.

One of the careers that interested Rhonda was that of a pipe fitter. She applied and was accepted as an apprentice pipe fitter. She trained to install and maintain piping systems, including those used for heating, cooling, and sprinkling. Rhonda climbed scaffolding and worked outside on new buildings. She had variety and independence. The major drawback to Rhonda's new career was that she was a woman. She was the first woman with whom many male pipe fitters had ever worked. She had to prove herself by working harder and better than many of her male counterparts. But the effort was worth it. Rhonda completed her apprenticeship and became one of the most sought-after pipe fitters in the area. Her advice? "You have to believe you are good enough—and you will be."

According to the U.S. Department of Labor, women entering nontraditional careers earn an average of 30 percent more than women in traditional female careers. Only 3 percent of women in the workforce are presently in skilled trade and technical occupations.

Nontraditional careers for women often offer higher salaries and better chance for advancement. Those advantages are important for career satisfaction. However, nontraditional careers often require additional training, especially the added time needed to receive a professional degree.

The Bureau of Labor Statistics (BLS) usually applies the term *nontraditional careers* to women because of discrimination and inequity of pay in traditional women's careers. However, men also work in nontraditional careers, particularly in the healthcare field and certain areas of education.

Gender equity creates opportunities and changes stereotypes. Do not ignore a career opportunity because you think the career is for the opposite sex. Consider traditional *and* nontraditional careers. You will have a better chance to find your *P*A*T*H to Success*.

Workplace Expectations

Occupations are constantly changing. Changes in demographics and technology are the major reasons for the change. After World War II, companies that manufactured goods were the major employers in the United

Real People / Real Careers

Raul Tellez / *Owner, Operator—Custom Garment Industry*

Manufacturing facilities come in various sizes—from facilities several blocks long to a storefront facility. Raul Tellez and his wife, Cathy, own and operate a clothing manufacturing company—one that custom-imprints products. From shirts and posters to coasters and mouse pads, Raul's company creates and manufactures individual designs on absorbent surfaces to customers' specifications.

Choosing to be a clothing manufacturer was a decision that took Raul some thought. He knew that his ambition was to be an entrepreneur and own a franchise. The best franchises fill a place where the needs are not met. Many companies design and manufacture products for other companies, but not for individuals and smaller orders. Also, the company appealed to him because it included

Raul

personal design done very cost effectively by designers.

The manufacturing industry was not Raul Tellez's first choice for a career. After he graduated from college with his bachelor's degree, he continued through law school. However, Raul wanted the independence of business ownership. His knowledge of law and economics is a great basis for his business plan, giving his company a strong foundation.

Being the first member of his family to graduate from college, Raul Tellez is now making a positive impact on his community with the new manufacturing facility. "My business is near where I live. I am my own boss—and get to work daily with my family. This company is the first to market this type of manufacturing. I'm in on the ground floor of a successful business."

For more information about:

* manufacturing careers

* manufacturing certifications

Access **www.cengage.com/school/iyc** and click on the appropriate links in Chapter 4.

Source: *Personal Interview,* August 2011

States. Previously, the farming industry was the largest employer. Agriculture remains a major industry today, but in off-the-farm careers, such as agriscience and agribusiness. Even though manufacturing companies produce more than one-fourth of the goods in the United States, they are no longer the largest employers. In fact, manufacturing employment growth is declining rapidly.

One of the reasons manufacturing jobs have decreased is because of advances in technology. For example, in the past, machine operators set machines manually. Then they physically operated the lathes and drills. Today operators simply program a computer to run the machines. In this case, workers still produce the same product. However, the skills needed for the job have changed a great deal.

Since 1970, service occupations, particularly professional and business services, healthcare, and social services, outnumber manufacturing occupations. Service industries provide more services in less expensive ways. For example, nurse practitioners, who receive more training than registered nurses but less than doctors, can provide basic medical care at a lower cost.

Changes in occupations will affect many careers—including yours. Workers in nearly all occupations must be computer literate. They must be able to adapt to increasingly complex computer applications. New technology means an increased need for employees who have higher reading, communication, technology, and math skills. Those skills play an important role in developing a career and in getting a job.

Workplace Trends

In today's workplace, skills, not educational background, may decide who will be employed. With a need to fill positions, especially those using new technology, companies are more willing to hire employees who have training. For example, someone with specialized job skills may be employed over a college graduate. According to the BLS, many of the largest industries choose specialized training ahead of a college degree when they are searching for people to fill highly technical positions.

For example, the BLS predicts that many of the fastest-growing careers in the next ten years will be healthcare assistants and dental workers. Neither of those careers requires a bachelor's degree.

Why healthcare? People are taking better care of themselves. They want to live longer and enjoy good health. Healthcare assistants are less expensive to employ than doctors.

Another workplace trend is contracting or outsourcing work. Work previously done by employees is sent to other businesses that specialize in particular skills. A business can save money by hiring specialized workers for a project instead of hiring a full-time employee with benefits. Commonly contracted work includes security services, grounds maintenance, payroll services, advertising services, and computer repair.

Teams Many employees today are learning different ways to work. Instead of being closely supervised, they are expected to identify and solve work-related problems on their own. They manage their own work schedules and work closely with coworkers and customers. Working in teams is a workplace certainty.

Robert Kneschke/Shutterstock.com

Companies must respond quickly to changes in technology, customer demands, and global competition. Workers who complete specific tasks as a group usually include the teams. Each team member may be skilled in one area, such as technology or finance, and work more efficiently.

Team members need skills that fit more than one situation or cross training. In cross training, employees prepare for several workplace roles, rather than just one job. Many manufacturing plants use cross-trained teams to avoid problems when a team member is absent. Because it helps with staffing changes, cross training is a major trend in today's workplace.

Why is the trend toward teams important for you? Although employers want to know what specialized skills you have, they also want you to be skilled in many other areas. Your interpersonal skills, such as communication and cooperation, are often more important than your technical skills when you are a team member.

Skill Sets Workers may have to change quickly to pursue new opportunities. To adapt well to change, they must develop their transferable skill sets. As discussed in Chapter 1, skill sets combine the ability to perform tasks that transfer to various careers. For example, if you know how to run complicated computer applications and complex machinery, you can transfer more easily from one career cluster to another or from one work site to another. The advantages of a thorough knowledge of adaptable skill sets will help you, especially if you are in an industry that is declining or if your employer relocates or goes out of business.

Sommara loved working with computers. When she was not working with computers, she interacted with people. Sommara decided that nursing would be a good career field for her because she would be able to work with people and computers. In addition, her research showed that registered nurses were always in demand.

After finishing nursing school, Sommara chose to begin her career in the cardiac intensive care unit at the Ohio Clinic. She also thought she would like the work schedule because the 36-hour, 3-day work week would give her four days off to work on computers.

However, after two years, Sommara realized that nursing was not for her. Her work in the cardiac unit simply did not allow enough opportunity for her to work with computers—her passion.

Sommara applied for work at the local cable company to install high definition and wireless systems. Now, interacting with both people and computers gives Sommara the satisfaction she needs. She also gained the experience needed to pursue working for a computer consulting firm in two years.

Skill sets are valuable resources that provide you with options when changes occur in the workplace. Improve your skills to adapt to future trends in career fields. In addition to technology skills, effective communication, research, and math skills are skill sets that will be in high demand in the future. As you create your *Internal Career Design*, keep in mind that your skill sets and your ability to work in teams are important to achieving career success in the future. Be adaptable by having skill sets that fit several careers.

Lifelong Learning

Learning the basic skills of reading, computing, writing, and listening is no longer enough. To understand changes in technology and the workplace, education will help you prepare for career success. For example, many classes explore real-world problems common in the working world.

For you to be successful in the changing workplace, your education cannot stop with high school, college, or your first on-the-job training. Your education must continue throughout your working life. **Lifelong learning**, constantly improving your education and training, is necessary for nearly all occupations. In fact, 85 percent of all careers require lifelong learning, education beyond high school graduation. The jobs that do not require more than a high school degree are mainly service industry jobs. They include restaurant servers and cashiers, where employees start at low pay and have little opportunity for increased wages or better positions.

Lifelong learning does not necessarily mean going to a traditional school. One option for continuing your education is **virtual learning**, using educational materials and courses available on the Internet. This type of education provides solutions for people whose schedules prevent them from physically going to a university or another facility.

ACTIVITY 4.2

Learning from Others

In this activity, interview a member of another generation about workplace trends.

1. Choose an adult to interview from one of the generations listed below.

   - Millennials, born between 1982–1998

   - Generation X, born between 1961–1981

   - Baby Boomers, born between 1943–1960

   - Silent Generation, born between 1925–1942

2. Interview the person by asking the following questions:

   - What is (was) your career field?

   - What is (was) your last job title in that field?

   - What were your family's expectations for you? That you succeed as well as they did or better than they did? Explain.

   - Would you describe your culture as traditional? Why or why not?

   - Are (were) men and women treated differently in the workplace? Why or why not? How?

   - What are (were) your employer's expectations of your attitude toward your career and family?

   - Do you think you had freedom in choosing your career? Why?

3. Use the results of your interview to prepare for a discussion to share the results as a class.

Goals
- Explain the advantages and disadvantages of global careers.
- Describe entrepreneurship and the characteristics needed for owning a business.
- Discuss how workforce trends are changing the ways people work.

Terms
- e-commerce, p. 93
- outsourcing, p. 94
- offshoring, p. 94
- entrepreneur, p. 95
- telecommuting, p. 96
- job sharing, p. 97

Portfolio

Real Life Focus

What would you do if your employer asked you to work overseas? How you answer these questions may help you to decide. Remember: The answers refer to international situations.

- Why do you want to work overseas?
- What qualifications/skills do you possess that will make you effective overseas?
- What working conditions do you anticipate will be different in another culture?
- Have you been separated from your family or your loved ones for extended periods?
- Have you ever had to cope with loneliness?
- How would you occupy your spare time?
- How important is privacy for you? Have you ever lived in situations where you have not had a lot of privacy?
- Do you make friends easily?

The answers to these questions will give you insight as to whether or not you want to work overseas, according to *The BIG Guide to Living and Working Overseas*.

The Global Effect

In the past, most businesses in the United States competed with other businesses within the United States. Today, U.S. businesses have fierce competition from countries all over the world. The U.S. economy links to economic and political changes in nations around the world. Indeed, what happens in China or India can affect the entire United States.

International trade has expanded the world's marketplace. Modern communications technology, such as the Internet, has made today's workplace a global one. The global marketplace has caused several changes that affect employment in the United States.

- To expand their markets, many U.S. companies have formed partnerships with companies in other countries. Those changes have increased the companies' need for employees.

- Other U.S. companies have moved their manufacturing plants to countries that pay lower wages than those in the United States, decreasing the number of American workers.

- Having a larger market in which to sell their products, many U.S. industries such as financial services, software publishing, and healthcare services have seen significant job growth. However, some of the work of those industries is completed overseas.

How would the trend toward a global marketplace affect you and your career? The American workplace has seen increased cultural diversity in both customers and employees of U.S. employers. Knowing how to interact with workers from different cultures and knowing how to speak different languages are important skills for today's employees. Those skills also will become important for future employees.

Career FACT

The top spoken native languages in the world are Mandarin Chinese, Spanish, English, Hindi (Indian), and Arabic.

There has been a shift with fewer Hindi native speakers. Instead, Spanish and English have moved up the list to a close 2nd and 3rd.

English is the top language spoken around the world by non-native speakers. In most countries, it is the choice for a second language.

—*Ethnologue*

Global Career Opportunities

Businesses must consider whether they can market beyond their local area. U.S. companies sell products and perform services in other countries. But they also import materials from companies worldwide. Many businesses believe that global marketing is necessary if they want to remain competitive and attract new customers.

For example, a company in the United States may form a partnership with a company in another country. Both companies profit from such an arrangement because it allows them to reach more customers. A company in the United States might make an agreement with a foreign government to set up an office or a plant in the foreign country. The foreign country benefits from increased employment. The U.S. company benefits from lower manufacturing costs and a larger market for its products or services.

As one business owner stated, "Anything that can be made or sold in my state can be made or sold anywhere else. My company will make products in my state only if the talented workforce is here."

E-commerce, or electronic commerce, is the buying and selling of goods and services over the Internet. E-commerce is changing the way people shop. Because of e-commerce, companies must change the way they do business. Companies should offer both web-based and in-store retailing. When people shop less often at retail stores, the demand increases for package delivery services such as the U.S. Postal Service and UPS.

How does the global marketplace affect you? It provides you with more career opportunities. For example, you may consider working for a U.S. company in one of its plants or offices located in a foreign country.

Another career option is to work for a foreign company abroad. Medical research continually creates new products and procedures. Those innovations create specialized skills needed both in the United States and abroad. Many foreign companies employ healthcare workers from other countries to fill the positions. As a temporary worker, you often can obtain a visa to work in another country in a specialty occupation.

If you work in another country, you may be starting a new career. You also are entering a new culture, perhaps with a different language. Even if you work for a U.S. company, you will need to adjust to living in another culture. Skilled training provides you with the chance to work all over the world. Each culture has different attitudes, values, and behaviors. People base their behaviors on their culture's viewpoint. To be successful in a job in a foreign country, you will need to adapt your behavior to the culture in which you work and live.

Working in another country is an excellent way to learn about and understand another culture. You can expand your knowledge both in the working world and in your personal life. Seeing other cultures and learning other languages offer challenging opportunities. Working abroad may have some disadvantages, such as adjusting to a new culture and being separated from familiar surroundings, friends, and family. However, if you think of the disadvantages in advance, you will have a more accurate picture of working abroad. A realistic view can increase your chances of success.

Consider

What would you do to prepare for a career overseas?

Pete Saloutos/Shutterstock.com

What are some advantages of working overseas?

Exporting Jobs

One downside of global opportunities is that global careers create competition. **Outsourcing** in the job market is when a company hires workers outside the company. It does not use its own employees to do the work, but rather those in another country. **Offshoring** is relocating a business or part of the business from one country to another. More than 3.4 million jobs will relocate offshore in the next ten years, according to Investors.com. The work will move to India and other locations. For example, doctors are monitoring patients remotely—whether they are 10 miles or 10,000 miles away. Radiologists in India read X-rays and CT scans overnight for U.S. hospitals. Careers that leave the United States are often entry-level positions.

When you research a career field, you need to pick a career that will stay in the United States—if that is where you want to work. How can you choose a career that is "safe"? How can you adapt to change if your position or company moves out of the United States? Here are a few suggestions:

- Pick a career that involves face-to-face contact, such as law enforcement, hands-on healthcare, or auto mechanics.

- Choose a career that requires you to know the culture. Examples are advertising, entertainment, and electronics.

- Do not stop learning. Be aware of new trends. Take courses to increase and update your knowledge. The more education a career needs, the less likely it is to be offshored.

- Focus on learning skill sets instead of many specialized skills. If you overspecialize and your career is offshored, you may find that looking for a new job is more difficult.

- Add more courses, such as entrepreneurship, communication, and marketing. Those courses offer flexibility to changing careers or workplaces.

- Check to see if a career you are considering is on the BLS web site of jobs to avoid that could go overseas. Access **www.cengage.com/school/iyc**, Chapter 4, for the information.

According to the Population Reference Bureau, the countries with the largest population (in order) are China, India, United States, Indonesia, and Brazil. Much of the world exists outside the United States. Why not expand your career options and explore that outside world?

Entrepreneurship

Have you dreamed of being an **entrepreneur**, a person who creates a business? Starting your own business is a way to combine your passions, skills, and values into a career that you control.

Being an entrepreneur is not a career choice. You choose your career. Then you set the goal of starting your own business as part of your career plan. That goal is one of the ways to reach your P*A*T*H to Success.

What do you need to be a successful entrepreneur?

Digital Vision/Jupiter Images

In her culinary class, Natasha learned the skills of cooking basic recipes and working with new flavors and types of food. However, her passion was always desserts. At first, she used her skills at home for family celebrations. When Natasha's aunt found out about her pastry skills, she hired her to make the desserts for her book club meetings. Natasha's aunt was very pleased with the desserts and told her friends about Natasha's skills. Soon she had so many baking and pastry orders that she was working several evenings a week and most weekends.

Although Natasha was still in high school, she wanted to start a business. With her teacher's help, she created a business plan. The plan included start-up costs, expenses, and projected income.

Sometimes school and work competed for her time, but Natasha persisted and kept the business going. When she graduated from high school two years later, she had a successful, established business. She was even able to hire an employee so she could start her associate degree in pastry arts.

Running a business involves more than having a great idea. You must be prepared to eat, sleep, and breathe your business 24/7—24 hours a day, 7 days a week. Your business is your passion. Successful entrepreneurs share many qualities. They need these characteristics to start the business and to keep the business going. If you have most of the following traits of a successful entrepreneur, you should consider starting your own business one day.

- *You believe in your business.* You are the only person who can make your business successful.

- *You are motivated to set goals and create the steps to reach them.* Starting your own business requires planning, including the education needed and start-up funding—and five years into the future. Your plan will also help you set limits.

- *You have a support system.* An entrepreneur cannot be afraid to ask for help. Businesses often fail because owners end up asking for help too late—when the business is already doomed to fail.

- *You have good organizational skills.* You must be able to organize your tasks, set priorities, and stick to them. Another organization tool is time management.

- *You see problems as challenges and are willing to develop alternative solutions.* An entrepreneur sees an unfulfilled need, creates a solution, and starts a business. Skill and hard work keep the business going.

- *You are enthusiastic, persistent, and optimistic.* Your passion drives your enthusiasm to start a business and to manage your career.

Different Ways of Working

Trends show that the traditional workweek is being redefined. Alternative work schedules are becoming less unusual. Many employees no longer work five 8-hour days each week. Instead, some work four 10-hour days or three 12-hour days, working full-time for fewer than 40 hours a week. Healthcare facilities often have employees with alternative work schedules to provide patients more personal care.

Telecommuting

Many employees are not required to go into the office every day. **Telecommuting**—when a company links its offices to employees at another location—has become increasingly common. Originally designed to help a company cut costs, these arrangements help employees balance work and family life. Many telecommuters prefer this way of working even though they may average more than 40 hours a week on work at home and/or in the company office.

There are advantages and disadvantages for employees also. They are in control of their working hours and constant supervision. However, working too much or too little may be the price. Having privacy and freedom may seem ideal; however, interruptions from family and other distractions may take over. In-home work space should be dedicated to work *only*.

Flexible Work Arrangements

Part-time workers and job sharing are ways to avoid the usual 40-hour, 5-day workweek. In **job sharing**, two employees split a full-time position and pay. They may not receive benefits, depending on company policy.

Other types of work arrangements include independent or contract workers. They are employees hired to work on certain projects. The company gets the work done and avoids paying these workers benefits.

Flexible work arrangements offer benefits and drawbacks. These positions allow workers to balance their careers and personal lives better. However, some employers may not treat the workers as they treat their regular employees. These jobs do not guarantee steady or lasting work.

ACTIVITY 4.3

Leadership

Do You Have What It Takes to Be an Entrepreneur?

In small groups, decide on a project or business that you could start while you are still in school. As a group, take this quiz to see if you have what it takes to be an entrepreneur.

1. How do you feel about taking risks?
2. Are you a self-starter, or do you need someone to advise you?
3. Are you a leader?
4. Are you self-confident and have willpower?
5. Can you live with uncertainty, or must you know what is ahead?

6. Do you handle pressure well?
7. Do you feel that you are an individual or a conformist?
8. Are you creative?
9. Do you multitask well?
10. Are you competitive?

Portfolio

When all the groups are finished working, reporters will share with the class the group's business idea, along with quiz results.

Roger Jegg – Fotodesign-Jegg.de/Shutterstock.com

Chapter Summary

4.1 Futurecasting

- Demographics can help predict the trends that affect future careers and lifestyle.

- Knowledge of technology is vital for the technological changes affecting careers in the future.

- By using various sources to research trends, one can make predictions about the future workforce to plan for a career that will be there when education and training is finished.

4.2 Workplace Trends

- Workplace diversity is respecting others' differences, especially with regard to culture, disabilities, and age.

- Gender equity in the workplace provides both men and women with equal opportunities, including both traditional and nontraditional careers.

- Education is key for careers now and in the future. Having skill sets that transfer among careers will help with continuous employment, as will lifelong learning.

4.3 Working Differently

- Knowing which careers could possibly be outsourced and offshored will help prevent possible unemployment problems. However, working globally can provide career options and opportunities.

- Owning one's own business is a dream for many people—a dream that can become a reality if one realizes the pluses and pitfalls.

- Flexibility in work schedules and locations is a trend that will make an impact on future careers and lifestyle.

Chapter Assessment

Vocabulary Builder

Match each statement with the term that best defines it. Not all of the terms will be used.

1. Buying and selling of goods and services over the Internet *g*
2. Physical or mental impairment that greatly limits major activities *c*
3. How one says or writes something, when one says or writes it, and why one says or writes it *a*
4. Relocating a business from one country to another *n*
5. A company hires workers outside the company *o*
6. Equal pay and freedom from employment discrimination *f*
7. Courses related to Science, Technology, Engineering, or Math *q*
8. Person who creates a business *h*
9. All people aged 16 and older who are working or actively seeking employment *k*
10. Educational materials and courses available on the Internet *t*
11. Optional courses *e*
12. Constantly improving education and training throughout life *l*
13. Careers with one gender of 25 percent or fewer workers *m*
14. Occurs when people act on their prejudices negatively *d*
15. General direction or change over a period of time *s*
16. Changes needed to the job or the work environment to provide assistance to do the job properly. *p*
17. Making predictions based on trends *i*
18. Two employees split a full-time position and pay *j*
19. A company links its offices to employees at another location *r*
20. A workplace includes a variety of workers with different backgrounds, viewpoints, experiences, and ideas *v*
21. Information about a population *b*

a. communication style
b. demographics
c. disability
d. discrimination
e. electives
f. equity
g. e-commerce
h. entrepreneur
i. futurecasting
j. job-sharing
k. labor force
l. lifelong learning
m. nontraditional careers
n. off shoring
o. outsourcing
p. reasonable accommodations
q. STEM
r. telecommuting
s. trends
t. virtual learning
u. workforce trends
v. workplace diversity
w. workplace trends

Review What You Have Learned

22. What are some of the trends that affect your everyday life?
23. What are some reasons for the technological revolution?
24. How do you make sure that your passions and talents lead to a career that will have a future?
25. Explain the negative influence of discrimination on the workplace.
26. How can an employer benefit from hiring a person with a disability?
27. How does gender equity affect the workplace?

Goals

- Explain why you need to make a career decision now.
- Describe the career decision-making process.
- Identify the benefits of making a good career decision.

Term

- decision-making process, p. 107

Portfolio

Real Life Focus

Writing down what is most important in your life will help you understand why you need to start career planning now. This activity will help you prioritize your activities. Use the *Real Life Focus* form, Lesson 5.1, found at www.cengage.com/school/iyc, Chapter 5 for this activity.

1. Inside each of the nine boxes, write one of the nine most important things in your life.

2. Number the boxes from 1 to 9 to show what is most important in your life. (Number 1 is the most important. Number 9 is the least important.)

3. Using a different color, number the boxes from 1 to 9 again. This time, number the boxes to show how you currently spend most of your time. (Number 1 is the most time; number 9, the least time.)

4. Compare the results from each set of boxes. What did you learn from the comparison?

Looking at the results, you may need to change your priorities. You should be spending more time on what is most important to you.

Deciding Now

Career planning is more than dreaming about what you want to do for the rest of your life. You have investigated the influences on your career choice and explored assessments. You have considered workplace and workforce trends and looked at how workforce diversity and the global marketplace have expanded your career options. You realize that career planning involves more than knowing your likes and dislikes from an interest inventory.

Currently, you are acquiring skill sets that give you the flexibility to pursue several types of careers. Now you can begin developing the specialized skills needed for a specific career within a career cluster.

The secret to choosing a satisfying career is to make your choice based on your *P*A*T*H to Success* and your personal goals. Then you must develop and follow a plan. Planning allows you to be in charge of your career.

Rather than going through life waiting for the right career to find you, you can plan for the career that will give you satisfaction. The time is right. You can select the career and decide the direction your career will take.

The Decision-Making Process

Throwing a dart at a list is *not* the way to choose a career. You need to have an organized, logical method to make an informed career decision. The **decision-making process**, based on the steps for problem solving, offers a way to plan carefully. The following course of action will help you discover your *Internal Career Design*, the ideal career for you.

1. **Recognize that you must make a decision.** Choosing a career now allows you to focus on preparing for your future education and skill training. Doing nothing is much worse than deciding something now. Keeping your career choice in mind, you can select activities and classes that will help you prepare for your future career success. Your decision will give you a head start in preparing for the average eight careers you may likely have from ages 18 to 42.

2. **Identify the benefits of making a good decision.** Follow your *P*A*T*H to Success* to choose a career created from your passions, attitude, talents, and heart. Choosing a career based on your *P*A*T*H* and your ideal lifestyle will provide you with satisfaction in both your work and personal life.

3. **Consider all possible choices.** Do not rush into a decision. Examine each career cluster. Look carefully at the passions, attitude, talents, and heart associated with each cluster. The clusters show some of the possible careers in a field. You then can select the cluster that matches your personal *P*A*T*H*.

How do you answer these questions?

✔ Am I passionate about the career?

✔ Can I succeed in the courses needed for the careers listed in the cluster?

✔ Do I understand the positives and negatives of the cluster? Of the careers within the cluster?

How will your research help you make your career decision?

RapidEye/iStockphoto.com

Career FACT

In 1971, an accounting professor at Portland State University in Oregon saw Carolyn Davidson, a graphic design student, drawing. He was interested in her work and commissioned her to create a logo for the company he co-founded, Blue Ribbon Sports.

Carolyn created a "swoosh" logo and sold it to the professor, Phil Knight, for $35.

Why is this important? Blue Ribbon Sports was soon renamed Nike. When Carolyn Davidson left Nike in 1983, Phil Knight presented her with a ring with the swoosh in diamonds – and an envelope full of Nike stock certificates.

—Interview with Phil Knight
The Oprah Winfrey Show, April 2011

4. **Make a decision.** Select the career cluster that best matches your *P*A*T*H to Success*. Then identify several careers within the cluster that are closest to your passions, attitude, talents, and heart and that match your lifestyle preferences. Consider the education and training needed for each career. Although you may change careers throughout your working life, your passions and talents— and your *Internal Career Design*—are not likely to change.

5. **Create a plan to carry out your decision.** Your plan will outline your goals and the steps necessary to achieve your goals. Above all, your plan will help keep you on track. It will show how each step takes you closer to your career goal.

6. **Monitor the success of your decision.** Check your plan and your progress regularly to make sure you are on track. By watching your plan closely, you can modify it before you go too far in the wrong direction. Adjusting your plan might be necessary if you need to make any changes in your goals or in the steps you need to achieve them.

Consider

What important decisions have you made in your life? What steps did you use to make those decisions?

Benefits of a Good Career Design

Enjoying your career will give you a sense of success and help you live a more satisfied life. You will see a career not only as a way to earn money, but also as an important, positive part of your life.

To have a fulfilling career, create your choice based on your *P*A*T*H to Success*. Each part of the *P*A*T*H to Success* is important in discovering your ideal career.

■ **Passion** is what fascinates you. Your passion is what made you happy as a child. Passion is what you love to do now. You never object to spending more time with your passion.

■ **Attitude** involves your emotions. A positive attitude will make you feel as though you can accomplish anything.

■ **Talents** are those abilities that allow you to do something well. The satisfaction of working in a career field that matches your talents will encourage you. It will advance your career and help you explore new challenges.

■ **Heart** refers to what you feel is important about a career. Being happy is encouraging. Your life feels more worthwhile than if you work in a career that is not a good fit.

Map out your *P*A*T*H to Success* to discover your *Internal Career Design*. Your passions, attitude, talents, and heart will guide you as you begin your career journey.

Matt Nodro is getting discouraged. Many of his friends have already chosen a career direction. Matt talked to his counselor again and realized that he needs to focus more on a career path that is similar to his P*A*T*H to Success. Then he can adjust his course schedule to relate directly to his career. Matt believes his future will be clearer after he makes a career decision.

Matt charts his passions, attitude, talents, and heart, making his own P*A*T*H to Success. He also describes his ideal lifestyle to prepare for a more satisfying life. After he completes his chart, shown in Illustration 5-1, Matt feels much better. He knows he is on his way to finding a career that will allow him to enjoy his passions.

Illustration 5-1: Matt Nodro's Chart

Passion (Interests)	Doing creative work Taking photographs Working with digital drawing & editing technology Reading
Attitude (Personality)	Artistic Sensory Precise
Talents (Skills/Strengths)	Verbal communication skills Ability to compose photographs Writing ability Ability to enhance photographic images
Heart (Values)	Likes to work alone Is thoughtful and modest Considers family important
Ideal Lifestyle and Climate and Community Preferences	Prefers solitary workplace Must live near mountains and waterway Prefers location with seasons

Charting the Course

Record the results from the following activities you stored in your Career Portfolio. Use the chart for this activity from www.cengage.com/school/iyc Chapter 5.

- Passions (Interests): List the results from Activity 3.2, bottom left of the *Coat of Arms,* page 61.
- Attitude (Personality): List the results from the *Web Connection*, Chapter 3, upper right of the *Coat of Arms*, page 56.

- Talents (Skills/Strengths): List the results from Activity 3.2, page 61.
- Heart (Values): List the Work Values results from the *Web Connection*, Chapter 3, lower right of the *Coat of Arms*, page 56.
- Ideal Lifestyle Preferences: List the results from the *Real Life Focus*, Lesson 2.2, page 34.

The results of the chart will help you discover the career cluster that fits you best for Activity 5.2.

GG Pro Photo/Shutterstock.com

Goals

- Explain why self-understanding must happen before you choose your career.
- Analyze the career clusters to compare them with your P*A*T*H to Success.

Term

- self-understanding, p. 111

Real Life Focus

At one time or another during their school career, students ask, "Why do I need this course?" Many of the skills you learn in your academic classes are in demand by employers.

Look at the skills listed below. Why would employers need future employees to have these skills?

- Math and Science Skills
- Language Arts Skills
- Teamwork Skills
- Problem-Solving Skills

Which career clusters would emphasize the above skills?

The Starting Point

This time of your life is supposed to be exciting because you have so many options. However, sometimes having many options is the problem. Should you listen to the advice of others? Sometimes listening to others makes you even more confused. Some people may warn you that the future is unknown, so be cautious and do not plan too much. Others will tell you to take risks; after all, you can always change careers. Some people may advise you to go to college or to pursue career and technical training in or after high school. Others may recommend finding a job as soon as possible after high school graduation.

So how do you begin narrowing your focus to choose a career? How can you choose a career?

Self-Understanding

You cannot select the right career if you do not know yourself. You need to achieve **self-understanding**, the true knowledge about yourself. Self-understanding sounds easy. After all, who spends more time with you than you? But achieving self-understanding is not a quick and easy process. At first, you may have more in-depth knowledge about a friend or a family member than you do about yourself.

Self-understanding means more than identifying your positives and negatives. True self-understanding means working on building your strengths *and* improving upon your weaknesses. You need to do both to gain insight into the best career area for you.

You *can* make an informed career decision. But first, you need to understand yourself by accepting your qualities, both strengths and weaknesses. You want the basis of your decision to be your *P*A*T*H to Success*.

Consider

What are your strengths? What weaknesses do you need to improve upon?

How can informal assessments, such as job shadowing, help you match your P*A*T*H to a career?

Goodluz/Shutterstock.com

Assessment Results

In previous chapters, you considered many factors that influence your career decision. The advice you received and the results of the assessments are guides that will help you discover your career match. You explored various career options through informal assessments such as informational interviews, job-shadowing activities, and service learning projects. You have gained additional insights through these experiences.

When you have a good understanding of your *P*A*T*H to Success*, you can match your formal and informal assessment results and your experiences to the career cluster descriptions on pages 114–117. After you choose a career cluster, additional informal assessment experiences will confirm that the cluster and careers you chose are right for you. Everything that makes you a unique individual will help you create your *Internal Career Design*.

Career Clusters

As you learned in Chapter 1, a *career cluster* is a group of careers in one broad area. Under the umbrella of each career cluster are many different types of careers. For example, the Arts, A/V Technology, and Communications cluster includes web designers, graphic artists, television producers, sculptors, architects, entertainers, and broadcasters. Although those careers may seem very different, they have some common interests and skill requirements. On the other hand, individual careers within a career cluster often vary in the amount of education and training needed, the work setting, work values, and other factors.

Now that you are beginning to create your *Internal Career Design*, you need to analyze the career clusters to find the career path that most suits you. Illustration 5-2 on pages 114–117 describes the characteristics of the 16 career clusters. The charts list just a few career options for each cluster.

■ First, look for your passions as you begin to study each cluster. Your passions will start you along the pathway to your ideal career.

■ Next, think about your attitude, talents, and heart.

■ Explore some of the careers listed, as well as others, by using the tools in the Web Connection on page 121.

Look at all of the career clusters before you choose. Review all of each individual cluster's characteristics before accepting or rejecting it. Compare the cluster's traits to your own. You may even find that your best match is a cluster you did not expect to fit you at first glance.

ACTIVITY 5.2

Portfolio

Investigating Career Clusters

Use the 16 career cluster charts at www.cengage.com/school/iyc, Activity 5.2. Do this activity in small groups.

- Answer each of the groups of questions *yes* or *no* for each career cluster.

- Put checkmarks by the *P*A*T*H traits* in each career cluster that match the results you charted for Activity 5.1.

- Use the results from the charts to choose the career cluster that best fits you.

Answer the following questions in career cluster groups.

1. Which cluster is your best match? Why?

2. What other clusters are also good matches? Why?

3. List two or three careers you want to explore in your primary career cluster.

Leadership

Designate a class recorder. As each team's reporter gives his or her group's results to the class, the recorder will list the careers the class will explore. After the list is posted, discuss possible informal assessment ideas.

iofoto/Shutterstock.com

Illustration 5-2: Career Clusters

Passions

- Planning and organizing
- Working with hands or using technology
- Working outdoors and/or with animals

Attitude

- High energy
- Common sense

Talents

- Technology skills
- Problem-solving ability
- Math and science ability

Heart

- Likes to work independently
- Likes to learn how systems work

Some Career Areas to Consider

- Wildlife Manager
- Meteorologist
- Veterinarian Assistant

Passions

- Working with hands
- Designing or building
- Working with tools

Attitude

- Self-motivated
- Detail-oriented

Talents

- Mechanical ability
- Math and science ability
- Thinking skills

Heart

- Likes to work with people
- Needs standards and rules

Some Career Areas to Consider

- Plumber
- Construction Inspector
- Civil Engineer

Passions

- Being creative and original
- Using music, art, drama, or writing
- Applying technology

Attitude

- Persistent
- Creative and unique

Talents

- Innovative style
- Technical and mechanical ability
- Art, music, drama, or writing ability

Heart

- Likes to create original ideas or objects
- Needs variety in activities

Some Career Areas to Consider

- Web Page Designer
- Telecommunication Director

Passions

- Creating order
- Knowing the proper procedures and standards
- Valuing consistency

Attitude

- Organized
- Honest, dependable, and responsible

Talents

- High energy level
- Good with words
- Organizing and leading ability

Heart

- Likes to work with people
- Likes to coordinate projects

Some Career Areas to Consider

- Personnel Recruiter
- Customer Service Supervisor

Illustration 5-2: Career Clusters *(continued)*

Passions
- Interacting with others
- Leading or teaching
- Understanding others' needs

Attitude
- Caring
- Outgoing

Talents
- Ability to work with all types of people
- Planning and organizing ability
- Good verbal skills

Heart
- Likes to help people
- Likes to work closely with others

Some Career Areas to Consider
- Nanny
- School Psychologist
- Teacher or Teacher's Aide

Passions
- Finding solutions to problems
- Working with math
- Respecting ethics

Attitude
- Detail-oriented
- Logical thinker

Talents
- Record keeping skills
- Ability to handle money with accuracy
- Calm under pressure

Heart
- Prefers working inside
- Is admired by others

Some Career Areas to Consider
- Loan Officer
- Tax Preparation Specialist
- Insurance Agent

Passions
- Working with people
- Solving problems
- Helping others

Attitude
- People-oriented
- Caring

Talents
- Ability to speak in public
- Communication skills
- Ability to lead and facilitate

Heart
- Likes to improve how things work
- Likes to communicate with all types of people

Some Career Areas to Consider
- Border Inspector
- Military

Passions
- Working with people
- Using math, science, and technology
- Researching and investigating

Attitude
- Caring
- Sensitive

Talents
- Excellent memory
- Ability to adapt to all kinds of people
- Detail-oriented

Heart
- Likes to solve problems
- Values wellness activities

Some Career Areas to Consider
- Dietetic Technician
- Nurse Practitioner

Illustration 5-2: Career Clusters *(continued)*

Hospitality & Tourism

Passions
- Planning and organizing
- Meeting new people
- Influencing others' decisions

Attitude
- Sociable
- Dependable

Talents
- Ability to work with people
- Outgoing personality
- Communication skills

Heart
- Likes detailed projects
- Likes to travel

Some Career Areas to Consider
- Caterer
- Reservations Manager
- Event Planner

Human Services

Passions
- Working with people
- Fascinated with human nature
- Helping others

Attitude
- Dependable
- Respected by others

Talents
- Communication skills
- Ability to work with all types of people
- Understanding of human nature

Heart
- Wants to understand others' situations
- Wants to make things better for others

Some Career Areas to Consider
- Nail Technician
- Consumer Advocate
- Social Worker

Information Technology

Passions
- Solving problems
- Trying new technology
- Improving how things work

Attitude
- Analytical
- Curious

Talents
- Ability to work with technology
- Scientific-minded
- Detail-oriented

Heart
- Likes to work alone
- Likes challenge of solving problems

Some Career Areas to Consider
- Digital Media Engineer
- Help Desk Specialist

Law, Public Safety, Corrections & Security

Passions
- Solving problems
- Working with details
- Helping people

Attitude
- Confident
- Analytical

Talents
- Ability to relate to many types of people
- Ability to communicate by writing and speaking
- Ability to make quick decisions

Heart
- Is trustworthy
- Is caring

Some Career Areas to Consider
- Corrections Officer
- Court Reporter

Illustration 5-2: Career Clusters *(continued)*

Manufacturing

Passions
- Putting things together
- Repairing equipment
- Making decisions

Attitude
- Precise
- Logical

Talents
- Problem-solving ability
- Math, science, and technology ability
- Ability to imagine a final product

Heart
- Likes to work with hands
- Likes to be accurate

Some Career Areas to Consider
- Industrial Maintenance Technician
- Machine Operator
- Environmental Engineer

Marketing

Passions
- Organizing projects
- Seeing the big picture
- Working with details

Attitude
- Outgoing
- Organized

Talents
- Communication skills
- Sociable
- Leadership abilities

Heart
- Likes to interact with people
- Likes to study people and trends

Some Career Areas to Consider
- Sales Representative
- Merchandise Buyer
- Public Relations Manager

Science, Technology, Engineering & Mathematics

Passions
- Building and repairing things
- Working with tools
- Working with hands

Attitude
- Curious
- Quiet

Talents
- Math, science, and technology ability
- Problem-solving ability
- Mechanical ability

Heart
- Likes to work alone
- Likes to investigate the "why" of things

Some Career Areas to Consider
- Mechanical Engineer
- Toxicologist

Transportation, Distribution & Logistics

Passions
- Driving or working on vehicles and equipment
- Analyzing problems
- Working with hands

Attitude
- Individualistic
- Practical

Talents
- Belief in oneself
- Detail-oriented
- Mechanical ability

Heart
- Takes pride in accomplishments
- Is calm under pressure

Some Career Areas to Consider
- Air Traffic Controller
- Logistics Specialist

Creating Your *Internal Career Design*

Goals

- Explain how to make your career decision.
- Construct a plan to carry out your career decision.
- Set goals to meet your career plan.
- Monitor the progress and success of the decision.

Terms

- career satisfaction, p. 121
- monitor, p. 124
- career maturity, p. 125

Portfolio

Real Life Focus

To choose a career, you need to know how your skill sets match with careers that may use those skills. It is also very important to know which skill sets will adapt to your changing careers throughout your working life. Use the chart at www.cengage.com/school/iyc, *Real Life Focus*, 5.3.

Update this list regularly to help you set goals and plan your career journey.

- List your current skill sets in the top left column. These skills transfer from one career to another.
- List careers that use those skill sets in the top right column.
- List careers that use any specialized skills that will help you in a specific career area in the bottom left column.
- List careers that may use the specialized skills in the bottom right column.

Make the Decision

After you have considered each career cluster in the Real Life Focus, decide which one is the best match for you. Next, explore various careers within the cluster you chose. Select the career or careers that best match your unique qualities.

When he analyzes the career clusters, Matt Nodro knows that he should disregard clusters that require strong math and science skills. Matt does well in those subjects. However, he does not want to use that knowledge every day. Design technology and photography require only some scientific and mathematical knowledge.

Matt's passion for design technology and photography leads him to a career in the Arts, A/V Technology, and Communications or the Information Technology career clusters. Matt uses a checklist, shown in Illustration 5-3, and his P*A*T*H to Success to make sure his choice is right for him.

Matt primarily likes to work alone. His work values assessment shows the same results. Many careers in the Arts, A/V Technology, and Communications cluster fit Matt's ideal workplace. The Information Technology career cluster does not have the creativity aspect that Matt needs.

Create questions using the *P*A*T*H to Success* traits for each career cluster. If you answer *yes* to most of the questions, like Matt, the cluster is a good match for you. Check the *P*A*T*H* traits. The more checkmarks you have, the more the cluster is a good match for you.

You may find part of one career cluster that closely matches you and another cluster that fits a different part of you, as Matt did with Arts, A/V Technology, and Communications and Information Technology. If so, your best option may be to choose a career directly related to one career cluster with some characteristics of another cluster.

Jo Ann has two major passions—working outdoors with plants and working with people. Her interest inventory supports her passions. Her work values assessment shows that she is very thorough. Her skills assessment shows that she has skills in science, psychology, and writing. Jo Ann also loves to solve problems.

Jo Ann analyzed all of the career clusters. She believes the Agriculture, Food, and Natural Resources career cluster may be the best fit for her P*A*T*H to Success. She knows that she will not consider a career in farming or forestry because she lives in the suburbs of a major city. Her lifestyle choices are to continue to live in a similar place.

So Jo Ann decided to explore landscape design. She plans to job shadow a landscape architect. She knows she would enjoy a career in landscaping, but she is concerned she would not be interacting with other people enough.

Jo Ann also is considering teaching landscaping in another career cluster she is exploring, the Education and Training cluster. By teaching landscape design, the Agriculture, Food, and Natural Resources cluster would still be her primary career cluster. Together, the two clusters match Jo Ann's P*A*T*H to Success.

Careers often cross two or more clusters when they have characteristics from more than one cluster. Matt's design career crosses two career clusters. Jo Ann's teaching is in the Education and Training cluster. However, a teacher's subject matter may be included in another cluster. Another example, engineering, can also cross into many clusters, such as environmental engineering or civil (construction) engineering. If your career choice crosses clusters, your primary career cluster will be the one that best matches your *P*A*T*H to Success.*

Illustration 5-3: Matt Nodro's Checklist

ARTS, A/V TECHNOLOGY, & COMMUNICATIONS CLUSTER CHECKLIST

	Answer yes or no.
• Is sharing information one of your passions?	No
• Do your talents include creativity, imagination, and originality?	Yes
• Do you prefer expressing yourself in art, photography, graphic media, audio, or writing?	Yes
• Do you use photographic enhancement technology?	Yes
• Is performing your preference?	No
• Do you like to communicate ideas?	Yes

Passions (Interests)	**Check _P*A*T*H_ matches.**
• Taking photographs	√
• Being creative and original	√
• Using imagination	√
• Composing photographs for in artistic activities	√
• Sharing information and ideas	

Attitude (Personality)	
• Self-motivated	√
• Sensitive	√
• Determined	√
• Creative and unique	√

Talents (Skills/Strengths)	
• Innovative style	√
• Knowledgeable about latest technology	√
• Art, music, drama, or writing ability	√
• Gift for recognizing details in surroundings, including colors and shapes	√

Heart (Values)	
• Likes to create original ideas or objects	√
• Likes to make beautiful things	√
• Likes to work alone	√
• Needs variety in activities	√

Create the Plan

Deciding which career cluster to use for your *Internal Career Design* is the beginning of your career journey. Next, you will research the different aspects of the cluster. Then you will explore one or two careers further. After your research, you will need to evaluate the careers. When you are confident you have made the right decision, you will create a plan and goals to guide you on your career journey.

Portfolio

The career cluster you chose is the best match to your *P*A*T*H to Success*. Now research some careers that interest you. The investigation will give you information to narrow your career choices within your career cluster. You should also focus your education and training.

You will need to do the following:

■ Investigate the education and training needed for entry-level and higher-level positions. You need to know what education and training will qualify you for the career you chose.

■ Research the workforce and workplace trends influencing your career to get a view of the future. The predictions will help you realize how your chosen career may change in the next 10 to 15 years. The Web Connection on this page provides many web sites to explore.

■ Investigate the employment outlook, earnings, and possibilities for advancement in your career area. The amount of money you earn will influence your lifestyle research. When you develop your talents, you affect your **career satisfaction**, the pleasure that comes from working in a career that allows you to use your passions. Explore several careers within your career cluster.

■ Make an inventory of your skill sets. These skills can be assets for several careers and may transfer across career clusters. Identify the skill sets you have now. Add to your inventory as you acquire new skills. Include records of situations in which you have used your skill sets effectively. For example, keep copies of test scores, photos of work, and outstanding papers in your Career Portfolio.

■ Begin a list of your specialized skills. This list will include the different equipment, technology, and talents you have to help you work and advance in specific careers. Your research into various careers will identify specialized skills you will need in the future for your chosen career. Starting early will give you a head start on your career pathway.

Web Connections

Researching your career cluster will give you the information you need to set your career planning goals in Chapter 6.

Use Career Transitions to research your career cluster. Find the following information about each career you chose.

- Description of the work
- Education and training requirements
- Working conditions
- Employment outlook
- Workplace and workforce trends that may affect the career. Similar skills sets among other career researched
- Future trends for the career

For additional links to websites that will help you with your research, access the Web Connections link for Chapter 5.

www.cengage.com/school/iyc

Matt Nodro researched the Arts, A/V Technology, and Communication cluster. In particular, he looked at product design and photography careers. He has design skills other than photography. Not only can he produce, but also Matt creates designs using digital software.

In addition, Matt knows that learning additional software will enhance both his creation and production specialized skills. His research confirms that those trends will continue in the future. Matt keeps records of the technology he uses and has samples of his designs and photographs.

Besides investigating a career in product design, Matt researched a career in advertising. His grades in English showed that he could excel in writing. That, plus design, made Matt decide to investigate advertising. He researched the need for advertising copy designers in Colorado, where he wants to go to college and eventually work. Matt hopes to be able to concentrate solely on his photography some day. However, for now, he is happy to have found a career path that will allow him to develop his passions.

Real People / Real Careers

Doug Teets / *Real Estate Title Services—Co-Owner and Title Examiner*

Owning his own business was not Doug Teets' first choice as a career. In high school, his goal was to be a journalist, but because of family circumstances, college was not an option after graduation. The lack of an education led Doug into jobs he did not really enjoy. Those jobs did not pay very much—or the companies were financially unstable. Fortunately, his job search led Doug to a job with good pay, working with real estate titles. Eventually, he started his own business, and title services became his career.

To be a real estate title examiner means researching property records for real estate transactions. The transactions include sales, refinances, wills and estates, and foreclosures. As the business co-owner, Doug primarily manages expenses and hires (and fires) employees.

Doug's love of journalism and English prepared him well for his career. He learned to pay attention to detail. Both classes encouraged the use of technology, particularly for layout and design. Doug states, "I have always like technology and been good with it. Over the years, I have been able to bring technology into my business and gain advantages because of it. Computer training has given me a competitive advantage in an industry that is seriously behind the times."

His advice on owning his own business? Doug insists, "If you can't do something you love, do not lose hope. Find something you are passionate about and slowly bring your skills and interests into it. But do not start your own business too soon. It is easy to work a job, see your boss, and think that you could do much better. That is not always the case. It is best to learn from mistakes while working for someone else. When you are confident and ready, go out on your own. However, plan well financially. There are things you need to watch out for that you did not even know about. Ignorance will not protect you."

For more information about:

* title and real estate careers

* business ownership

Access **www.cengage.com/school/iyc** and click on the appropriate links in Chapter 5.

Source: *Personal Interview*, September 2011

Photo courtesy of Doug Teets

Evaluate the Decision

You need to evaluate your career decision based on your research. Make sure that all aspects of the career meet your expectations. You should answer *Yes* to the following questions about the career cluster and the careers you have chosen:

✔ Will you find enjoyment in the career?

✔ Is the product or service needed and valued?

✔ Will you respect the kinds of people working in the career field?

✔ Will you appreciate the work your career involves?

✔ Will you have opportunities for personal growth? Have you planned your career path beyond an entry-level position?

✔ Does the career have the work environment that is best for you?

✔ Will you have the contact with people that matches your work values, such as working alone, interacting with people, creativity?

✔ Will you make enough money to support your desired lifestyle?

✔ Will you have enough leisure time to spend with family and on activities?

✔ Will you be able to live in the area you want while working in this career?

✔ Are you aware of the challenges you may come across in your career? Do you know solutions to some of those challenges?

✔ Have you investigated the employment outlook of the career?

✔ Have you researched workplace and workforce trends affecting the career?

By answering *Yes* to most of these questions, you will know you have chosen the career cluster and the career well matched for you. If you have two or more negative answers, you may need to investigate further or research another career or another career cluster.

Jaimie Duplass/Shutterstock.com

Consider

What might happen if you set goals for your career plan without evaluating your decision?

Set Goals

You can begin to set goals and create a plan to achieve your goals after you have completed the evaluation of your career cluster and potential career. You may have created some goals already. If so, you are moving right along your career pathway. If not, you can focus on the goals necessary to achieve your *Internal Career Design* to meet your graduation requirements.

Your goals may include choosing electives in your career area. These courses will help you discover whether the career is a good fit for you. Part-time jobs, job shadowing, and other informal career assessments discussed in Chapter 3 will help you sample a career too. These activities also help you develop skills that support your career goal.

Setting goals and creating an action plan are the next steps for your career journey. These are the steps that guide you toward making your dreams realities. In Chapter 6, you use the information from this chapter and from your Career Portfolio to set goals. You will create timelines to help you set an action plan and complete your goals.

Monitor Success

The career you choose now is probably the first of eight careers you will have from ages 18 to 42. Basing your first choice on your *P*A*T*H* builds a firm base for all of your career choices.

After you have made your career decision and created your plan, you need to **monitor**, or keep track of, the success of your decision. Then review your career plan periodically to check if you are on the right track.

Your Career Portfolio

twohumans/iStockphoto.com

What should you have in your Career Portfolio to showcase your specialized skills?

Your Career Portfolio contains samples and other items important to your career choice and career path. Besides including the results from specific activities marked with the Portfolio icon, you should include:

- Records or copies of accomplishments, such as certificates, badges, and letters

  - Newspaper articles, programs, and brochures about your activities. If your name does not appear in the document, keep it anyway. Make notes of a brief description about your participation.

  - Photos of projects and achievements

  - Letters about your activities and achievements

  - Copies of anything showing your specialized skills, such as drawings, test scores, and assignments

  - Samples of your work saved electronically. For example, music, drawings, photographs, computer files, project demonstrations

Your school may offer each student access to a web-based career-planning system similar to the Career Portfolio. Take the opportunity to use it by collecting the items listed above and storing them electronically on the web site.

Why should you save those items in your Career Portfolio? They offer evidence of your achievements. The collection will help you remember what you have done.

It is very important for you to keep your Portfolio up-to-date. It will help you plan your career. Use the Portfolio whenever you need to explain your talents to others. Later, you can use it for school admissions and job searches.

Check Progress

Checking your progress along your career journey keeps you moving in the right direction. Review your progress from time to time.

1. Ask yourself the following questions:

   - Does my career choice match my passions?

   - Do I feel positive about my career choice?

   - Are my goals part of my career plan?

   - Do I have the motivation to meet the timelines of my goals? Am I meeting the timelines?

   - Does my career decision continue to match my *P*A*T*H to Success*?

Chapter 6 provides you with the tools to set goals, create Action Plans, and develop timelines for each Action Plan.

2. Analyze your answers to the questions in Item 1. If you answered *No* to any of the questions, decide what you need to do to change your answer to *Yes*. Perhaps you should consider changing your career choice.

If you discover that your career plan is not taking you in the right direction, make a change. You need to be flexible to adjust to new experiences and situations. You may need the courage to stay in pursuit of the career of your dreams. You may meet resistance from some of the people who influence you. However, you need to make your *own* choice.

Career maturity is using the path you created to make an informed career decision. With career maturity, you use self-knowledge and self-motivation to create your *Internal Career Design*. When you continue on your *P*A*T*H to Success*, you gain career satisfaction from your career journey that allows you to use your passions.

Learning from Others

Job shadow someone who is working in your career cluster. The closer the person's career is to your career choice, the better. Your family or teachers can help you find someone if needed.

1. Before you go, create a list of questions to ask the person about an average day in his or her career. Also, include questions about the person's career goals. In addition, add questions similar to those in the bulleted list on page 123. Your teacher will check your list.

2. Share your information with the class when you return.

Chapter Summary

5.1 Start the Plan Now

- Making a career decision now allows a person to choose courses, add skill sets, and increase specialized skills.

- The decision-making process has six steps: (1) Recognize that one must make a decision. (2) Identify the benefits of making a good decision. (3) Consider all possible decisions. (4) Make a decision. (5) Create a plan to carry out the decision. (6) Monitor the success of the decision.

- A fulfilling career will result if a person's *P*A*T*H to Success* is the basis for his or her career.

5.2 Career Decisions

- Self-understanding is necessary before one can make an informed career choice.

- The 16 career clusters are groups of careers that have common interest and skill requirements. Studying the clusters for career possibilities will give one the understanding to make an educated career choice.

5.3 Creating Your *Internal Career Design*

- Using the characteristics of each career cluster will help a person create a career plan that best matches one's *P*A*T*H to Success*.

- Evaluating possible careers in a chosen career cluster will help narrow the choices.

- Setting goals will help create plans for education and training and additional skill sets and specialized skills.

- To help with planning, a person should organize the contents of the Career Portfolio, which contains evidence of achievements. Reviewing the success of the decision periodically will help monitor the success of the career plan.

Chapter Assessment

Vocabulary Builder

Match each statement with the term that best defines it.

a. career maturity
b. career satisfaction
c. decision-making process
d. monitor
e. self-understanding

1. The pleasure that comes from working in a career that allows one to use his or her passions
2. To keep track of the success of the career decision
3. Using one's career path to make an informed career decision
4. The true knowledge about oneself
5. Offers a way to plan carefully, based on the steps for problem solving

Review What You Have Learned

6. Why is it so important to start career decision-making now?
7. Describe the six steps of the decision-making process.
8. How is the P*A*T*H to Success important in making a career decision?
9. Why is self-understanding important when choosing a career?
10. How should one use assessment results to choose a career?
11. Explain the process of choosing a career cluster.
12. How can one career cross two or more career clusters?
13. Describe how one can research careers to narrow the choices.
14. What is career satisfaction?
15. How can one make sure he or she is on the P*A*T*H to Success?
16. How does one achieve career maturity?

Case Challenges

Each case study describes a person's P*A*T*H to Success. After reading each case study,

- decide which career cluster fits each person best.
- list at least three careers the person might choose.
- include reasons for your decisions.

There are no right or wrong answers.

17. As a child, Runi's favorite birthday gift was a box of interconnecting building pieces. She drew her structures before she built them. Analyzing the curve of a bridge or the height of a tower was a test of Runi's problem-solving abilities. She just started learning the computer drawing program for creating her plans.

18. Maddie gets along with everyone. She never seems to play favorites. Maddie is usually chosen as a group leader because she gets every team member to work together. Also, Maddie has patience and listens to everyone's opinion before asking the group to make a decision.

19. Ram observes his surroundings carefully. He is a sensitive person and needs to have alone time to absorb his environment so he can recreate it using his imagination. Ram feels the need to express the meaning of his observations in creative ways.

20. When a group at school needs a hard worker, someone usually calls Aesha. She is always calm in the midst of chaos. Always able to help, she seems to find solutions to problems. No one was surprised to learn a few months ago that Aesha is a member of the Explorers and helps the fire department's emergency team.

Make Academic Connections

21. LANGUAGE ARTS Each profession has its own language, specialized terms used to communicate about their work. For example, people in education use terms such as *differential instruction* and *program of study*. The legal profession uses terms such as *appellate* and *judicial review*.

- Identify ten specialized terms used in your chosen career. You may need to ask someone in that career for assistance.
- Define each of the terms.
- Write a memo to a fictitious coworker using at least five of the specialized terms.

22. SPEECH In nearly every career, you will have to speak before a group. Develop a three-minute informative presentation on your chosen career or a topic related to that career. Using technology will enhance your project.

Workplace Connection

In small groups of career cluster teams, research several careers within the cluster that interests the group. Each team member should research one career.

23. Survey three to five people employed in the career cluster, asking the following information.

- Type of work involved in the career
- Working conditions
- Educational background, personal qualities, and skills needed for the career
- Employment outlook
- Earnings
- Related careers, including advancement

Portfolio

24. Share your survey results with the class. Discuss the careers each group researched.

Blogging: My Career Choice

In this blog entry, you will tell the story of how you made your career decision. Explain the six steps of the decision-making process. Include the methods you used to focus on the choice of a career cluster or clusters. Then lead the reader through your choice of a specific career.

Blog

Setting Goals

Lesson 6.1 Self-Motivation
Lesson 6.2 Action Plans
Lesson 6.3 Time Management

pressureUA/iStockphoto.com

POSITION
6/6

HEALTH
99%
+0'03.50
TO RECORD

LAP
2/3

What Do You Know

1. What are some goals you need to complete your career plan?

2. What is your most daring career dream? How could you accomplish it?

Even as a very little boy, Ed loved to play video games. He was like many children who thrived on the mechanical motions and skills that increased his chances at winning a game. From handheld devices to those with full-body motion control, Ed loved electronic games.

When Ed read about a contest that combined video games with learning, he was intrigued. Students were to create a video explaining how an electronic game helped them understand a course taught in school.

In his video, Ed explained how gaming improved his ability to learn vocabulary for various classes. He developed a playable model where the characters in the game would respond only to the scientific terms of particular classes, such as physics or zoology.

Ed's experience drew him into the world of Science, instead of his former goal of teaching English. He liked the precision required for the technology and the testing required to produce a model. Ed also knew that gaming could be an important asset in education.

To his great surprise, Ed won the contest. Along with the prize of a notebook computer, Ed received a large scholarship—if he majored in some form of scientific research. Ed realized that changing his future goals from teaching English to scientific research related more directly to his *P*A*T*H to Success*. After consulting with his family, his physics teacher, and the contest advisor, Ed revised his career goal and applied to the university that underwrote the scholarship.

Planning a Career in . . . Science

Change or routine. Working with people or alone. Research or field work. These are the varied working conditions in Science. Careers in Science cover many industries, from food to medicine to chemistry to space exploration. All the careers require knowledge of Science, Math, and Technology.

Gathering, creating, processing, and sharing data defines the basis of a Science career.

Employment Outlook

- Demand for Science breakthrough areas, such as genetics and medicine.

- Best for those in Science programs or applied science programs trained in the latest technology and research processes.

Career Possibilities

- NASA Technician
- Chemist
- Science Visualization Graphics Expert
- Biotechnologist
- Criminal Lab Technician

Needed Skills

- Strong science, math, and technical skills.

- Excellent communication.

- Curiosity and persistence in uncovering the truth.

- Education needs vary from career and technical education to a Ph.D.

What's It Like to Work in Science?

Square watermelons ship better. Featherless chickens grow 25 percent faster. New cholesterol-reducing drugs increase life expectancy by 1.5 years.

From new agricultural techniques to developing medical breakthroughs, Science is at the forefront.

Science careers include those in physical, environmental, and human projects. Science skills, with a foundation of math and technology, use the real world. Understanding the process and applying the skills is necessary for discoveries and research.

A career in Science offers you a variety of workplaces from a hospital to a lab to a crime scene or a space station. A career in Science requires a love of detail and accuracy, making it a good career choice.

What about You?

Was the Science Fair one of your favorite activities? Does it bother you when people are not accurate and precise? Do you thrive on change? Or do you need routine? Answering *yes* to any of these questions will open up a career in the many Science work environments.

R. Gino Santa Maria/Shutterstock.com

Self-Motivation

Goals

- Identify how self-motivation is needed to set goals.
- Understand the differences between long-term, medium-term, and short-term goals.
- Describe why timelines are necessary when setting goals.

Terms

- self-motivation, p. 133
- procrastinate, p. 133
- long-term goals, p. 133
- medium-term goals, p. 133
- short-term goals, p. 133

Portfolio

Real Life Focus

Imagine that you are 30 years old. What would you like to accomplish by then? Use the categories:

- Education
- Career
- Family
- Home

How long would it take to complete each item on your list?

- Highlight in yellow those goals that would take more than 5 years to complete.
- Highlight in green those goals that would take between 1 and 5 years.
- Put a star beside those goals that would take less than 1 year.

Save this list to use for Activity 6.1.

Goals to Set

You want to dream big, but how do you make that dream happen? You need to plan how you will reach your ideal career. After all, in Chapter 5, you discovered your *Internal Career Design*. What strategies should you follow? What goals should you set? How can you stay motivated to reach your goals if you run into problems with your plan?

When Angela created her career plan, she decided to follow her sister, Nieca's, path and work with her in public relations. Nieca advised Angela to begin her plan now and take as many writing classes as she could fit into her schedule. Nieca also suggested that Angela write for the school newspaper to get the prime internship in public relations.

Angela took Nieca's advice about her classes and activities. However, she just did not feel motivated to work hard writing for the school newspaper. Instead, she wanted to run track and spend time with the

*other athletes. Whenever Angela felt discouraged, she would call Nieca.
Nieca would always encourage Angela and tell her to keep trying.*

*In her senior year, Angela lost the public relations internship to another
student. Instead of being discouraged, however, Angela was determined
to succeed in activities that were her passion. She found a part-time job
with the professional baseball team in her town and used her writing
skills in the team's public relations office.*

Self-motivation is the determination to stay on track and avoid distractions. Achieving the goals you set for your career—and your life—requires self-motivation. It helps you take responsibility for managing your life. Instead of feeling as though events are out of control, self-motivation gives you the energy to take charge. That control will help you feel good about each success that brings you closer to your goals.

People need to be self-motivated to stick to their career planning. Without self-motivation, you may **procrastinate**, or delay, planning. You also may find that events in your life distract you from thinking about your career plan and cause procrastination.

Consider

What strategies do you use to motivate yourself in school?

Set Your Goals

Setting goals is an important part of your life. Career goals are not the only important goals you must consider. You also need to set goals for your personal, school, and work life based on your values and other influences.

Examples of personal goals you may set include staying physically fit and being honest. School and work goals could include having ethical behavior and doing your best to have perfect attendance. The principles for setting and meeting goals are the same whether they are career goals or personal goals.

Types of Goals

Breaking your goals into parts according to how long you think it will take you to complete them is a way of managing them. **Long-term goals** are goals you expect to achieve in five or more years. Some examples are planning education and training or getting married. **Medium-term goals** are goals you expect to achieve in one to two years. They might include running for student office or managing your study time more efficiently. **Short-term goals** are goals you expect to achieve in less than one year. Some short-term goals might be starting the English project when it is first assigned or auditioning for the school musical.

You may have a long-term goal of owning your own business in your career field. To reach that goal, you first must set and meet short-term and medium-term goals. The shorter-term goals act as steppingstones to the ultimate goal. One important medium-term goal may be to manage a business similar to the type you wish to own. A short-term goal may be to take a job as an assistant or a technician in a related business.

Kirstin wanted to work in a European country since she began German and French language classes. She took a stand on many issues, so she decided her best college major would be international economics. In her classes, Kirstin was usually the first to volunteer to speak about economics, politics, and other interests. She spent many hours working on her language skills and spent time conversing with her foreign language teachers. Kirstin's excitement lasted long after the talking stopped.

For two summers before college, Kirstin went on school trips to France and Germany. During her trips, Kirstin really enjoyed conversing with the natives and learning their customs. During her junior year, Kirstin began working as a volunteer with English for Speakers of Other Languages (ESOL) students. The work was valuable. It gave her a realistic picture of using a foreign language and working with those people whose native language was not English. After her first year of volunteering, Kirstin revised her school schedule, adding more language courses to advance her knowledge.

All of Kirstin's research and experience shaped her desire to work with foreign languages. Her desire is to work directly with foreign languages, rather than indirectly as she would with international economics. She is confident that her career plan is on the right track.

Kirstin's goals began early. She recognized that reaching her long-term goal would mean setting and revising short- and medium-term goals along the way.

Strategies

Your goals must be useful, or you will ignore them. When you create your goals, you want to complete them successfully. Make sure that each goal has the following criteria.

How could a trip be a step for completing a career goal?

jan kranendonk/Shutterstock.com

■ *Realistic.* You should write goals that you know you actually can accomplish. If science is your weakest subject, should you really plan a career as a registered nurse?

■ *Challenging.* You need to make an effort to accomplish your goals. Why write a goal that does not motivate you to action?

■ *Positive.* Avoid negative words when you create your goals, such as "Do not take zoology." Positive statements motivate you to succeed.

■ *Measurable.* Each goal should have a specific, measurable outcome.

To be successful with your goal setting, you will need to pay attention to *each* of your goals. Create goals that fit together well. Then decide which goals have the highest priority for your career and your personal life. For example, suppose you set two goals—to learn to speak Spanish fluently and to learn to cook Spanish cuisine. While you can achieve both of these goals, they are really unrelated. Cooking Spanish-influenced food and speaking Spanish require different strategies for success.

Putting your goals into writing will help you identify what you want to achieve. Written goals also increase your personal commitment. The special attention that you give to your goals motivates you to work hard to reach them. The satisfaction of accomplishing even a short-term goal can inspire you to work hard to achieve your next goal.

Review and revise your goals periodically. You grow as a person. As you change, your goals also will change.

Timelines

To reach most long-term goals, you must complete a number of short-term and medium-term goals. Each long-term goal should consist of steps or activities that you need to complete before you can achieve that goal. Set an estimated target date for accomplishing each step or goal. The dates will help you plan more effectively. The following guidelines describe how to develop a timeline for a long-term goal:

1. Determine how much time you need to meet each step or goal.

2. Divide the time you need into smaller parts. Are days, weeks, or months needed for reaching your short-term goals? How much time will it take to achieve each medium-term goal? How many months or years will it take until you reach your long-term goal?

3. Use a calendar or planner to schedule the day, month, or year you want to complete each step.

4. Write down your timeline. Include all of the steps necessary to reach your long-term goal.

When Kirstin prepared the timeline below, she made sure that each of her goals was specific. Some goals will require additional parts, or steps, for her to complete. For example, the medium-term goal of spending a summer working in Germany will probably require Kirstin to research the types of jobs available, learn how to apply for work in a foreign country, earn money to pay for the trip, and so on. As time passes, Kirstin will need to revise her timeline to include additional short-term goals.

Kirstin's Timeline

	Target Date:
My Long-Term Goal:	
Teach German to Americans in Berlin	10 years
Medium-Term Goals:	
Intern for the American consulate in Germany	9 years
College major – German	5–8 years
Semester in Germany	6 years
German Sister Cities volunteer	1–2 years
Finish 4 years of high school German	1 year
Short-Term Goals:	
Research colleges with German language major	Now
Tutor a German-speaking ESOL student	Now

ACTIVITY 6.1

Leadership

Long-Term Ambitions

Creating goals for your career path requires many steps. To help you with this long-term goal, you will need the list you created for *Real Life Focus* on page 132. Working in small groups will help you brainstorm ideas and check the reality of the goals you created.

1. What are some of the terms that might describe you at age 30?

- Employee
- College graduate
- Apprentice
- Married
- Girlfriend/boyfriend
- Employed overseas
- Employer
- Professional
- Entrepreneur
- Single
- Parent
- Engaged

2. Working backward, write down the steps needed for you to reach the items you listed in Item 1 to create your possible career path. Some suggestions are:

- Master's or Doctorate degree
- Bachelor's degree
- Associate degree
- Internship
- College courses
- High school courses
- Service learning
- Job shadowing
- Entry-level job
- Activities
- Summer job

Save the results to use for Activity 6.2.

humonia/iStockphoto.com

Action Plans

Goals

- Recognize the influences that could affect your Action Plan.
- Describe the steps and criteria for developing a career Action Plan.
- Develop strategies for overcoming roadblocks.

Terms

- Action Plan, p. 137
- backup plan, p. 140
- roadblocks, p. 141

Real Life Focus

Considering not only deadlines, but also the importance of what to finish first is important in setting goals. What are the priorities in this story?

It is Friday afternoon, and you have a long list of things to finish before Monday. The weekend is your time to recover from the week, sleep in, and get a head start on next week. This weekend is especially full since you are a volunteer coach for your school's basketball team. Your team has a weekend game, as well as a tournament that starts Monday evening.

Of the following activities, mark the order of those you would complete this weekend. Mark those you would postpone or cancel with an X. Your basketball duties are not on the list.

- Bathe the dog.
- Read materials for Tuesday's English exam.
- Practice the piano for your Thursday lesson.
- Wash the car.
- Arrange your CDs.
- Do laundry.
- Eat pizza with friends Friday night.
- Attend a concert on Sunday.
- Write thank-you notes for gifts you received 3 weeks ago.
- Iron your school clothes.
- Drive your sister to the mall Sunday.
- Watch a TV show Sunday evening.

Why did you choose what you did? Why did you eliminate or postpone certain things?

To complete your goals, you need to create Action Plans. An **Action Plan** shows how to get from where you are now to where you want to be. It is a list of steps to your goal, directing a way to the future. An Action Plan details everything you need to know to reach a goal. Your goal is the starting point and destination for your Action Plan. An Action Plan lists the skills and knowledge you need to reach your destination. Following are some important points you should consider as you develop an Action Plan.

Remember Your Influences

The influence that someone or something has on you can give you motivation and purpose for setting your goals and making an Action Plan. That influence can affect your decisions. Remember the influences discussed in Chapter 2 and think about how they can affect your plan.

P*A*T*H to Success

Use your passion, attitude, talents, and heart—your *P*A*T*H to Success*—as the basis of your goal to accomplish your *Internal Career Design*. Your Action Plan should describe how you plan to use your strengths and talents to fulfill your passion. For example, if math is your passion, your Action Plan might identify the steps you need to take to develop a career as an actuary or a meteorologist. Remember your talents and passion when you develop your Action Plan.

Stay true to your values. They are your guides through life. Remember the list of your values that you created for the Web Connection activity in Chapter 3? Consider them when you develop an Action Plan.

Leatha loved biology and its research. She especially enjoyed studying animals. She knew her career focus should involve biology and research. Her biology teacher, Mr. Braun, sent her to interview as a lab technician for the university biology lab.

After a successful interview, Leatha toured the lab. There, she discovered that the university used animals for testing. Even though the job seemed ideal and paid more than she would make working for a veterinarian, Leatha turned down the job offer. She loved animals. But she did not want a part in harming them, even for the purpose of research.

When life situations, such as career decisions, are in conflict with your values, you experience tension. Let your values guide you as you make decisions for your career and your future.

People

In creating your Action Plan, you may turn to others for information, advice, or assistance in getting a job or an internship in your career field. Your Action Plan may include a list of people you can go to for advice and assistance. Include their contact information with phone numbers and e-mail addresses so you can reach them when you need to talk or meet with them. At least one of these people may become a mentor to you.

An important step for a successful Action Plan is finding a mentor. As discussed in Chapter 2, a mentor is a person who offers experience and knowledge to help you complete your Action Plan and follow your career journey. Mentors are experienced people you can turn to when you have a decision to make or a problem to solve. They will make themselves available to suggest positive approaches, to point out pitfalls, and to make suggestions.

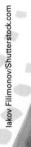

Most mentors develop a caring relationship over time to provide guidance. Some mentors are teachers, relatives, or employers. As you advance in your career, you will meet mentors whom you respect and who listen to and help you. Successful people know that mentors make a difference.

Consider

Who might serve as a mentor for you? What questions would you like to ask this person?

When you have an internship in your career cluster, you will gain an understanding of the day-to-day responsibilities and career possibilities in your career area. You may receive positive benefits from your employer. He or she may not only offer you career experience, but also advice, possibly even becoming one of your mentors.

Working with others in a business situation increases your interpersonal skills, as well as your career knowledge. Both are important to your long-term success.

However, you may decide that this cluster is not the area for you. Great! You now have the opportunity to search for a well-matched career before you have spent time and money in education and training.

What can I learn about careers at an event such as a career fair?

arindambanerjee/Shutterstock.com

Trends

An Action Plan should futurecast to see what the career you are considering will look like in 10 or 15 years. The U.S. job market is in a constant state of change. As you read in Chapter 4, some industries disappear, move overseas, or change radically while others will take their place. Some career fields have too many workers for the number of available jobs. Others cannot find enough people to fill the openings.

The career cluster interested you before you chose a specific career to pursue. If the trends do not offer a successful future for your career choice, make sure you look at the entire range of careers in that cluster. For example, suppose your passion is helping others and you are planning a health career. Many people automatically think *doctor* when they imagine a career in the health care field. However, health care careers include medical researchers, nurses, massage therapists, medical equipment designers, acupuncturists, and technicians in all areas. The more career choices there are within your career area, the more you will need to expand your Action Plan.

Steps to Action

Understand the steps of your plan: put first things first. Following through in the right order is a key factor in career planning. Figure out what steps will produce results that will lead you to the next step. Careful planning is the only way to make sure you will have the career you want.

These guidelines offer suggestions for creating a successful career plan.

- *Research your career.* Gather information from web sites, magazines, newspapers, family, friends, teachers, counselors, and businesspeople in your career field. Listen and read any information that will help you in your planning, including career workforce and workplace trends.

- *Identify possible ways to reach your ideal career. Then select the best one.* Most careers have several education and training paths: on-the-job training, an associate or bachelor's degree, career and technical training, apprenticeship, or military service. Evaluate each alternative. Which one best fits your needs? Then create a schedule around your career plan by choosing courses and outside activities that will help you reach your goals.

- *Divide your career plan into small steps.* Your dream will seem more within your reach if you divide your career plan into many small steps. Each step you complete is progress toward your success.

- *Decide which steps will be easier if you get help.* Many people can assist you with your planning. For example, your counselor, teacher, or coach can offer useful web sites for learning about your ideal career. Family members, friends, businesspeople, and others will be glad to talk to you about your career choices.

jane/iStockphoto.com

- *Begin with your goal and work backward to reach your ideal career. Be sure to set deadlines on your timeline.* Planning works best when you look at your future and work backwards from there. For example, if you know you want to start your career by age 22, what type of training and experience will you need to meet your time frame?

- *Put your career plan in print.* Seeing the words helps you identify any gaps or problems. You can see larger sections that need to break into smaller steps. Picturing your career plan motivates you to take action. A printed plan also helps you remember all of your ideas and notes.

- *Check your plan's progress periodically. Make revisions as needed by adding, revising, or deleting steps at any time.* Even the best futurecasters cannot truly read the future. Plan to review your progress every few months. At that time, decide if you need to modify your plan.

- *Be flexible.* You need to create a Plan B, an alternative or **backup plan**. Sometimes unexpected circumstances may cause you to revise your plan. For instance, what if your family moves to another state? Will your new school offer the classes you need? Will you need to enroll in a training program that requires more time to finish? Your backup plan may require you to add summer school or online courses to your education plan.

Roadblocks

In Jamaica, when people talk about roadblocks, they mean things thrown in the road to prevent cars from traveling. In career planning, **roadblocks** are barriers that may slow or stop the progress of your Action Plan. Some of the common roadblocks to career success are difficulty with school, family issues, procrastination, lack of money, and competition.

You can anticipate some roadblocks based on your goals and Action Plan. Other roadblocks, such as an illness in the family that causes an interruption in your education, cannot be anticipated.

When you anticipate a roadblock, prepare by looking for possible barriers to reaching your goals. Develop backup plans for overcoming each roadblock.

When Shaheen was in the seventh grade, her counselor, Mr. Christos, met Shaheen and her parents for a scheduling conference. Mr. Christos urged Shaheen to begin a foreign language in the eighth grade. By starting a language early, Shaheen would have four years of a language completed before her senior year. Many universities require four years of a foreign language for admission. But Shaheen wanted to attend the state university a few hours from her home. She insisted she would need only two years of a language, the state university requirement. Shaheen created her long-term schedule with her starting a foreign language in the eleventh grade.

The summer before her sophomore year, Shaheen received a scholarship to attend a science camp at Montgomery, a prestigious university. The professors admired Shaheen's work at the camp and offered her an assistant's position at the camp the following summer. After completing that summer successfully, Shaheen would be eligible for a full tuition scholarship at Montgomery.

After the summer ended, Shaheen told Mr. Christos about her plan to go to Montgomery instead of the state university. Mr. Christos looked up Montgomery's admission requirements and saw that the school had a four-year foreign language requirement. Since Shaheen was starting her sophomore year, she had created her own roadblock.

Now Shaheen had to decide how to overcome the problem of having only three years of high school left. She knew she would be accepted at the state university with only two years of language. However, she could try to take online foreign language courses to increase her number of foreign language credits.

Shaheen decided that she preferred to attend Montgomery. She reworked her timelines and Action Plan steps for her career goal, creating a backup plan. Shaheen promised herself she would not delay anything else that could affect her future—and she would listen to the advice of others.

How can I prepare for unforeseen roadblocks to my career planning?

The following strategies can help you overcome roadblocks:

■ Ask for help from someone who understands your situation. For example, if your family does not have the financial resources to send you to college, discuss your options with your guidance counselor.

■ Break a roadblock into smaller parts, and try to find a solution for each.

■ Create a backup plan for the major steps of your Action Plan, just in case.

Portfolio

ACTIVITY 6.2

Learning from Others

An Action Plan will help you determine the steps and events needed to reach your long-term goals. The Plan lists what you need to know to achieve a goal.

1. Select one long-term career goal and one long-term education goal from the goals you listed in the *Real Life Focus*, page 132.

2. Create an Action Plan for each of the goals you selected in Item 1. Include necessary details.

3. Write down two things you can do immediately to work on your education goal. Examples include completing an assignment, increasing your grade in one class, and improving your attendance.

4. Now write down three specific skills you need for the career cluster you chose in Chapter 5. Suggest

how you can obtain those skills. For example, if your career area is digital design, skills could include mastering a digital drawing program.

With a family member or another adult, brainstorm several roadblocks that might interfere with your career goal. Consider different types of barriers—financial, educational, personal, family issues, and other problems.

Then work with this person to create a plan to overcome each of the roadblocks you listed. For example, if lack of money for education or training is a roadblock, list several sources of income, such as grants, scholarships, loans, work, part-time classes, or military service.

val lawlwess/Shutterstock.com

Time Management

Goals

- Describe how to prioritize activities to achieve goals.
- Explain scheduling short and long projects to achieve good time management.
- Discuss how time wasters can interrupt time management.

Terms

- priorities, p. 143
- time wasters, p. 145

Real Life Focus

Knowing your habits will help you determine how well you manage your time. Answer the following with *yes*, *no*, or *sometimes*.

- I have a place where I always study.
- I have a regular schedule for studying.
- I plan my social life around my assignments.
- I answer texts and phone messages only after my studying is finished.
- I avoid distractions by turning off music or TV.
- I use a calendar to schedule my school, work, and home life.
- I start assignments when they are assigned, not when due.
- I make time for fun and household chores every day.
- I spend at least 20 minutes a day with my family.
- I review for my classes constantly, not just before a test.

Your teacher will tell you the scoring system and what your score indicates about your time management skills.

Do you often find that there are not enough hours in the day to complete everything you want to do? How often are you late in finishing homework? Do you ever have any time for yourself—to do what you love to do? How can you find better ways to use your time?

Set Priorities

The time management skills that you create as a student will help you for the rest of your life. The best way to begin is with good study habits. Setting blocks of time for studying, reviewing weekly, and studying at regular times each day will help you develop a habit.

The items of greatest importance on your schedule are your **priorities**. You are in school, so studying is your number one priority. Here are some other points to consider.

- **Eat right, get plenty of sleep, and exercise.** You are smarter and more creative when you have sleep. Sleep-related issues are the most common reason people are late for school. Do not hit snooze often.

- **Learn to set priorities.** Your commitments that are fixed are the things you must do during the day, often at certain times, such as going to class, play practice, and religious services. Commitments that are flexible are daily activities that can be done on your own at various times, such as doing homework and listening to music.

- **Do not be a perfectionist.** You can spend more time than necessary trying to be perfect. Know when to stop working on a project.

- **Avoid procrastination.** If you delay finishing an assignment, it is not any easier to complete. You waste time having to restart the task.

- **Learn how to schedule.** Take a few minutes to make a schedule. It often will save you time.

- **Set deadlines.** Setting a date to finish a task forces you to manage your time so you can meet the deadline.

- **Reward yourself for successes and achieved goals.** Set aside some time for yourself.

Real People / Real Careers

Christopher Gaskey / *Materials Scientist*

If there really were fortunetellers who could read crystal balls and foretell the future, they would have predicted Chris Gaskey's future career. As he played with Legos as a boy, little did Chris realize that he was developing skills for his future career as an engineer. Chris was a natural student; he loved all school subjects. However, his favorite was science—much needed for a STEM career. Also, Chris's family influenced his career decision. His father was an engineer and encouraged Chris on his career path.

These factors led Chris to choose Engineering as his college major. After excelling in science and math in high school, Chris knew that he would do well in Engineering. Besides, having an engineer as a father helped him realize what the career entailed. Chris felt he would do well—and he did. Exploring why things work and what causes them to fail led Chris to complete his Masters in Materials Science.

Chris is now in the specialized engineering field as a Materials Scientist. A Materials Scientist determines ways to strengthen or combine materials for use in a variety of products and applications. Chris performs failure analyses, reporting his results to service departments and customers for a large company that specializes in engines and related equipment, such as fuel systems.

Why Engineering? Chris's love of analyzing problems to create solutions, his even temperament, and his love of science led him to the perfect career. As Chris explains, "Engineering was a good fit for my personality and also a good fit for my strengths."

For more information about:

* engineering careers, including Materials Scientists
* STEM careers

Access **www.cengage.com/school/iyc** and click on the appropriate links in Chapter 6.

Source: *Personal Interview,* July 2011

Photo courtesy of Christopher Gaskey

Scheduling

In scheduling, setting priorities is most important. There is always more to do than you have time to do it. To head off problems, consider keeping a time management diary for a few days as explained in the *Workplace Connection* activity at the end of the chapter. You will be surprised at how little time you spend on what is considered important.

If you find that your priorities are not being fulfilled, you may need to limit your commitments. Typically this means cutting back on some of your activities, but you may have to say *no* to new ones.

When you do have a huge project, how do you tackle it? Do you know where to start? Do not let the size of the project keep you from getting organized.

Web Connections

You can manage time in many different ways. Explore some suggestions on different web sites. Access the Web Connections link for Chapter 6. Study at least two web sites of those given. Make a list of time management suggestions and forms that will help you.

As a class, share the suggestions you wrote. Have several students record the information to create a class list of time management tips.

www.cengage.com/school/iyc

- Break the large project into smaller chunks.

- Decide the steps for each of the smaller parts.

- Set deadlines for each smaller task—and meet the deadlines.

- Continuously look for ways to improve and simplify your task management.

- Take notes on the progress, including suggestions for improvement. You may have a similar project again.

Consider

How will scheduling help you meet your goals?

Time Wasters

Before you can manage your time effectively, you need to find out how you are spending your time. Keep track of how you spend your time for a week. Then you will know how you can save time. You also will learn what are your **time wasters**, the distractions and interruptions that cause you to go off your schedule and lose track of time.

Television, music, texting, social networking, video games, and phone conversations are typical time wasters. Here are some others you may not be aware of.

- Multitasking is one of the best ways to waste time. Switching between tasks means doing each less well and actually takes more time. You will also make more errors. If you create deadlines, take breaks, and keep to your schedule, you are less likely to waste time.

- Lapses of time add up. You may be spending too many minutes on some tasks at the expense of others.

- Consider using electronic devices, such as texting and phone calls, as rewards instead of time wasters. For example, for every 45 minutes of work, take a 10-minute break for yourself.

- Time wasters often occur when you have been working too long on one task. Take a break. Get some air, take a walk, or play with the dog. In fact, a University of Michigan study showed that walking in a greenspace, such as a park, improves your mind's recall and focus. Try taking a walk in the morning before your next test.

ACTIVITY 6.3

Portfolio

Managing Your Time

Use the blank *Weekly Time Planner* at www.cengage.com/school/iyc, Chapter 6. After reviewing the time management tips from this chapter, design a schedule using the *Planner*. Your schedule should allow time to meet your responsibilities at school, home, and work, plus time to relax during the course of a week.

Chapter Summary

6.1 Self-Motivation

- Self-motivation is the determination to stay on track and to avoid distractions.

- Long-term goals are completed in five or more years. Medium-term goals are finished in one to two years. Short-term goals take less than one year to complete.

- Each goal should have a timeline so a person can monitor the goal's progression.

6.2 Action Plans

- Influences such as one's *P*A*T*H to Success*, various people, and trends can affect one's career goals.

- An Action Plan details what a person needs to know to reach a goal.

- If one anticipates a roadblock, he or she can prepare for it by including backup plans for overcoming possible barriers in the Action Plan.

6.3 Time Management

- Setting priorities allows one to realize and complete the most important things.

- Scheduling in the priorities, then the regular daily and weekly activities and chores, allows one to see where there is free time.

- Time wasters, such as texting, phone calls, and television, need to be controlled so that the schedule is completed first.

Chapter Assessment

Vocabulary Builder

Match each statement with the term that best defines it.

a. Action Plan
b. backup plan
c. long-term goals
d. medium-term goals
e. priorities
f. procrastination
g. roadblocks
h. self-motivation
i. short-term goals
j. time wasters

1. The distractions that cause a person to lose track of time
2. Goals a person could expect to achieve in five or more years
3. A list of steps to a goal
4. Goals a person could expect to achieve in one to two years
5. The determination to stay on track and avoid distractions
6. Delaying planning
7. The items of greatest importance on one's schedule
8. Goals a person could expect to achieve in less than one year
9. An alternative plan
10. Barriers that may slow or stop the progress of planning and time management

Review What You Have Learned

11. Why is self-motivation important when planning career goals?
12. How can you manage the long process of finishing high school to achieving a career goal?
13. How can you make sure your career plan is going in the right direction?
14. Why is having long-term goals, medium-term goals, and short-term goals important? Why not set just long-term goals?
15. Why should a goal have a timeline?
16. Why is having a mentor so important for career planning?
17. What are the steps to creating an Action Plan?
18. Why is a backup plan necessary?
19. What roadblocks are common for students?
20. Explain some tips for managing time.
21. What are typical timewasters for students? How can they be avoided?

Case Challenges

Develop strategies to meet the following goals. Label them short-term, medium-term, or long-term goals. Write the first step for each.

22. Miguel wants to get his homework finished on time.
23. Jason wants to make new friends.
24. Flavia wants to save money to buy her prom dress.
25. Eduardo needs to arrive at school on time.
26. Ben wants to break the habit of reading new texts and answering them immediately.

Make Academic Connections

27. TECHNOLOGY The misuse of technology is a big timewaster. In pairs, contact two businesses. Interview someone in management or human resources to find out what technology timewasters they encounter. Then discuss how the company manages the timewaster. One of the businesses you interview should be a retail store or restaurant. Each group will create a presentation of their findings for the class.

28. LANGUAGE ARTS In pairs, each partner interviews the other about his/her career choice. Ask questions similar to both parts of Activity 6.1. During the interview, ask questions until you have determined the *Identity* of the other person.

After you and your partner finish both interviews, make a business card for your partner on an index card. Put your partner's name, then create a logo or symbol to represent your partner's identity. After all the pairs of students are finished, each pair will introduce each other's career goal to the class using the business card.

Portfolio

Workplace Connection

Discovering how you spend your time can help you improve your time management skills. For this activity, you will use the *Time Analysis* form available www.cengage.com/school/iyc, Chapter 6.

29. Complete the chart today and for the next two days—3 days total. Use the categories above the chart to write in the activity for each hour. For example, in the 6 AM – 7 AM box, you may put Sleep. If you used only part of an hour for a category, split the hour with a diagonal line. For example, 30 minutes for Sleep and 30 minutes for Meals.

Portfolio

30. Count how many hours you spent in each type of activity each day. Put it in the blanks beside the category. Each category has three blanks, one for each day.

31. Answer the questions. Save the results in your Career Portfolio.
* How do I spend the majority of my time each day? The least amount? Is this helpful for me? Why or why not?
* What are my time wasters?
* Are there differences among the 3 days I charted? Is this important or a coincidence? Why or why not?
* Should I make any changes in how I use my time each day? If so, what are they? Why should I make those changes?

Blogging: Plans into Action

Explain how you will put your career goal into action. Describe the steps of your Action Plan in a story that starts now and finishes in the future. Include the results of the *Real Life Focus* on page 132 and Activities 6.1 and 6.2. Be as detailed as possible. The length of each entry should be an average of two or three paragraphs.

Blog

Understanding Finances

Stanislav Komogorov/Shutterstock.com

What Do You Know

1. How do you think your career plays into your financial plans?

2. Do you have plans for working part-time now to save money for the future?

Spencer enjoys repairing and restoring things around the house. He watches all of the home shows on TV and has a subscription to *Build It Yourself* magazine. He believes a career related to construction would be something he would enjoy. People tried to convince Spencer to be an architect because he likes to draw buildings and house plans and is taking a drafting class in high school. He thinks he might enjoy the building aspect more than the design aspect of construction, but he's not sure.

Working with his teachers, counselor, and family, Spencer began to think more carefully about his career goals and investigated various careers related to architecture and construction. He began to work on weekends with his uncle who builds houses to get an idea of everything involved with building a home. Spencer also got a job for five hours per week with a family friend at an architectural firm. The part-time jobs gave Spencer an understanding of the differences between building a home and the underlying principles of planning and design. The jobs also helped him save some money.

These invaluable experiences led Spencer to obtaining an associate degree in Construction Technology. This degree helped him develop skills in construction, engineering, and business. He learned how to analyze plans and blueprints, interpret building codes, and inspect others' work. Today, Spencer works as a Building Inspector with a company building schools. Spencer supervises the construction of computer labs within the schools. He is enjoying his work and is considering going back to school to become an architect in the future.

Planning a Career in . . . Architecture and Construction

Take your passion for Architecture and Construction and build it into a career. Architecture and Construction is one of the career clusters.

Many professions associated with this career cluster are available to you through the achievement of a high school diploma. However, many require an associate, bachelor's, or master's degree and/or additional certifications. Pathways in this career cluster include Construction, Maintenance and Operations, and Design/Pre-construction.

Employment Outlook

- Architecture and construction make up one of the largest industries in the U.S. with over 9 million jobs.
- Many jobs are being added and there will be a large demand to replace workers who have been in the industry for many years.

Career Possibilities

- Carpenter
- Electrician
- General Contractor
- Building Inspector
- Project Manager

Needed Skills

- Math and technical skills.
- Attention to detail.
- Judgment and decision making.
- Time management.
- Accurate recordkeeping.

What's It Like to Work in Architecture and Construction?

Those who enjoy working in the area of construction like to solve problems and work with their hands. No matter where you work, what you do is important to others' lives.

Construction is a career in which you may start work directly out of high school, but some college courses and associate or bachelor's degrees will give you more opportunities in the field. Building inspectors get a lot of on-the-job training. They must learn things specific to their state or county, such as ordinances, regulations, building codes, and standards. They may do this by working with an experienced building inspector or be required to learn on their own.

As they inspect and monitor sites to ensure the safety of others, inspectors confirm compliance with the standards. Through the use of compliance software, they keep accurate records of their inspection.

Each building could be an adventure. You must be motivated to learn on your own and earn a state-issued license or certification if necessary. You will need to work independently, be ethical, have initiative, and analyze issues that may arise.

What about You?

Do you like solving problems and analyzing issues? Do you like to work with your hands? Construction has many areas in which you can work.

Goals

- Determine the difference between wants and needs.
- Explain the need for checking accounts.
- Explain the need for savings accounts.

Terms

- needs, p. 152
- wants, p. 152
- check, p. 153
- checking account, p. 153
- FDIC, p. 153
- checkbook register, p. 154
- online banking, p. 155
- debit cards, p. 155
- savings account, p. 155
- compounding interest, p. 156

Real Life Focus

Did you ever buy something you really wanted and then figured out that you really didn't need it? When thinking about your finances, it's important to determine the difference between your wants and needs. Which of these are wants and which are needs?

- Clothes
- Eyeglasses
- Car
- Movie
- Dining Out

Your career decision will impact the amount of money you will have to buy things you need and want. Everything you buy reduces the amount of money you could save. It's important to carefully think about purchases you make so that you do not overextend yourself and get into debt. Do you want to buy something right now? Is it a want or a need? Consider your choices carefully.

Difference Between Wants and Needs

Everyone has wants and needs. **Needs** are things that are necessary for you to live your life. They are things you cannot do without. Particular needs we all must have to live are food, shelter, and clothing. These are our basic needs. However, when people go beyond the expense of these basic needs and begin to buy more than they need, they are doing so because of their wants. For example, we all need food to survive, but when you visit a restaurant for every meal and spend a lot of money doing so, this is a want. Spending money for wants decreases the amount of money you have to save for your future.

Wants are things you desire, demand, or would like to have for reasons beyond survival and basic comfort. They are not absolutely necessary, but you believe they would be nice to have. Wants include music, movies, and games.

Diego says things like, "I need that skateboard" or "I need that pair of jeans." But what does he really need? He needs nutritious food, a place to live, and transportation. What he may want is new jeans, games, and travel. What are your needs and wants? How can you save your money to make sure you can have both?

You should not only determine your needs and wants, but organize them by most important to least important. By prioritizing your needs and wants, you will be able to begin to establish your financial goals. Keep in mind that your needs and wants will change over time, but to manage your money wisely, determining your needs and wants is the first step. Creating a two-column table is the easiest way to get started. Simply write "Needs" at the top of one column and "Wants" at the top of the other column. Then, begin to list all of your needs and wants. You may begin to determine that you have more wants than needs. You can give up some of your wants now so that you can save money to have a more financially stable future.

As you review your needs and wants, organize and prioritize them so you will be able to analyze how they will affect your savings, spending, and financial goals. This will help you move toward your financial goals.

Career FACT

Financial planning is essential to your career planning as well. Financial planning, like career planning, is ongoing. As your life goals and financial status change, you must review your needs, your wants, and your spending. Follow these three steps to put you on the right track for financial and career success.

- Plan Financial and Career Goals
- Prioritize Needs and Wants
- Save and Spend Wisely

When you fail to plan, you plan to fail.

Consider

How can you concentrate more on your needs (instead of your wants) and save more money for your future?

Checking Accounts

You will need money to buy things included on your needs and wants list. In addition to cash, you can use checks, online banking, and debit cards to pay for items.

Checks

A **check** is written to order the bank to take money from your account to pay the person or business noted on the check. To start a checking account, you will need to give the bank money as an initial deposit. A **checking account** is a service provided by banking institutions to allow you to deposit and withdraw money. The **Federal Deposit Insurance Corporation (FDIC)** is federal insurance designed to protect your money. Some accounts may be FDIC protected, protected by another agency, or may not be protected. There may also be limits on the amount of money that may be protected. Make sure the checking account you start is protected.

When you open a checking account, you will be asked for identification and personal information. Checks will be sent to you along with a checkbook register. A **checkbook register** provides you space to track your checking account deposits and withdrawals. You may be provided with temporary checks until the personalized checks are mailed to you. Checking accounts help keep your money safe. They are also a convenient way to pay others and help you budget your money as you review the check register. Illustration 7-1 shows the parts of a check.

Illustration 7-1: Parts of a check

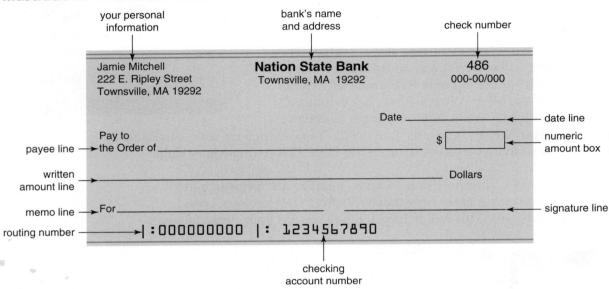

The check number helps you keep track of which checks you have written. The payee is the person or business to which you write the check. The amount of the check must be written in both numbers and words. The check number, payee, and amount will also be included in your checkbook register to keep an accurate account of your transactions. Illustration 7-2 shows a checkbook register.

Illustration 7-2: Checkbook register

Number	Date	Description	Debit (−)	Credit (+)	Balance
					$1150.00
1010	12/10/11	Jackson's Car Service		$200.00	$ 950.00
1011	12/15/11	Nancy's Nook		$ 50.50	$ 899.50
1012	12/22/11	Lance's Skiing Lodge		$348.22	$ 551.28
	12/30/11	Pay - Business Corporation	$756.90		$1308.18
1013	01/10/12	NSS Housing Mortgage		$980.00	$ 328.18

To write a check properly, make sure you use a pen, write legibly, complete all parts of the check, and sign your name exactly as it appears on the check. Checking accounts can help you manage your finances, but they must be used properly. For example, you must keep accurate records of the balance in your account so you do not write checks for more than you actually have in the account. If you do this, it is called "bouncing" a check. There will be penalties and fees associated with bouncing checks. However, some banks provide overdraft protection, which eliminates the fee for bounced checks if you have a savings account with the bank as well. Then, if you bounce a check, the bank takes the money out of your savings account to cover the amount of the check.

Online Banking

As stated earlier, checks provide a convenient way to pay others. You may pay your bills with checks, but you may also have the option of online banking. **Online banking** provides an option for paying bills over the Internet. To set up your online banking account, you will need to access the bank's web site. You will be asked to enter a special personal identification number (PIN) and/or password.

Once your account is established and specific companies have been identified as ones that accept online payments, you will login to your online banking account and select the payee from a list and enter the amount to be paid. The bank will transfer the amount to the business and your bill will be paid electronically. This may save you time, but it will definitely save paper and money as you will not have the check, envelope, and stamp to mail the payment to a business.

Debit Cards

Debit cards can also be used to buy items and withdraw money from your checking account. **Debit cards** are cards that allow for immediate deductions from your checking account. You may use debit cards to pay for items in a store or obtain cash through an Automated Teller Machine (ATM).

Keep in mind that some banks may charge a fee for a checking account or for a certain number of withdrawals. You may be required to maintain a minimum balance in the account or be charged a fee for online banking. Also, some accounts will pay interest if you maintain a large balance in the checking account. These are all important questions to ask the bank representative when you set up your checking account.

Savings Accounts

Saving money impacts the needs and wants you can accumulate in the future. Savings accounts are different than checking accounts. A **savings account** is a bank account on which you earn interest. You can withdraw money from a savings account, but savings accounts are designed for you to save money for the future. There are a variety of types of savings accounts such as traditional or money market accounts. The differences between these types usually include the minimum balance required, percent of interest, and how many withdrawals you can take within a specified timeframe.

With any account (checking or savings), make sure you ask the following questions.

- Is a minimum balance required?

- Are there fees for this account?

- Does the account pay interest?

- Are there any other restrictions on this account?

Web Connections

Web sites offer valuable information about saving money.

Click on the Web Connections link for Chapter 7. Search at least two of the sites listed. As you are reviewing sites, write down ideas that may help you become better at saving money. Share your ideas with the class.

www.cengage.com/school/iyc

As with a checking account, you will open your savings account with a deposit. You may receive a register or other documentation with this account as well so you can keep track of future deposits and withdrawals. To help you save on a regular basis, you can set up automatic deposits from your employer directly into your savings account. If you choose this option, you will need to provide your employer with your account number and additional information.

Interest on savings accounts is compounding interest. **Compounding interest** is interest that is calculated on the balance, additional deposits made, and interest earned. See the example in the table provided below.

Year	Beginning Balance	Deposit	Interest Earned (3%)	Ending Balance
1	$0.00	$50.00	$1.50	$51.50
2	$51.50	$50.00	$3.05	$104.55
3	$104.55	$50.00	$4.64	$159.19

With compounding interest, you will save at a faster rate. To secure your financial future, you should be saving now. If you begin to save early in life, you can save more for the future. For example, suppose 15-year-old Yoko opened a savings account with a $50 initial deposit and deposited $20 per month for 40 years in an account that earned 5% interest. When she is 55 years old, the amount in the savings account would be over $30,000.

Everyone should have a personal goal for saving. The main thing is that you should save more than you spend and save on a regular basis. Developing good saving habits helps you begin to build wealth, which will help you be in a better financial situation in the future. It is not that difficult. You just need to start now and continue your savings on a regular basis. The following tips can help you become a good saver.

- Develop a budget and stick with it.
- Save first before you consider any spending.
- Think before you spend. Consider your needs versus your wants.
- Track how you spend money and review your budget.

How much money should you be saving? It depends on your specific circumstances, but typically you should be saving 5–10 percent of what you earn. But you must consider the following questions: How much do I earn? How long do I have to save? How much savings do I want for my retirement? What am I saving for? Remember, you are saving for your needs, wants, education, retirement and many other things. But, most importantly, you are saving for your future!

ACTIVITY 7.1

Learning from Others

In this activity, you will work with your family to develop a prioritized list of family needs and wants. There are many things to think about to develop a comprehensive list and analyze how to save more money. Work together with family members to create the list. Then discuss what needs and/or wants can be postponed or eliminated to save more money. Follow the steps below to determine the amount of money your family can save for the future.

1. Using a spreadsheet or notebook paper, list all family needs and wants.
2. Assign a monetary value to each need and want.
3. Organize and prioritize the list by placing the most important items at the top and the less important items at the bottom of the list.

4. Answer the following questions.
   - Are there any wants we can eliminate or postpone?
   - Are there any needs we can eliminate or postpone?
5. Using the answers to these two questions, rewrite your list. You will then be able to compare the two lists and determine a more realistic amount your family can save each month.
6. Be prepared to share your information and the answers to your questions with the class.

Photodisc/Getty Images

Financial Planning

Goals

- Examine your financial goals.
- Develop a budget to live within your means.
- Identify common money mistakes.

Terms

- financial plan, p. 159
- budget, p. 159
- income, p. 159
- fixed expenses, p. 159
- variable expenses, p. 159
- credit card debt, p. 161

Real Life Focus

Do you think people can spend more money than they earn? Why do you think credit card debt is a problem in the U.S.? Do you have a personal budget or a family budget? Many people find that it is easy to spend more than they earn. If you do the following, are you spending more than you earn?

- Carrying credit card debt.
- Finding it difficult to pay your bills.
- Paying on a second mortgage on your home.

Think carefully about your financial goals, living within your means, and making sure you don't spend more than you earn. Once you get into debt, it is hard to get out—and it may take a very long time to do so.

Financial Goals

Developing your financial goals is the first step in financial planning. It is important to think about and develop your short-term goals (under one year), medium-term goals (one to two years), and long-term goals (five or more years). Just as you developed a list of your wants and needs, you should do the same with your financial goals. Making a list of short-, medium-, and long-term goals helps you categorize and organize your financial plan. Once your list of goals is complete, then you must do the following:

- Prioritize your goals.
- Estimate the cost of each goal.
- Set a deadline for achieving the goal.
- Determine the amount you need to save monthly to reach your deadline.
- Identify what actions you need to take to reach the goal.
- Review your progress to ensure you are on track.

Therefore, planning is essential. Financial planning will help you determine a budget and live within your means. A **financial plan** is a blueprint containing your personal goals, a timeline for reaching your goals, and an understanding of how to save to reach the goals. Keep in mind that your goals may change and alter your financial plan, but your financial plan guides your success. Also, understand that your financial success depends on clear, concise goals and an organized strategy for achievement.

Financial planning is very personal. You have different goals than your friends and family. Developing your personal financial plan not only helps you prioritize your savings and spending, it helps you develop key components for your budget. Building a monthly budget will help you stick to your financial plan and begin to achieve short-term goals. Once short-term goals are achieved, you will feel more motivated to work toward medium- and long-term goals.

You do not need to do all of your financial planning by yourself. Professional financial counselors can help you if you need it. But their services cost money. Consider all of these factors to make your financial future more secure.

alexskopje/Shutterstock.com

How will you develop a budget to meet your needs?

Consider

Why is it important to regularly review your financial plan? What are some situations that may occur that would alter the path of your financial plan?

Budgeting to Live Within Your Means

Creating a budget to live within your means will help you save money and not spend more than you earn. A **budget** is basically a spending and savings plan. A budget is based on monthly income, expenses, and savings. These three components help you establish a habit of earning, spending, and saving. A budget can also help you determine if you are off track and spending more than you earn or not saving as much money as you could.

Income is the amount of money you earn. Income is usually a set amount. People typically bring home the same amount of pay each month. However, if an individual is self-employed or works part-time, his or her pay may vary each month. When you create your budget, calculate a monthly average income. This fixed income helps you establish a baseline amount of money you have available to pay the bills, spend on wants, and save.

Monthly expenses can be either fixed or variable. **Fixed expenses** are expenses that are the same amount each month. Examples of fixed expenses include house, car, and insurance payments. **Variable expenses** are expenses that may be different amounts each month. These include groceries, clothing, utilities, and fuel. When reviewing your budget, look at your expenses and see where you can cut back to save more money or maybe just break even.

> Kristy works part-time at the movie theatre and brings home $80 per week. Her short-term goal is to buy a new laptop to use for school. She needs to save $40 per week to meet her goal in a timely fashion. She spends $10 per week on gas, $20 per week on car insurance, and an average of $15 per week on music. She also spends $25 per week on going out with friends and $10 per week on eating out. She is spending every penny she is earning and she is not saving any money. She has to cut back somewhere. She wonders what choices she can make to save $40 per week to get her laptop.

Your budget should list all income such as your salary and interest you may be earning on savings accounts. All of your expenses, fixed and variable, should also be listed. Expenses may include many more items than those previously mentioned. Make sure you list all expenses on your budget, such as house payment, car payment, insurance, taxes, utilities (telephone, electricity, water, etc.), childcare, clothing, food, gas, gifts, and entertainment. Once you have a complete list of income and expenses, subtract the total amount of expenses from your total income. This is the amount of money you can save.

Your budget provides you with important information to make good decisions about spending and saving. You can create your budget on paper, electronically using budgeting software, or on an Internet-based budgeting web site. But no matter how you develop your budget, make sure you review it monthly. Reviewing your budget every month allows you to make sure you are not overspending or to make adjustments. Your budget should be flexible enough that you don't feel confined, but it should encourage you to live within your means.

Common Money Mistakes

Everyone makes mistakes sometimes. One mistake that many people make is getting into debt. However, there is good debt and bad debt. The term *good debt* is used for investments that will create value later or generate long-term income. Good debt typically includes buying a home and paying for education. But people can sometimes borrow too much for these items. They can get into trouble with debt by developing enormous student loans or taking second mortgages on their home. Your mortgage is what you owe on your house. When people have too much debt they cannot pay, they may go bankrupt or lose their home, car, or business. This creates bad debt.

Bad debt typically includes credit cards, car title/payday loans, IRS debt, and loans to finance a vacation. Credit cards are owned by various companies and banks. Credit cards provide individuals the ability to purchase something before they have to pay for it. When you purchase something on a credit card, your account is charged immediately, but you may not get the bill for a few weeks. Credit card bills are due every month. If you do not pay the entire amount of your credit card bill every month, you will

be charged a finance charge. Car title/payday loans are loans the borrower typically gets from a company (other than a bank) where the borrower provides their car title as collateral for a loan. Therefore, if the borrower does not pay the loan back, the company takes their car.

Credit card debt is the amount you owe on credit cards that you cannot pay. Credit cards may have interest rates over 20 percent. Unlike your savings account, which pays you the interest, with credit card debt you pay the credit card company the interest on the amount you have not paid. You pay this interest each month. The average family carries almost $8,000 in credit card debt. They could be paying $2,000 per year in interest. Many people find themselves in situations where it is very difficult to get out of debt.

Credit card debt is probably the most common money mistake people make. It occurs when people live outside their means and buy things they cannot afford. They are spending money they do not have. Personal finance is very much based on your behavior. It is based on your spending behavior and your saving behavior. As you know, it can be difficult to change your behavior. The easiest way to avoid credit card debt is to pay for items you buy with cash or a check whenever possible. If you use a credit card, pay the balance due in full each month. Credit card debt can build quickly because of common money mistakes, such as:

■ Emotional or impulsive spending

■ Persuasive advertisements or sales techniques

■ Buying without researching

■ Borrowing at high interest rates

■ Skipping payments on credit cards or loans

■ Not having a financial plan and budget

When you spend money based on an emotion or impulse, you will regret it later—especially if it was a big ticket item that you cannot return. Be careful not to let advertisements and sales people talk you into buying something you don't need or cannot afford. When you feel emotional or that you are being persuaded to purchase, step back and take time to make your decision. There is no purchasing decision you have to make immediately. Always do your research before you buy anything. There may be a better deal or another product that would be cheaper.

Be careful when borrowing money. Loans can have high interest rates or interest rates that increase over the duration of the loan. These types of loans are very dangerous because your payments will increase. You may not be able to afford the higher payments. Also, never skip a payment on a loan or credit card. Fees will be applied, your interest will continue to grow, and you will become further in debt. As we have discussed, you must have a plan and a budget to stay on track. This will help you live within your means and save for the future.

What will you do to avoid common money mistakes?

Piotr Marcinski/Shutterstock.com

■ *Homeowner's insurance:* Protects you, your home, and your belongings if they are damaged or destroyed.

■ *Life insurance:* Provides cash payments to your loved ones in the event of your death.

Investigating Credit Cards

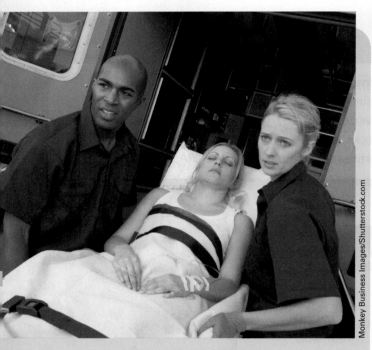

How will you pay without insurance?

Monkey Business Images/Shutterstock.com

■ ***Disability insurance:*** Provides part or all of your income if you cannot work due to a disability.

■ ***Long-term care insurance:*** Provides for expenses for individuals for extended care.

Janessa did not have medical insurance. She had a motorcycle accident, broke her leg, and bruised her back. She was taken to the emergency room. The cost of the emergency room visit and x-rays was $2,800. Her leg had to be put in a cast and special prescription drugs were given for the pain. She also had to visit her doctor twice for follow-up appointments and one last time for the cast to be removed. All of these charges totaled almost $9,000. Without insurance, she is responsible for all of these expenses. This will impact her financial plans for the future.

Believe it or not, Janessa's example would be considered a fairly inexpensive medical situation. The cost of open heart surgery, for example, could be over $100,000. Think about how this would impact you financially. However, medical insurance is not the only type of insurance you should consider to protect yourself from financial loss.

You may pay for insurance monthly, bi-annually, or annually. Most insurance is well worth the cost. For example, suppose you pay $150 per month for health insurance through your employer. The following examples show how paying for insurance is beneficial to you financially.

■ You go to the dentist for a cleaning and checkup.
  - Cost with insurance: $20
  - Cost without insurance: $50
  - A savings of $30

■ You go to the eye doctor for a checkup.
  - Cost with insurance: $75
  - Cost without insurance: $150
  - A savings of $75

■ You have a prescription for allergies that you get from the pharmacy each month.
  - Cost with insurance: $25
  - Cost without insurance: $85
  - A savings of $60

Your health insurance saved you a total of $165 on these three procedures.

Health problems are not the only situations that could cause you to go bankrupt or be in a financial bind for a long time. Other types of insurance protect you from natural disasters, car accidents, fire in your home, and many other catastrophes. What if you lost everything in a tornado, earthquake, flood, or fire? How would you be able to afford to replace everything without insurance?

You should anticipate life changes and risk in your life. Make sure you include insurance in your budget.

Saving for the Future

As you develop your short-, medium-, and long-term financial goals, saving money is going to play a huge part in reaching your goals. By carefully planning, prioritizing, and developing a timeline for reaching your goals, you will see more clearly how much money you need to save and how quickly you may need to do so. Establishing a savings routine and commitment is key to reaching your financial goals.

What are some major long-term goals for which you may be saving? You may possibly be saving for a car, your education, or a place of your own. Let's analyze just one of those goals: Your education.

The average cost of one year at a private college is estimated to be $38,000. The average cost of one year at a public college is $17,000. This includes tuition, fees, and room and board. You can estimate an additional $5,000 for textbooks, supplies, transportation, and other expenses per year. Most students do not finish their degrees in four years, but rather need five or six years. The longer you take to graduate, the more financially difficult it may be. However, using these estimations, graduating in four years from a public university would cost approximately $90,000.

How do you prepare for this type of financial commitment? Typically, students rely on their savings, employment, financial aid, and loans to help them attain their educational goals and pay for their education. Time is of the essence. The sooner you begin to save, the less you will have to borrow. It is less expensive to save for your education than to borrow money. Remember, when you save money you earn interest, but when you borrow money, just like credit cards, you pay interest plus the principal amount you borrowed. This can be very costly.

This is why many times families begin to save for their children's future. For example, suppose your family saved $50 per month from the time you were born until you were 18 years old and earned 5% interest on the savings. In this case, there would be enough money to pay for approximately one year of your education: $18,000. If your family saved $200 per month during the same timeframe with 5% interest, the savings would grow to approximately $72,000.

Now is the time to save! The sooner you begin, the more money you will have to pay for your education no matter at what level. Review your career goals and investigate what type of higher education you'll need to get the job you want. Will you need to earn a particular type of certification? Will you require an associate or bachelor's degree? The more education you need to complete to reach your career goal, the more money you'll need to save.

Paying for classes is not the only thing to think about when you are saving for your education. You will need to consider these questions as well:

■ Will you be going to school in-state or out-of-state? The cost of going to school out-of-state is substantially higher than in-state tuition.

Whatever your career goals, you will probably need to further your education after high school. How do you plan to pay for your education?

©Jeff Greenberg/Alamy

- Will you be living on-campus or off-campus? Typically is it cheaper to live on-campus.

- Will you go to school part-time or full-time?

- Will you work while you are in school?

All of these factors will impact how much you'll need to save. Starting to save now will help alleviate the need to borrow money later and be in debt when you graduate. Here are a few tips to help you cut expenses and begin saving now.

- Consider going to a community college and then transferring to a four-year university if necessary to achieve your career goal.

- Review colleges that are close to home so that you can commute easily and live at home to avoid paying for room and board.

Real People / Real Careers

Joe Harrison / *Project Manager—Residential Remodeling*

"I want to stay in construction for the rest of my working life," commented Joe Harrison. Though construction was not Joe's first career choice, it is his passion now.

Joe played football well in high school, so when he was offered a football scholarship, he took it with the goal of becoming a teacher. Becoming a teacher was a good choice for Joe, a people person. But what was missing was hands-on work. His father worked in construction, so Joe knew the demands of the career. Doing construction work and relating to customers was more gratifying.

The construction industry has many facets. Joe chose residential remodeling—so he has to know how to do everything. Joe apprenticed as part of various crews in areas such as roofing, siding, and carpentry. Knowing all aspects of the business led to his current position as project or production manager. He directs each crew, assigns the jobs, orders the parts, and constantly moves to his firm's various job sites.

Knowledge of construction does not stop with on-the-job training. Joe has to keep up with the changes in regulations, design trends, and technology. For example, LED and CFL lighting made home lighting more energy efficient and created design challenges. The removal of lead and asbestos requires that only certified personnel can work with those renovations.

Construction careers require much customer communication. Joe emphasizes, "You are speaking with the customer, both as a construction crew member and in my current position as project manager. Having excellent English and speech skills is important. I should have studied math more in school. I use math quite a lot every day."

For more information about:

* construction careers
* construction management

Access **www.cengage.com/school/iyc** and click on the appropriate links in Chapter 7.

Source: *Personal Interview,* August 2011

- If you live on-campus, carefully consider a meal plan.

- Find low-cost (or no-cost) entertainment options: visiting friends, hiking, skateboarding, and so forth. Check for student discounts at museums, zoos, and movie theaters.

- Avoid eating your meals out—it adds up quickly. Buy store-brand groceries instead of brand names. Make a list before you shop and stick to it.

- When you want to buy something, always ask yourself if you really need it. Avoid impulse buying. Learn how to shop for bargains.

- Use free campus or low-cost city transportation or bike to school if possible. You won't have to pay for parking.

- Find roommates to share living expenses.

- Don't get into credit card debt. Pay your bills on time. Always.

- Make a budget and stick with it.

- Apply for financial aid, student loans, grants, and/or scholarships. You will learn more about these in Chapter 9.

Without a plan for saving, you may not be able to attend the school of your choice or you may have to delay your education. You don't want this to happen. Develop a savings plan now so that you do not get into debt. Large debt will impact your financial plans for the future. Make sure you set your financial goals, set up a budget, open a savings account, pay yourself first, and control your expenses. When you get a paycheck, put money into your savings account first—pay yourself. The best advice to save for your education is to start saving early to minimize the amount you will need to borrow. If you need more money for your education, apply for financial aid and scholarships that do not have to be repaid.

Consider

What might happen to your financial goals if you have $50,000 worth of student loan debt when you graduate?

Investing

Keep in mind that you are not just saving for your education, but other needs, wants, and retirement. You must invest for your future. An **investment** is putting money into something with an expectation of a financial gain. Some investments are risky and some are more secure.

Risky investments typically have the possibility of a higher return, but you may also lose money. Buying stocks is one example of a risky investment. **Stocks** are shares in a company. When you invest in a company's stock, you own part of the company. If the company makes money, your stock will increase in value. But if the company loses money, you will too. If you buy stocks, you should invest in multiple companies to minimize the risk of losing all of your money. This is called *diversifying* your investments.

Safer investments include putting your money in a secure, FDIC-protected savings account or **certificates of deposit** (CDs). CDs are short- or long-term, interest-bearing investments offered by banking institutions. You invest your money in a CD for a specific time frame. There are penalties for withdrawing your money before the time frame is complete. And even though your money is safe and earning interest, the risk you take is that you may need the money before the time frame is complete.

Investing is especially important for long-term financial goals such as education or retirement. There are some tax sheltered investments in which you may choose to participate. **Tax shelters** are investments designed to reduce the amount of your income that can be taxed. Therefore, if you earn $45,000 per year and you invest $10,000 per year into a tax sheltered investment, your income taxes will be based on only $35,000. Examples of tax sheltered investments include 529s, 401(k)s, and IRAs.

- **529 Plan:** A 529 plan is an educational investment account. This investment is designed to help your family prepay tuition or save for your education. These plans are operated by a state or educational institution. They allow families to set aside money now for future college costs. There are two types of 529 plans: (1) prepaid programs and (2) savings programs. The prepaid program typically allows those saving for college to purchase credits at certain participating colleges for future tuition. The savings program allows individuals to save for any college.

- **401(k):** A 401(k) is a retirement savings investment that allows individuals to save for retirement and defer taxes until the money is withdrawn later. If an employee contributes to a 401(k) sponsored by an employer, the employer often matches the employee's contribution to a certain amount. Therefore, the amount of the 401(k) will increase more quickly. This is a great benefit to ask about when applying for full-time employment. Funds can be withdrawn when an individual reaches the age of 59½. This is an investment for the future.

- **IRA:** An Individual Retirement Account is an overall term for a retirement plan with tax advantages for retirement savings. There are several types of IRAs, such as Traditional IRA, Roth IRA, and Simple IRA. Each type of IRA has specific rules, regulations, and tax benefits. Funds cannot be withdrawn from these accounts until you are 59½ or you will pay a penalty. Save for your retirement now!

A general rule of thumb is to save 5–10 percent of your income annually. However, investing should be planned carefully. The following are guidelines for investing for the future.

- Investigate investment opportunities carefully.

- Begin to save early.

- Keep saving.

- Diversify your investments.

Finding Money in Your Budget

As you have learned, developing a flexible budget and saving for your future are connected. Review Callie's college budget below. She is spending approximately $200 more than she earns each month. If she continues to do this, she will be in debt $2400 by the end of the year. She can't continue to live like this. What can Callie do to save enough money per month to break even and not spend more than she earns? Be prepared to discuss your answer in class.

Monthly Budget	
Income	
Scholarship	$300.00
Job at Justin's Steakhouse	$500.00
Total Income	**$800.00**
Expenses	
Gas	$30.00
Groceries	$30.00
Eating Out	$50.00
Entertainment	$200.00
Tuition (Mom and Dad supplement tuition)	$300.00
Books	$20.00
Rent (Sharing apartment with 3 others)	$180.00
Utilities	$40.00
Cell Phone (Typically go over on my texting limit and pay additional fees)	$80.00
Car Insurance (Car is paid off)	$70.00
Total Expenses	**$1000.00**
Total Savings	**−$195.00**

Chapter Summary

7.1 Finances 101

- It is important to determine and prioritize one's wants and needs. One's wants and needs will affect spending and savings goals.

- A checking account is a safe place to keep money. It is important to keep an accurate checkbook register and review spending each month.

- A savings account earns interest and helps one save for the future. Compounding interest adds up quickly.

7.2 Financial Planning

- Developing one's financial goals is the first step in financial planning. It is important to develop short-, medium-, and long-term goals. It is never too early to begin financial planning.

- Creating a budget will help one save money and live within one's means. Budgets should include income, fixed expenses, and variable expenses. Total Income − Total Expenses = Savings!

- Avoid common money mistakes such as carrying credit card debt, buying without researching, borrowing at high interest rates, and being an impulse buyer.

7.3 Preparing for the Future

- Purchasing insurance offers financial protection. Financially, purchasing insurance is a smart move as one can get compensated for losses. Insurance should be included in every budget.

- Establishing a savings routine and commitment is key to reaching one's financial goals. The best advice is to start saving early and minimize borrowing money.

- One must invest in the future. An investment is putting money into something with an expectation of a financial gain. Remember, some investments are risky and some are more secure.

Chapter Assessment

Vocabulary Builder

Match each statement with the term that best defines it.

1. A blueprint containing your personal goals, timeline for reaching your goals, and an understanding of how to save to reach your goals

2. The amount of money you earn

3. A spending and savings plan

4. A written order to the bank to take money from your account to pay a person or business

5. Investments designed to reduce the amount of your taxable income

6. Coverage you can purchase to provide reimbursement or replacement in case of loss

7. Expenses that are the same amount each month

8. Something you desire, demand, or would like to have

9. A service provided by banking institutions to allow you to deposit and withdraw money

10. A bank account on which you earn compounding interest

11. Retirement savings investment with deferred taxes until the money is withdrawn later

12. Expenses that may be different amounts each month

13. Cards that allow for immediate deductions from a checking account

14. Federal insurance designed to protect your money

15. Something that is necessary for you to live your life

16. Short- or long-term, interest-bearing investments offered by banking institutions

17. The amount you owe on credit cards that you cannot pay

18. Interest that is calculated on the balance, additional deposits, and interest earned

19. Space to track your checking account deposits and withdrawals

20. Putting money into something with an expectation of a financial gain

21. An educational investment account designed to help you prepay tuition or save for education

22. Option for paying your bills over the Internet

23. Overall term for retirement plan with tax advantages

24. Shares in a company

a. 401(k)
b. 529 plan
c. budget
d. certificate of deposit
e. check
f. checking account
g. checkbook register
h. compounding interest
i. credit card debt
j. debit card
k. FDIC
l. financial plan
m. fixed expense
n. income
o. insurance
p. investment
q. IRA
r. needs
s. online banking
t. savings account
u. stocks
v. tax shelter
w. variable expenses
x. wants

Review What You Have Learned

25. What is the difference between wants and needs?

26. Why should you open checking and savings accounts?

27. What is the first step in financial planning?

28. What should be included in your budget?

29. What are some of the common money mistakes people make?

30. Why should you purchase insurance?

31. What are some ways you can save money?

32. How can you invest in your future?

Case Challenges

After reading both case studies, analyze each situation. Do the individuals have a good financial plan? If yes, explain why. If not, suggest actions they can take to be more prepared.

33. Jake and Damon are thinking about starting a summer lawn mowing business together. Right now Jake charges $20 per yard and typically cuts 2 yards per month. Damon cuts 3 yards per month and charges $25 per yard. If they purchase a new mower, weed eater, and edger, they believe they could cut 8–10 yards per month together. They think the investment in the new equipment will be worth their while and they will be able to save a lot of money this summer.

34. Landon's friend's dog had puppies and Landon wants one. He has already picked out the one he wants and named her Speckles. His mom and dad told him it would be his total responsibility to take care of the dog. This means he'll have to pay $30 for the dog, pay the veterinarian to get shots for the dog, and buy dog food, a leash, and other items for the dog. He has $50 in his savings. He gets an allowance of $10 per week if he keeps up with his chores of mowing the lawn and taking out the trash. He's going to buy the dog and use the other $20 in his savings to pay for the other things.

Make Academic Connections

35. **BUSINESS**   Interview someone who works in finance (i.e., banker, financial planner, etc.) and then develop a top ten list for the best ways to save for your future. Describe how you could implement these techniques and begin saving for your future now.

36. **MATH**   Purchasing a home is a huge financial investment. When you get a home loan, you will pay interest on the amount you owe. To calculate how much you'll pay for your home plus interest, you can use an amortization table. Search the Internet for an amortization calculator. Use it to answer the following questions.

- If you purchase a home for $200,000 at 5% interest for 30 years and have a good credit score, how much will you have paid at the end of the 30 years?
- How much of what you paid over the 30 years is interest?
- Do the same for purchasing a car for $18,000 over 5 years at 1% interest. How much would you pay for the car over 5 years and how much of that would be interest?

Workplace Connection

Understanding your financial goals is important. Start thinking about your future. Complete the following statements.

Portfolio

37. When someone asks you the following, what will you say? How much money do you hope to have saved in 10, 20, and 30 years?
- In 10 years, I hope to have saved . . .
- In 20 years, I hope to have saved . . .
- In 30 years, I hope to have saved . . .

How do your answers relate to your financial goals? What are you doing now to ensure your financial plan becomes a reality?

38. Complete the simple financial goal worksheet below to help you establish how to reach one of your financial goals.

Goal	Timeframe	Total Cost	Monthly Amt. to Save	Ways to Reach Goal

Blogging: Financial Goals

Blog

As you continue to blog or journal about your career plan process, reflect upon your financial goals and what you have learned in this chapter. Blog about how your financial goals have changed or how they have remained the same. Explain why you believe your financial goals have changed or remained the same. Access www.cengage.com/school/iyc and click on the appropriate links in Chapter 7.

Capstone Project: Part 2

This step of the **Capstone Project** will use the choices you made in the last three chapters. In Chapter 5, you chose a career using the decision-making process. In Chapter 6, you made plans to put your career goal into action. Chapter 7 led you to consider financial goals and decisions.

This Capstone Project assignment is to write your project proposal. You will describe the scope of the project and its goals. Using the references you chose for the Capstone Project, Part 1, you will explore current ideas and related areas of study.

The Topic or Challenge is: *Why I Chose _____ for My Career*

Your written one-page proposal must include the following elements.

Portfolio

- Project title.
- Career description.
- Brief outline of references chosen in Part 1. Include online, print, and potential interviews in your outline.
- How you propose to discuss the career.
- A brief project timeline. Your teacher will give you suggestions or specific dates.

Keep in mind that the Capstone Project completion includes:

- A written paper.
- An oral presentation.
- Use of visuals and/or technology, such as a poster, film, or PowerPoint presentation.

Your teacher will give you the specific requirements.

Decisions

Considering Career Preparation Choices

226552472/Shutterstock.com

What Do You Know

1. What is the advantage of long-term planning for your career?

2. How might your activities at school and in the community help you in making career plans?

Jackie has lived in the Washington, D.C. area all her life. She loves living in the home of the U.S. government. But for Jackie, the Metro—D.C.'s train and bus transportation system—is her favorite part of the city.

As a young girl, Jackie learned to ride the Metro transit system. She and her friends would travel all over the area to visit relatives or go shopping. And Jackie didn't just enjoy riding the Metro, she loved how the Metrobus and the Metrorail systems intermingled. Other parts of the Metro system interested Jackie. The Metro accommodated people with disabilities and those who spoke languages other than English. The system also had a great reputation for safety.

When beginning her career planning, Jackie researched the Metro well, for she knew she wanted to work there. She spent time job shadowing several people in the Red Line office and started working there part-time.

Jackie realized that her career path was to work in the Transit Accessibility Office helping persons with disabilities. She would start her career preparation path with electives in sociology and psychology. Her postsecondary education could begin at a community college with concentrations in social work or psychology. After transferring to the university for her bachelor's degree, Jackie's future would be to major in government planning with additional courses to learn about persons with disabilities.

Planning a Career in . . . Government

A career in Government may make you think of the mayor's office or the FBI or BMV. People who work in these agencies have careers in Government, but so do people in any career that is paid with public funds.

Government careers span many areas, from water quality inspection to occupational safety to helping farmers with crop problems. Every career cluster includes government workers. In fact, the Government career cluster is a secondary career cluster for many positions.

Employment Outlook

- Average growth in federal government employment, excluding public education and hospitals.

- Higher than average growth in state and local government positions.

- Strong demand for public safety services and assistance to the elderly.

Career Possibilities

- Translator
- Urban Planner
- Building Inspector
- Transportation Security
- Internal Revenue Service

Needed Skills

- Solid background in academics, communications, and information technology.

- Leadership and teamwork skills.

- Ability to problem solve.

- Strong ethics and sense of responsibility.

What's It Like to Work in Government?

Name nearly any career, and you will find a corresponding career paid by a federal, state, or local government. In a Government career, you are working for your satisfaction—and for the public.

Government careers can be anywhere: embassies in foreign countries, airports and subways, U.S. borders and customs, and military bases are just a few examples. From the animal control employee to the President of the United States, they are all Government workers.

The majority of Government positions have job security. However, when budgets are cut, tax increases are not passed, and services reorganized, Government workers may lose jobs.

Many positions in hospitals, public schools, and universities are part of the Government career cluster. So are accountants for the IRS, police officers and firefighters, and highway workers. They are all public employees.

A career in Government may not be your first career cluster choice. However, the career you choose may have Government as its secondary cluster. You will be working *for* the public. That is very satisfying for many. And you?

What about You?

Are you interested in serving the public? Is being in a government position a first or second career cluster? Are you proud of your strong ethics? A career in a Government position may be in your future.

David Glider/Shutterstock.com

Goals

- Explain how your goals influence your career preparation choice.
- Describe why it is important for you to examine all the career preparation options.

Term

- career preparation, p. 178

Portfolio

Real Life Focus

Deciding the influences that are important in achieving your career goal will start you on the road to your career path.

Trace your hand. Then do the following to your drawing. Be prepared to give the reasons for your choices.

1. Inside your palm, write 5 names of people who influence your career path.
2. Next to each finger, write 5 places that you spend a lot of time.
3. Inside each finger, write one activity you do in each place to help you on your career pathway.

Follow Your Goals

You have determined your ideal career cluster and have researched some careers. You have set goals for achieving your career path. Now you need to examine the **career preparation** or education and training options that are available for your career path. By considering the options, you will find the right path for your career. Some professional careers require at least four years at a college or university. Other careers may have several different career preparation options. Alternative education options are more common today, even for careers that previously required traditional attendance at a college or university.

Clarissa has worked part-time bagging at Veggies and Things Market since she was fourteen. Next summer she hopes to have a full-time job as a clerk at the organic produce grocery. In her junior year, she can begin the career and technical program in culinary arts. The program will earn Clarissa college credits during her two years before high school graduation.

Clarissa is considering working full-time at Veggies and Things after she graduates from high school. She learned that there are prep cook positions in the catering department that start at a high hourly rate. Clarissa is sure she would start at an even higher rate because of her experience working in the grocery.

Clarissa knows that another alternative is to delay working full-time at Veggies and Things until she finishes an associate degree in culinary arts. She can continue to work part-time while attending college full-time. Also, the college program is a cooperative (co-op) program. Clarissa will be paid while she works, and she earns college credit at the same time. After earning her degree, she would be eligible for higher pay and more responsibility in Veggies and Things' catering department.

Another alternative is to use Veggies and Things' tuition reimbursement program. The company will reimburse for college tuition if Clarissa is working full-time at the market. Earning a college degree would take Clarissa longer with this alternative, but she would not have any tuition costs if her grades were a C or better. Clarissa has some serious decision making to do.

Consider

How does setting your long-term goals help you decide which career preparation options to choose for your career path?

Real People / Real Careers

Alex Brown / *Emergency Preparedness & Safety Coordinator*

Alex Brown's interest in aviation began with machines, Legos, and hand tools. As he grew older, he added model rockets. With a love of math, science, and *Top Gun*, Alex became fascinated by airplanes—the noise they made, their speed, and the technology inside.

In his senior year in high school, Alex started taking flying lessons. At Embry-Riddle University, Alex majored in Aerospace Studies. He intended to become a pilot, but his colorblindness prevented him from becoming a commercial pilot. After taking several safety courses, Alex realized that he wanted to pursue that aspect of aviation.

His university required an internship or a thesis for college graduation. After interning for the FAA at Embry-Riddle working with Next Generation airspace technology, Alex interned for a jet-leasing company, assisting in the executive offices. After graduation, he started his career with a smaller commercial airline doing everything

but flying the planes. Two years later, Alex began his current position with a large metropolitan airport authority. Though he is in the Transportation career cluster, he is a government employee. He is responsible for duties at three airports: an international airport, a cargo hub and charter terminal, and a general aviation airfield.

Why safety? For Alex, designing new ways to protect persons and property is important. The industry uses checklists and gathers, shares, and analyzes information to improve aerospace safety. Alex is also interested in the forensic side of looking at wreckage, gathering evidence, determining a sequence of events, and developing a probable cause to prevent or reduce future accidents.

With the support of his family, Alex pursued his passion. As he emphasizes, "My parents told me to look for a career that I would enjoy, not just one that would pay me the most. That the rewards would come from that enjoyment, dedication, and passion for what I was doing. They were so right!"

For more information about:

* occupational safety careers

* transportation careers

Access **www.cengage.com/school/iyc** and click on the appropriate links in Chapter 8.

Source: *Personal Interview,* July 2011

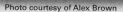
Photo courtesy of Alex Brown

-Antonio-/iStockphoto.com

Examine the Options

Before you can determine your career preparation path, you must investigate the options available to you. Although your career preparation path depends primarily on your career choice, you may find options that you have not considered previously. By being aware of the different preparation paths, you can choose the best way to reach your career and lifestyle goals.

More than one education and training path may allow you to reach your goal. For example, you might go directly from high school to your career. While you work in your career, you might receive on-the-job training or take virtual learning courses. Your employer may pay for advanced education. Your options may provide you with the same education and training as if you had gone from high school to a post-secondary school or to a formal training program.

As you look at the career preparation options available for your career path, ask yourself the following questions:

- When should I begin my career preparation?
- How long do I want to take for my career preparation?
- How will I pay for my career preparation?
- When do I want to start working?
- Do I want to combine work with education?
- Do I need to continue with my education after I begin my career?

ACTIVITY 8.1

Portfolio

Learning from Others

Interview a person in the career cluster you choose for Chapter 5, preferably in one of the careers from the *Web Connections* activity. Your teacher, counselor, or family can help you find a person to interview in person or over the telephone. Use the following questions as the starting point of your interview:

- What is your job title? Describe your job.
- How did you start in this career area?
- What was your educational pathway to your career?
- What are the most important skills needed for success in your work?
- If you could do it over again, would you change the way you prepared for your career? If so, how? Why?

- How has your career field changed since you started in it?
- How do you see your career field changing over the next ten years?
- What additional learning do you expect you will need to remain successful and to advance in your field?
- What advice would you offer students to help them make good career choices?

What conclusions can you draw from your interview?

Education & Training: High School Options

Goals

- Identify career preparation options for completing high school.
- Describe the alternatives for high school cooperative education.
- Define the ways you can jumpstart your post-secondary education while in high school.

Terms

- college prep courses, p. 182
- GPA, p. 182
- online learning, p. 182
- career and technical high school, p. 182
- certificate, p. 183
- internship, p. 183
- co-op (cooperative) programs, p. 184
- apprenticeship, p. 185
- advanced placement, p. 186
- articulation agreements, p. 186
- dual credit, p. 186
- dual enrollment, p. 186

Real Life Focus

Getting a jump on your career may shorten your career preparation path—or at least give you the foundation for courses you will take in the future. Look at the list of careers below. What high school courses will give a person a jumpstart and/or skills to do the work involved? How do the courses relate to the careers?

- Teacher
- Attorney
- Plumber
- Veterinarian Assistant
- Information Technology Help Desk
- Stockbroker

High School

Your high school may offer different options for completing your career path. Also, you may have the choice of different types of high schools to attend. You need to consider the options before you decide which career preparation path best meets your career, lifestyle, and budget needs.

Traditional High School

A typical high school has academic courses in language arts, social studies, math, and science that will give you a basic education. However, high schools also offer additional elective courses that will give you a head start on your career preparation.

Some high schools are designed with careers in mind and may be divided into career majors. Students choose a career pathway and take courses related to the career cluster. A series of courses may be available for careers in areas such as business, agriculture, technology, and health.

In addition, your high school may offer **college prep courses**. Those courses will help you with post-secondary (after high school) training, such as for advanced courses that will help you prepare to enter a college or university. Often, you need a teacher's recommendation or a certain **GPA** (grade point average) to take college prep courses.

Online learning courses are conducted through a web site with the teacher working with students from various high schools and communicating electronically. Some online learning may be in a blended course with students having face-to-face learning time with a teacher while taking the online course. Nearly 50 percent of high school students have taken an online course or used an online textbook.

Nearly every U.S. state has at least one virtual high school. Students do not attend classes in a school building. Instead, they take all their courses online. Students who choose this high school option will learn at their own pace.

However, online learning is not for everyone. Often there is little personal contact between the teacher and students. If you have strong time management skills and can work independently, online learning may be a good option for you. Always check the quality of the course or school before you start a virtual learning opportunity.

Career and Technical Education

Attending a **career and technical high school** or a specialized career-training high school can be an option for part or all of your high school education. During high school, you may enroll at a career center; at a career school within your regular high school; or at a magnet, or specialized, school. You may take a few career and technical courses and not an entire program.

With a career and technical major, you focus on one career area. These schools offer courses of study for many career areas. You take your academic courses such as math, English, and science. However, where you take these courses—either in the school you attend all day or at your home high school—depends on your school district's arrangement. There are many types of career and technical education course schedules.

Renata is passionate about technology, particularly how computers work. She knows her career will be in the Business Management and Administration career cluster. Renata loves courses that increase her knowledge of technology. The nearby career and technical campus offers a two-year career major working with various types of information technology.

However, Renata wonders if attending the career and technical school might limit her high school activities, which are very important to her. She enjoys being a cheerleader and a member of her school's environmental organization. If practices and

What are the options for taking career and technical courses in high school?

auremar/Shutterstock.com

meetings take place during the school day and she attends the career and technical school, Renata will not be able to participate in them.

Renata's counselor, Ms. Domet, suggested an alternative. Depending if she wants to work with computer software or hardware, Renata can take either Microsoft Office Specialist (MOS) or A+ computer service technician certification courses in her junior year at her home high school. Renata can complete the course work in one year and transfer to the career and technical school her senior year for additional specialization.

Another choice Renata has is to stay at her high school and complete the course work over two years. The course options would allow her to pursue her extracurricular activities.

You can accomplish the skills required for some careers in a certification course or program—one of Renata's options—or at a career and technical high school. When you complete the program, you take a test to receive a **certificate**. The certificate is an official document that proves you have successfully completed specific course content and have necessary skills. The certificate shows an employer that you have specialized skills and can perform a certain job. Certificates can be earned in many career areas, including cosmetology, culinary arts, welding, and childcare.

Consider

Why is setting your career preparation goals for high school so important? What are some of the roadblocks for completing the goal?

Cooperative Programs

Some specialized education and training options may be available to you while you are in high school. Internships, cooperative programs, and apprenticeships all combine education and work experience. They are great ways to combine schoolwork with the work world. Each option emphasizes work and education in different ways. The results of your experience will be different for each option.

Internship

An **internship** is a program that provides practical experience working in a specific career. As an intern, you may work after school or during the summer. If the internship is a required part of a class, you may be granted release time from school to work at the internship. Often high school internships are nonpaid, but they provide you with the experience of working in your career field.

In addition, an internship gives you the opportunity to research a career and the company before you commit to further education or training. As an intern, you learn about the work environment, the equipment, relationships between workers and supervisors, and other work issues, such as dress code.

If you are taking a class that requires an internship, your teacher may arrange an internship in partnership with a local company. If an internship is not available in your career field or if you do not qualify for the program at your school, you can plan an internship on your own. Talk to the owner or manager of a business. Offer to work for no pay in exchange for acquiring experience in your field. If the business owner is unfamiliar with internships, you may have to convince him or her that you will work hard and that the internship will benefit the business. Even if you do not earn credit, an internship is valuable for gaining skills and experience that classes cannot provide.

The rewards of being an intern are many. You get firsthand experience in a career field that interests you. You can improve your communication skills, identify your skills, and develop self-confidence. Although an internship may lead to a part-time or full-time job after you graduate, do not expect a job afterwards. However, you can expect to work with people who can write recommendation letters.

People who intern are often more satisfied with their career choice. Many are in the same career—and even the same company—several years later.

Cooperative Program

Co-op (cooperative) programs combine your high school courses with paid work experiences in a specific career field. You will attend classes at school part of the day and work at your co-op employer for the rest of the school day. Students receive school credit for participating in a co-op program and are paid for their work by the co-op employer.

In a co-op program, you take one or more courses to relate the class to your work experience. You apply the skills you learn in the classroom to the actual job in your career area.

You will develop a training plan with the school and the employer that outlines your goals and the skills and knowledge you will acquire. Co-op programs increase your classroom learning, improve your career opportunities, and provide career experiences as you earn money. Co-op programs involve a formal agreement between the student and his or her family, the school, and the employer. Usually, the three parties sign an agreement that outlines the responsibilities of each participant. The agreement may include the following points:

sjlocke/iStockphoto.com

- The job description and the work hours

- The evaluation methods used by the school, the employer, and the student to monitor and evaluate the student's progress

- The payment the student will receive

Both internships and co-op programs require planning on your part. You may need to find a work site that relates to your career path. The employer also should provide useful work experience. Research the organization's employee guidelines. Those guidelines, such as the dress code, absentee policy, and use of technology, apply to you as well.

Keep track of what you did during your experience. You will need the information for future education and work situations. You also will need to document the details for your resume and education applications. If you work closely with a supervisor, you often find you have a reference—and may develop a mentor relationship.

Apprenticeship

An **apprenticeship** is a program in which a person works as a skilled worker while learning a trade. At one time, an apprenticeship was the only way a person could learn some trades, especially in construction. Today, however, you can work as an apprentice in many different types of industries. For example, through an apprenticeship program, you can train for a career in the culinary industry or as an X-ray equipment tester.

Some apprenticeship programs are informal arrangements between a worker and an employer. However, most apprenticeships are registered state or federal government programs. Registered programs must meet government standards. Because the government oversees them, the programs provide high-quality training and protect the safety of apprentices. Additionally, most apprenticeships are union agreements. The union, not the business where you work, employs you. In fact, your work site may change when you finish a job.

For some careers, you begin apprenticeship training while you are still in high school. Two years in a career and technical program can lead to a journey-worker program, an average of four years after high school. For some careers, you must graduate from high school before beginning the apprenticeship, which can take up to six years. With either option, you will receive hundreds of hours of on-the-job training and hundreds of hours in the classroom. You earn money while you work. As you learn the trade and require less supervision, your pay gradually increases.

Monkey Business Images/Shutterstock.com

What is the advantage of being an apprentice for your career preparation path?

If you answered *yes* to the majority of these questions, you might consider going directly from high school to a career. Some companies encourage students to take this path. These companies need bright, trainable, entry-level workers, especially in technical areas. The high salaries available two or three years after leaving high school are appealing. Some high school graduates who would have gone on to post-secondary education join the workforce.

However, if you follow this path, you eventually may learn that the disadvantages of going straight to a career outweigh the benefits. Without additional education, your opportunities for career growth may be limited. Your technical skills alone will not determine your career success. Communication skills, business knowledge, and an understanding of global economic issues are vital to career advancement.

On-the-job training (OJT) is one way to continue your education while you work. In **on-the-job training**, you learn skills for a specific career under the supervision of an experienced worker. Often OJT combines some type of classroom training with hands-on instruction. OJT may take only a few days or may take a year or more. It requires less time than an apprenticeship.

Some form of OJT is necessary for nearly all jobs. An employer hires you because he or she believes you have the skills and ability needed to learn how to perform a job. Regardless of your training and education background, employers do not expect you to be able to perform a job expertly on your first day. Take advantage of any OJT opportunities. Additional training and education will help you achieve success.

Employers look for workers who know how to continue to learn and who are able to adapt to change. Education beyond high school helps you develop those skills. *Employers know this and, given a choice, will hire the better-educated person.* Some employers will pay for your education while you work full-time. Some form of education or training after high school is essential to help you achieve career success and reach your lifestyle goals.

Gap Year

The gap year is something to consider while you are planning your future. A **gap year** is a year between high school graduation and the start of your post-secondary education. Students take a gap year for various reasons, including travel, internship, work, and volunteer service. It should not be a year spent doing nothing, but time off with a purpose.

The option of students taking a gap year is becoming more popular. Nearly 15 percent of students in the United Kingdom and Australia take a gap year before starting their post-secondary education. If you are considering a gap year, ask yourself these questions:

■ What would be your goals for taking a gap year?

■ Will you apply for college your senior year, then defer, or delay, your admission? (If you explain the situation, some colleges will allow deferred admission.)

- Would you take a gap year to use the time to help you decide where to focus your education?

- What research will you do to prepare for your gap year?

- Do you have a reason for taking the gap year, or are you thinking of it as just a chance to take some time off?

The results of a well-planned gap year may help you learn more about your career and lifestyle goals. According to the book, *The Gap-Year Advantage*, the benefits of a gap year include helping students gain confidence and focus. The result is that students concentrate more in their next step on their career path—often pursuing post-secondary education.

Consider

Do the traditional ways that people prepare for a career in your chosen field apply to you? Why or why not?

Military Service

For many people, joining a branch of the military after high school is an option worth considering. They receive technical training while in the service. In addition, they are eligible for government education tuition assistance after they leave the service.

When Analise began her career planning, she knew exactly what her career would be. She wanted to follow her father's example and become an engineer, specifically a chemical engineer.

Analise always enjoyed research, especially the problem-solving aspects of science and math. She knew that her career choice would require at least a bachelor's degree. She also realized that she would have to work while she was in school so she could pay for her tuition and school expenses. Plus, Analise knew that engineering required much studying. It would be hard for her to work and attend school at the same time.

Ms. Fuller, Analise's counselor, suggested that she talk to an Army recruiter. Analise discovered that the Army would pay for her schooling. In exchange, she would agree to enlist in the Army for several years. Also, she would be working in areas related to her future career goal.

Several options are available for military service. In addition to the various branches of the military—Army, Navy, Air Force, Marines, and Coast Guard—you can investigate the National Guard and the Reserves. To enlist, you need to be a high school graduate, 18 years old, in good health, and a U.S. citizen.

DanielBendjy/iStockphoto.com

Military service may be more than an education option. You may decide that you want to pursue a career in the military. Talking to recruits in the Armed Services will give you information to make your decision.

Advanced Education

A **post-secondary education** is any type of education beyond high school. Besides a college or university option, some of the high school options discussed in Lesson 8.2 are available after you graduate. Co-op programs are available in colleges and universities. Career and technical schools have **adult workforce development** programs. There are one- or two-year post-secondary training courses and certification programs. In addition, virtual learning or an apprenticeship program may provide the training you want.

Web Connections

Web sites have information to explore career preparation options.

Access the Web Connections link for Chapter 8. Investigate at least two career preparation options for the career cluster you chose in Chapter 5. Answer the questions below for sites you investigate.

1. What are the benefits of the career preparation option?
2. What are some drawbacks to this option?
3. How can this option give me a start on my career?

www.cengage.com/school/iyc

Associate Degree

An **associate degree** is a degree earned upon completion of a program that usually requires the equivalent of two or more years of full-time study. The degree can be a final degree or a transfer degree for completing a bachelor's degree.

An associate degree is a way to prepare for a specific career. Many careers do not require education beyond an associate degree. For example, medical and veterinary technicians, computer service technicians, registered nurses, welders, and auto mechanics may need only an associate degree.

Also, if you decide you want more education after earning an associate degree, a college or university often will give you credit for courses you have taken in earning your degree. Most colleges have partnering arrangements with other colleges or universities, allowing for easy transfer of credits.

However, if you are thinking about attending a college to transfer for a bachelor's degree program, plan your transfer from the beginning. Talk to an adviser and focus on the future. The average tuition of a state college or university associate degree program is less than half the cost of a bachelor's degree program.

Also, being admitted into a **community college**, a government-supported college in your local area that offers associate degrees, may be easier than admission into a bachelor's degree program. The university may not accept you directly out of high school. However, transferring from one of its branch community campuses with an associate degree is a way to gain entrance in two or three years. The savings in time and money may be worth the transfer.

Bachelor's Degree and Beyond

A **bachelor's degree** is a degree issued by a college or university to a person who has completed undergraduate studies. Some careers require a bachelor's degree, which takes an average of over six years to earn.

Colleges and universities vary in the types of education and training they provide. Some colleges offer students a general education rather than training for a specific career. Other colleges provide specialized education in some career fields, such as artistic and hospitality careers. Most large universities offer both—a general education and training in certain career areas. Most importantly, keep in mind that college is not a career. You need to have a definite career goal that a college or university education will enhance.

Although less than 15 percent of careers *require* a bachelor's degree, the value of a college degree is clear. Starting salaries are often higher. Lifetime earnings are often greater for people with bachelor's degrees than for high school graduates without a post-secondary education. For each year of education you add, you increase your lifetime earnings an average of 10 percent. In addition, employers often prefer to hire candidates with well-rounded backgrounds and college degrees, even if a degree does not apply to a specific job.

Some professional careers require degrees beyond a bachelor's degree. For example, doctors, lawyers, and many university professors must have an M.D., J.D., or Ph.D. These degrees require two to four years of full-time study to complete. Some careers may require you to earn a master's degree for certain positions or for advancement. A master's degree takes an average of two full-time years to complete.

ACTIVITY 8.3

Pros and Cons

Identify the pros and cons for each of the following post-secondary options. Use two careers you chose in Chapter 5. You will be working in teams of students of similar career clusters.

- Work fulltime.
- Take a gap year.
- Get an education within your community.
- Enroll in an adult workforce development program.

- Work as an apprentice.
- Earn a certificate to document your career skills.
- Leave your community for your education.
- Graduate with an associate degree.
- Take courses for a master's degree.

Planning Your Career Preparation Path

Goals

- Explain how to analyze your career preparation options.
- Identify how to create a career preparation plan.

Term

- Plan B, p. 194

Real Life Focus

Your teacher will give your group a list of famous people, some current, and some from history. Each person in your group will choose one of the people and research his or her education, career, and accomplishments.

After your group members complete their research, you will role-play the person you chose. Act as the person, and ask the other group members about each other's careers and backgrounds. Try to identify the people your group members have chosen.

Analyze the Options

To begin to analyze your career preparation options, you must think about the path needed for your career and lifestyle goals. Research your career cluster thoroughly before you make any final decisions about your choice of career. Begin your research by:

- Exploring many of the ways people prepare for a career in your cluster. Check industry and career web sites for industries. Use specialized resources such as the BLS and career information systems provided by your school.

- Check with local employers to find out what they need from job candidates in your career cluster.

- Ask successful people in your career cluster which parts of their career preparation were most helpful and what they would change.

- Take advantage of the opportunities offered by your school to explore your career cluster. For example, your school may sponsor a career day or a career fair where you can interact with speakers who have jobs in your career field.

- Job shadowing can provide you with valuable information about your career choices. By job shadowing an employee in your career area, you can see what the career involves. You may decide whether the career would be a satisfying one for you.

- Service learning projects allow you to give to your community as you learn from the people you help. A service learning project may help you explore various careers in your career cluster.

- A final way to help you research your career area is to find a part-time job related to your career cluster. You not only can earn money, but also gain experience in your career field. However, be careful that your part-time job does not cause your grades to suffer or get in the way of spending time with your family. When students work more than 20 hours a week, including weekends, their grades may begin to drop.

Making the choices may seem overwhelming. However, planning can be less stressful if you prepare before you make the decisions.

Consider

What would you do if your career preparation plans took an unexpected turn?

Create a Career Preparation Plan

Each year in school brings questions about the next school year and its class schedule. Instead of asking, "Is it time to make a new schedule again?" consider planning your career preparation. Start with next year's schedule and plan until you begin an entry-level position in your career. You need to prepare with your *P*A*T*H to Success* in mind.

Remember the decision-making steps you learned in Chapter 5? Your career goal is at the end of the step. What you have accomplished so far is at the bottom, followed by next year's schedule.

When creating each step of your career preparation, ask yourself:

- Am I taking the correct math and science courses in the right order for my career goal?

- Am I scheduling elective classes needed for my career?

- Am I involved in activities that could relate to my career choice?

Starting your education and training plan now is a smart move. Over one-third of first-year college students need to take remediation "catch-up" courses in math or reading before they can start their college courses. Why? Because the students had not planned well in high school.

Avoiding remediation is important. So is having a **Plan B**, a career preparation backup plan. For example, the military may not be your first choice as a way to receive your career preparation. However, the military is a good backup plan if you do not have tuition and other education expenses. To many, joining the Armed Forces is better than piling up student loans.

Also, planning will save you time and money. More states are adding a workforce-readiness test or document to high school graduation requirements. Employers want the same high-level skills as colleges and universities want. If you have the skills an employer wants, then you chose the best career preparation options for your career path.

ACTIVITY 8.4

Portfolio

Career Preparation Timeline

The goal of reaching your career takes a series of career preparation steps, similar to a career ladder. Most career ladders require additional education and work experience throughout a person's working life.

1. Create your career preparation timeline using the guide from your teacher. Your starting point is what you are currently doing to achieve your career goal. At the end, write your career goal using one of the careers you chose in Chapter 5.

2. After you complete your timeline, create a Plan B for the same career. What if you receive no scholarships to help with the tuition? What if the employers you interviewed prefer certifications instead of degrees? Having a back-up plan in place is beneficial.

3. Save the results in your Career Portfolio to use in Chapter 9.

Micha Rosenwirth/Shutterstock.com

Chapter Summary

8.1 Finding the Right Path

- Career goals should influence the career preparation choices.
- Considering all the career preparation options requires examination of education, career, and lifestyle choices.

8.2 Education & Training: High School Options

- Career preparation options for high school include basic high school courses, college prep courses, online learning, career and technical education, and certificate programs.
- Cooperative education choices include internship, co-op, and apprenticeship programs.
- Post-secondary education choices include advanced placement, dual credit, and dual enrollment courses.

8.3 Education & Training: Options Beyond High School

- Working in a career is an option after high school graduation that usually includes job training.
- More students are taking the option of a gap year to concentrate on work or activities other than education.
- Military service is an additional option that helps pay for career preparation.
- Advanced education options include career and technical adult workforce development, apprenticeship, certification programs, and associate and bachelor's degrees.

8.4 Planning Your Career Preparation Path

- Through research, interviews, activities, and career events, one can analyze the various career preparation options.
- Using the career preparation analysis, one can create a career preparation plan, starting with today and ending with the career goal.

Chapter Assessment

Vocabulary Builder

Match each statement with the term that best defines it.

1. A degree usually completed in two or more full-time years
2. Any education beyond high school
3. Post-secondary career and technical education programs
4. Learning conducted through a web site
5. Grade point average
6. Career backup plan
7. Studying college-level material in high school
8. Specialized career training in high school
9. Government-supported local college that offers associate degrees
10. Education and training options
11. PSEO courses taken on college campuses
12. Program that provides practical experience working in a career
13. Combines high school courses with paid work experience
14. High school courses that help with post-secondary education
15. Advancing credit taken for both high school and college credit
16. Contracts between a high school and a college for coursework
17. College or university degree that takes an average of six years to complete
18. Learning career skills under an experienced worker's supervision
19. Learning a trade while working as a skilled employee
20. Document that is proof of completion of necessary career skills
21. A year between high school graduation and the start of post-secondary education

a. adult workforce development
b. advanced placement
c. apprenticeship
d. articulation agreements
e. associate degree
f. bachelor's degree
g. career and technical high school
h. career preparation
i. certificate
j. college prep courses
k. community college
l. co-op programs
m. dual credit
n. dual enrollment
o. gap year
p. GPA
q. internship
r. online learning
s. on-the-job training
t. Plan B
u. post-secondary education

Review What You Have Learned

22. What do you need to consider when choosing career preparation options?
23. What are the advantages of a career and technical high school?
24. Why take a certification course or program?
25. What is the difference between an internship and a co-op program?
26. Explain the different types of PSEO courses.
27. List the advantages and disadvantages of going straight to a career.
28. What are the benefits and commitments of joining the military?
29. What are some ways you can analyze career preparation options?

Case Challenges

Choose one or more options of career preparation most valuable for each student in the cases below. Explain the reasons for your choices.

- Bachelor's degree
- Associate degree
- Military service
- Internship
- Career and technical school
- Co-op program

30. Monica hopes to open a kennel. However, she is only familiar with a few breeds of dogs and knows she must expand her animal knowledge.

31. DaJuan has loved science all his life. He won a scholarship for his science fair project and had a nearly perfect SAT score. DaJuan knows that his education plan includes college with some type of science major.

32. Maya has always liked babysitting. Her summer job is working as a nanny for a set of triplets and teaching evening beginning swimming classes. Maya hopes to become an elementary school teacher.

Make Academic Connections

33. LANGUAGE ARTS In a persuasive presentation, convince your family to support your career preparation path.
- Provide specific reasons and support for why the career and the career preparation path is a good choice for you.
- Use persuasive language, building a rational argument.

Portfolio

34. MATH For each item, calculate the percentages, using the number of students in your class. The statistics are *national* averages.
- 25% of students will drop out of high school, and 75% will graduate.
- 50% will attend college, and 50% will not.
- 25% will complete a bachelor's degree, and 75% will not.
- 85% will take jobs that do not *require* a bachelor's degree. 15% will take jobs that *require* a bachelor's degree.

Workplace Connection

Between the ages of 18 and 42, people have an average of eight careers.

35. Develop a career preparation transition plan for changing from the career you used in Question 33 to another choice from your career cluster. Include additional education and skills you will need.

Portfolio

Blogging: My Career Preparation Pathway

In the first part of this post, describe your career preparation pathway. Begin with what you are currently doing, continue through high school graduation, and end with the completion of your initial post-secondary education. In the second half of the post, describe your Plan B, your backup plan.

Blog

Going from Here to Your Career

CLAUDIA DAUT/Reuters/Landov

What Do You Know

1. What steps can you take now for future career success in your chosen career?

2. What are some of the deciding factors for choosing your education/training path?

Madison Brown has a gift for languages. She realized she loved learning different languages when she began to study Spanish in seventh grade. Rather than take one language throughout middle school and high school, Madison decided that she would take three languages in her six years until graduation.

Spanish was relatively easy, so Madison chose Chinese for her next language. She understood that to become fluent in Chinese would take many years and trips overseas. Having a basic knowledge of the language gave Madison an appreciation for the difficulty of an English-speaking person learning an Asian language.

The last language that Madison chose to learn led to her career path. She began learning American Sign Language (ASL)—both signing and fingerspelling. How has ASL led Madison to realizing her career path? Because Madison began to understand the dilemma of those who are hearing-impaired. Working with ASL has given her an appreciation of the hurdles faced by people with hearing difficulties in a hearing world.

From that realization came Madison's career choice—speech-language pathology, previously known as speech therapy. Madison believes this career is the right one for her. However, finding the right place to continue her education after high school might be more difficult for her than most students. Why? Because Madison is a nationally ranked runner whose college acceptance depends on financial aid for her athletic ability.

Planning a Career in . . . Human Services

The Human Services career cluster includes any career that works with families and people's needs.

The diversity in this career cluster ranges from early childhood to family and community services. It includes careers in counseling and mental health as well as careers in personal care and consumer services. You may work with health issues, wellness, education, and personal appearance. However, in any Human Services career, you will be working with people.

Employment Outlook

- Strong demand for all types of Human Services careers.
- Personal Care and Early Childhood have a faster than average growth.
- Entry-level lower wage. Increases with experience and more education.

Career Possibilities

- Cosmetologist
- Consumer Advocate
- Nanny
- Religious Leader
- School Counselor

Needed Skills

- Knowledge of health and safety.
- Ability to apply information technology.
- Problem solving and communications.
- Certifications for most Human Services specialties.

What's It Like to Work in Human Services?

Choosing a Human Services career is like choosing from a restaurant menu that has many options. You can work with any age group—from infants to senior citizens. You may help people improve their consumer credit, conquer substance abuse, or strengthen their personal relationships. Focusing on personal appearance is another option if you are considering a career in personal care. Those careers include nail, hair, and skin specialists, plus massage therapists and personal trainers.

Many of the careers listed overlap with other career clusters, such as health, education, and finance. What a Human Services career emphasizes is working directly with people's needs.

Entry-level Human Services careers tend to have lower pay and longer hours. However, the more specialized you become, the higher the pay. In fact, many Human Services workers own their own businesses or contract their services.

There will always be a high demand for Human Services careers. If people are your passion, consider this career cluster.

What about You?

Do you like to work with people? Are you interested in helping others improve their lives? Is personal appearance important to you? If you answered *yes* to some of those questions, then consider a career in one of the aspects of the Human Services career cluster.

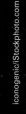

Career Preparation Path

Goals

- List the entry-level career path requirements.
- Compare the career path requirements with the career preparation options.

Term

- career preparation provider, p. 202

Portfolio

Real Life Focus

Consider the career preparation options described in Chapter 8. List the options that are appropriate for the two career preparation paths you chose in Chapter 5. You may use the form provided at www.cengage.com/school/iyc, Chapter 9.

Share the results with your career cluster group. Are there similarities? What were the reasons for each person's choices?

By now, you have created your *Internal Career Design*. You have identified the influences that impact your career choice. You have completed assessments to understand yourself. You have futurecast and researched various careers. You have also set goals and have begun to explore career preparation options. Now you can use all of that information to begin planning the path *you* will take to reach your chosen career.

Before you proceed, check that your career plan:

■ Is the basis for the four steps of your *P*A*T*H to Success*.

■ Will prepare you for various employment options.

■ Allows you to develop a wide range of transferable skills.

■ Will help you adapt to changing employment markets.

■ Includes plans for lifelong learning.

Your Career Choice Requirements

To begin planning your career preparation path, you need to review your *P*A*T*H to Success*. Then explore the education/training requirements and your current skills and experience for your career path choices. Your results will give you a starting point for putting your career plan into action.

P*A*T*H to Success

Your career path choices may require specific abilities and personality for you to be successful. For example, people in service careers, such as landscaping and music education, have the most success when (1) they are responsible, (2) they perform their job duties with independence, and (3) they work well with people. In addition, landscapers should enjoy working outdoors in most types of weather. People working in music education should enjoy making and teaching music.

Education/Training

Most entry-level positions require applicants to complete various types of education or training. For instance, someone without a high school diploma may get a job as a landscape laborer. However, a landscape designer usually needs to complete specialized training or earn an associate degree. In the music education field, preschool music specialists usually need a minimum of an associate degree. Teachers generally must have at least a bachelor's degree.

Skills and Experience

Each career cluster involves certain skills. For example, all landscaping jobs require the ability to operate and maintain hand and power tools. A music education career requires skills in reading music, playing instruments, conducting, and rearranging musical scores. You can acquire many of these skills before beginning your education and training.

Comstock Images/Getty Images

How much specialized education/training do you need for your career path?

In addition, different careers in each career cluster require different levels of skills. For instance, landscape designers must be able to identify various plants, analyze soil conditions, and understand the needs of specific plants. Entry-level landscaping jobs do not require as much knowledge and skill. Likewise, preschool music specialists do not need the same level of knowledge as music teachers.

The different career levels in each cluster may call for different levels of experience. In the landscaping career area, entry-level laborers may need to have experience using power tools. In contrast, landscape contractors usually need several years of more and more responsible landscaping experience. Sometimes, as in music education, advanced training or education may substitute for experience.

Consider

Do you think that the career plan you have now will be the same one you have all your life? Why or why not?

Options for the Career Requirements

After you figure out the requirements needed for your career cluster, you must decide how you will meet those requirements.

The career preparation options described in Chapter 8 will help you find your best path. Some careers, such as medical doctors, certified public accountants, and cosmetologists, require very specific training for people to become qualified. In other careers, people can follow a wider variety of preparation paths to become qualified. For example, those in successful information technology positions have an amazing variety of backgrounds. The education may be a combination of formal education, on-the-job-training, and earned certifications. However, all IT specialists have a curiosity for problem solving.

Illustration 9-1 shows how Madison Brown identified the career requirement options for each point—*P*A*T*H to Success*, education/training, and skills and experience. She included ways to prepare both while in high school and after graduation. Madison considered both her career in speech-language pathology and track.

If you are like Madison and will be pursuing your education while hoping to have your education financed by your athletic, music, artistic, or other ability, include your talent as well as your career requirements when considering career preparation options. You will choose the best **career preparation provider** to meet your education/training needs. The career preparation provider is any training program, school, institution, individual, or business that offers career preparation instruction.

Illustration 9-1: Entry-Level Requirements and Preparation Options for Madison Brown

Entry-Level Requirements for Speech-Language Pathologist

P*A*T*H to Success
- Loves to work with people
- Empathy for persons with disabilities
- Committed to lifelong learning
- Passionate about technology
- Open to constant change

Skills and Experience
- Clear and correct written and spoken communication
- Team leadership and participation skills
- Problem-solving skills
- Excellent communication
- Good listening skills
- Ability to multitask
- Attention to detail
- American Sign Language

Education/Training
- Bachelor's degree—required
- Master's degree—required
- Ph.D.—recommended for some positions

Match the Options to Your Career Plan

You have spent much time thinking about your *Internal Career Design* in the previous chapters. The classes you choose before you graduate from high school can help you meet your career goals. Before planning your education/training, consider the classes you will need in order to work in your top two career paths.

1. Remove the following from your Career Portfolio:

   - *Workplace Connection*, Chapter 1, Activity 29—Survey Your Strengths
   - *Workplace Connection*, Chapter 1, Activity 30—Transferable Skills
   - *Real Life Focus, Lesson* 2.2—Community and Climate Preferences
   - *Workplace Connection*, Chapter 2—Cultural Expectations
   - Activity 5.3—Investigating Career Clusters

   - *Web Connection*, Chapter 5— Career Research
   - Activity 6.1—Long-Term Ambitions

Portfolio

   Review your answers to each activity. Then choose an additional career path that would fit your *Internal Career Design*.

2. Use the Career Cluster Research form available at www.cengage.com/school/iyc, Chapter 9. Research and record the entry-level requirements for the two career paths you chose.

3. Match the career preparation options you selected for this lesson's Real Life Focus with the entry-level requirements you listed in your research and record your options.

OtnaYdur/Shutterstock.com

Goals

- Identify the factors in deciding on a career preparation provider.
- Explain the various types of financial aid available.
- Analyze the entrance requirements when selecting a career preparation provider.

Terms

- accreditation, p. 205
- campus culture, p. 205
- FAFSA, p. 207
- SAR (Student Aid Report), p. 208
- EFC (Expected Family Contribution), p. 208
- need-based, p. 208
- scholarship, p. 208
- grant, p. 208
- student loan, p. 208
- co-signer, p. 208
- work-study program, p. 208

Real Life Focus

If you were choosing a career preparation provider, what do you have to offer them? You will be selling yourself so that the program will choose you. Summarize your results from:

■ Your *P*A*T*H to Success*

■ Your education/training needs

■ Your skills/experience

Save the results to use throughout this chapter, especially for *Make Academic Connections*, Question 26.

After you know the requirements and preparation options for your career, you will need to investigate career preparation providers. To start your search, your guidance counselor can help you identify suitable career preparation providers. Also, your school media center or community library may have a special section devoted to career preparation. Additional information sources include web pages, online search sites, and other suggestions offered in Chapter 8.

Factors to Consider when Choosing a Career Preparation Provider

Your research should identify several career preparation providers whose courses meet the education/training requirements for your career. Which provider should you choose? Check different aspects of each provider (including reputation, accreditation, offerings, cost, and campus culture) to help you make a good choice.

Reputation

The reputation of your career preparation provider often influences potential employers. A program with a good reputation will reflect favorably.

A poor reputation may cause employers to wonder about the quality of your qualifications. Ask former students for their opinion of the education/training provider and the course of study you are considering. Check with those you have interviewed in developing your career plan. Call employers in your career path, introduce yourself, and ask for their opinion.

Over 100 years ago, educators realized that accreditation was important. They worked together to protect the quality of higher education. **Accreditation** is the measurement process they developed to make sure the schools and programs offered to high school graduates have a basic level of quality. Also, many professions and trades have set up state and national methods to evaluate schools and programs related to their professions.

Program Offerings

Career preparation providers offer different levels of education and training. For example, some may offer a certificate or an associate degree. Others may offer a bachelor's degree. Before you select a provider, make sure you understand the different options offered. Check that the available levels of education or training match your career goals.

Elenathewise/iStockphoto.com

> *Madison planned to enroll in a university that offers speech-language pathology as a major. She realizes that she cannot receive her certification from the American Speech-Language-Hearing Association (ASHA) without obtaining at least her master's degree.*
>
> *As part of her research, Madison interviewed Paul Carbo to learn about his education. During the interview, Paul mentioned that he earned his bachelor's and master's degrees in a combined program, usually a five-year program. He suggested that Madison check the ASHA web site to check each school's reputation.*
>
> *Madison also must check with the National Collegiate Athletic Association (NCAA) to see if the schools she is considering have good academic records for athletes and any violations in athletics.*

Review your career plan and your research. Decide whether the career preparation providers you are considering offer the education or training you will need for your chosen career path. For example, you may plan to get a certificate first and then a job in your field for several years. Then you may plan to study for an associate degree. Find out first if you will be able to transfer the credits earned at the certificate level toward an associate degree.

Campus Culture

The characteristics that give each school or training program its unique personality is its **campus culture**. When the time comes, you should make personal visits to possible career preparation providers.

Madison Brown grew up in a Maryland suburb of Washington, D.C. She preferred to attend a school in the South below Virginia. Several schools in North and South Carolina had accredited speech-language pathology programs, along with NCAA-sanctioned programs. Three schools particularly interested Madison. Fortunately, they were hosting open campuses for visiting students during her spring break week. The admissions counselors scheduled several activities, including attending classes.

During the school visits, Madison discovered that each campus had a unique campus culture. One was a community school with an enrollment of 70 percent local students. The second had an unkempt campus with few smiling students. The third gave Madison a good feeling. It was a smaller campus with out-of-state students comprising over 75 percent of enrollment. Both the speech-language pathology and the track programs were outstanding.

Madison talked about her visits with her family, school counselor, and coach. Ultimately, the visits supported Madison's decision to apply to the third school.

Real People / Real Careers

Louie Brockhoeft / *Certified Personal Trainer*

Louie Brockhoeft's love of sports started in elementary school. He played football, basketball, and baseball in high school and college. After college graduation, Louie had careers, but not related to sports. However, in his spare time, he continued to be a coach and a referee.

When Louie decided to pursue his passion, he wanted to become involved in health and fitness fulltime. Becoming a personal trainer was a natural fit. Louie was passionate about fitness. Using books and web sites, he consistently researched the human body's reaction to training, diet, and other wellness factors. With his majors in psychology and marketing, Louie had the education to support his work and real-world experiences.

Through the National Academy of Sports Medicine, Louie became licensed as a Certified Personal Trainer, which was required by his employer, a hospital-owned health and wellness center. Since then, Louie has chosen to increase his expertise by passing other certifications. Those certifications allow him to help people who have special problems, such as lower back and knee pain.

Several years ago, Louie and his business and personal training partner opened their own training studio. They developed a business plan, which included expanding their number of clients. They have so many clients now that they moved to a larger facility and added exercise classes.

Louie's career passion supports his clients. "My genuine desire is to help others reach their fitness and life goals. That desire keeps me learning the latest innovations and researching new strategies with my clients on a regular basis. I am passionate about health and fitness. It is a journey that takes time, dedication, and patience."

For more information about:

* certified personal trainers and similar careers

* personal care services careers

Access **www.cengage.com/school/iyc** and click on the appropriate links in Chapter 9.

Source: *Personal Interview*, 2011.

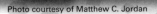
Photo courtesy of Matthew C. Jordan

As you narrow your career preparation provider choices, make sure you consider all aspects of the provider's campus culture. A campus culture that fits your personality and furthers your goals will help you relax and concentrate on your education. A variety of factors influences the campus culture of programs or schools, including the following:

- The mix and ages of resident and local students and full- and part-time students

- The type of provider (public school, private school, or workplace)

- The geographic and cultural origins of the students

- The geographic location, including the climate, of the school or workplace

- The number of students attending the school or training program and the size of the classes

All of these factors can affect the success of your education/training. During your visits, you may discover that the culture of some providers is not what you expected. In fact, a school or program you were not seriously considering may have just the culture you want. Or you may find that a provider you thought would be perfect is not.

If you are leaving home for the first time, the culture of your new school or program is especially important. You will not be close to your normal support group of family and friends. Being comfortable with your new surroundings is important to your success.

Financing Your Education/Training

Education/training costs vary widely and range from inexpensive fees to very expensive tuition charges. So you want to think ahead about what costs you will have. Keep in mind that accredited schools and programs often offer financial aid to qualified applicants. Tax returns and the FAFSA should be prepared as early in the year as possible. Early applicants for financial aid have the best chance of getting favorable aid packages.

Free Application for Financial Student Aid (FAFSA)

To apply for financial aid—whether it is need-based, scholarships, grants, student loans, or work-study programs—you and your family must complete a form called the **Free Application for Financial Student Aid (FAFSA)**. The FAFSA uses information from your parents' or guardian's income tax returns. Schools primarily give the best funding to students who submit their completed FAFSA by a specific date, possibly as early as February 1. That means that tax returns and the FAFSA should be prepared as early in the year as possible. Early applicants for financial aid have the best chance of getting favorable aid packages. Access **www.cengage.com/school/iyc** for the link to the FAFSA and other financial aid web sites.

You will receive the results of the FAFSA process in a report called the **Student Aid Report (SAR)**. The SAR shows the amount you and your family should contribute to your education or training as the **Expected Family Contribution (EFC)**.

Review the SAR carefully with your family. If you have any concerns or find any errors in the SAR, talk to a financial aid representative of the school. Based on unusual circumstances (such as high medical bills or unemployment) or the school's award criteria, the school often adjusts the results of the FAFSA process.

Types of Financial Aid

Financial aid can be need-based or in the form of scholarships, grants, loans, or work-study programs. Aid is also available from other sources, such as government agencies, private donors, and professional associations.

- Almost all **need-based** financial aid programs use the EFC as the basis for the amount and type of financial aid they offer students. Need-based financial aid depends solely on your financial need based on your family's income.

- A **scholarship** is money you do not have to repay that a school or an organization provides for your education. Scholarships may be awarded based on need; academic, artistic, or athletic achievement; or a combination. The scholarship may also consider need-based factors. If a scholarship is renewable from year to year, you must meet specific academic or other standards in order to continue to receive it.

  Scholarships are available from many sources, not just career preparation providers. For example, a professional organization may fund a scholarship for a qualified student who plans a career in that profession.

- A **grant** is money provided by government, schools, or private donors. For example, the Federal Pell Grant is a need-based grant for undergraduate students. You do not have to repay grant money, but you must meet the standards and qualifications set by the provider of the grant.

- A **student loan** is money *you* borrow that you must repay. Loans are available from the federal government, some state governments, and financial institutions. Government-sponsored loan programs offer lower interest rates and more flexible repayment options than commercial lenders. Although some federal programs loan money directly to students, most other loan programs require you to have an adult family member cosign a loan. The **co-signer** is the person responsible for paying back the loan if you do not.

- A **work-study program** provides money to pay students for qualified on- or off-campus jobs. Work-study programs are funded through a school and are awarded as part of a financial aid package. You must show financial need and apply for jobs approved by the school.

- Athletic financial aid has many regulations, based on NCAA criteria. Please check with your athletic director and/or coach for help.

How will you pay for your education/ training?

Monkey Business Images/Shutterstock.com

Money is indeed a factor for choosing a career preparation provider. However, schools that are more expensive may offer generous financial aid packages and have more student loans available. Refer to your answers for Activity 7.3. Prepare a similar worksheet for yourself.

Selection of Your Career Preparation Provider

Before you select your career preparation provider, be aware of these myths about furthering your education:

- *I cannot go to college because no one in my family has.* Not true. In fact, nearly half of high school graduates who go to college had parents who did not.

- *Small colleges are like high school.* Again, not true. Smaller colleges have professors with just as much education and expertise as larger universities. These colleges have an advantage over larger schools with more personal attention and smaller class size.

- *Prestigious schools are necessary for success.* No way. Yes, a few employers look for "brand name" programs, but the majority want a thorough education, along with good academic standing.

Consider

What particular information would you want to learn when visiting an employer, a school, or a program you are considering for your education/training? Why?

Regardless of the education/training path you select, you can improve your chances of being accepted into the school or program. Make sure your qualifications meet the provider's admission requirements.

Even though you may not have decided yet on a specific school or program, you probably have an idea of your career preparation needs. For example, you know that most schools or programs require you to have a high school diploma or its equivalent?

Determining the entrance requirements of the programs or schools you are considering will require research. You can begin by sending for brochures and view books from all of the programs or schools you are considering. You can review the web site of each provider. Many programs have YouTube videos explaining various features of the campus culture and some of the unique programs. You should ask your counselor and alumni for advice.

Carefully study all of the information you collect until you have an understanding of admission requirements. Then make a summary to help you see how you can benefit most from the options. You can use the summary to plan your remaining classes, after-school activities, and part-time and/or summer jobs. For example, Madison Brown summarized the entrance requirements as shown in Illustration 9-2 to plan her high school classes.

Illustration 9-2: Madison Brown's Summary of Entrance Requirements

Required for Admission

• Mathematics	4 years
• Laboratory Science	3 years
• Foreign Languages	4 years
	(4 years of one language or 2 years each of two languages)
• English	4 years
• Social Studies	4 years

ACTIVITY 9.2

Analysis of Career Preparation Providers

For this activity, you will investigate at least three career preparation providers—a local provider, a state-funded provider, and an out-of-state or privately-funded provider. Access www.cengage.com/school/iyc Chapter 9 for web site suggestions.

1. When researching, you may use Internet search engines. To customize the search, include your career path in the search phrase.

2. To verify the accreditation of a school or program, check the school web site or check the lists of recognized accrediting agencies on the Department of Education web site. To document the registration of an apprenticeship program, check the Department of Labor Employment & Training Administration web site or your state's Apprenticeship Office.

3. For each school or program, analyze the career preparation providers in the categories below:

   a. Provider Name

   b. Reputation/Accreditation

   c. Program Offerings

   d. Campus Culture

   e. Cost/Financial Aid

4. Determine the entrance requirements for each career preparation provider you investigate. List recommended or required courses, skills, and experience preferred by the provider. Summarize your results using Madison Brown's Summary of Entrance Requirements as an example. Refer to your chart from Activity 8.2 to update your course selection and your timeline from Activity 8.4 to keep your plan on track.

Image Source/Getty Images

Career Plan Implementation

Goals

- Modify high school courses to fit the career path.
- Describe getting ready for the next step, particularly the admissions process.
- Understand the total package from time management to use of social media.

Terms

- Common Application, p. 215
- early decision, p. 216
- early action, p. 217

Portfolio

Real Life Focus

An important factor in the admissions process is the activities you participate in, both at school and in the community.

Make a list of the school and community activities that you have participated in since middle school. Then create an additional list considering activities that will fit into your schedule and support your career choice.

Save the results to use in your application process.

Developing your career plan gives you the opportunity to explore your career possibilities and investigate your education/training needs, while learning more about yourself. During this process, you have:

■ Followed your *P*A*T*H to Success.*

■ Researched career clusters and pathways.

■ Interviewed or read about people who work in careers that interest you.

■ Investigated programs and schools that can help you succeed.

With a clearer idea of what is important to you and to your future, you can begin *implementing* your career plan.

High School

Many high schools offer a wide range of elective courses. Some also offer separate curriculum paths based on specific career goals. The summary of your entrance requirements will help you choose high school courses.

Each state sets its own requirements for the number and type of credits that students need to graduate. In addition, the average high school schedule allows students to take more credits than just those needed for graduation. You have the chance to gain practical workplace skills, as well as to meet basic requirements for advanced training programs or for college.

Course Selection

Choose a variety of courses that will provide you with a diverse background. As you learned in Chapter 4, consider more math, science, and/or technology classes when choosing electives. Also, resist the temptation to take easy electives. All of the courses you take should make a positive statement about you and your goals. Your guidance counselor can help you choose the classes that will be most useful for your future career.

Illustration 9-3 shows Madison Brown's credits and gives an example of how to use the High School Credits Tracker form. The Tracker will help you plan and track your advanced middle school classes and the four years of high school on one page. This tracking method shows when you have completed graduation requirements. You also can easily determine which entrance requirements you have already met and when to take the additional courses you need.

Photodisc/Getty Images

Plan Activities

Deciding among after-school activities such as sports, clubs, volunteer opportunities, and part-time jobs can be challenging. Many students have several strong interests and not enough time to do everything they would like.

To help you decide whether to participate in an activity, answer the following questions:

- How does the activity support my *P*A*T*H to Success*?
- Why is the activity important to me?
- How does the activity help me develop experience, knowledge, and skills that will support my goals?
- What effect will my participating in this activity have on my schedule?
- Who else will be affected by my being in the activity, and will they support my participation?

The answers to the questions will give you insight as to whether you want to join an activity or keep your participation in it.

Your activity choices should further your goals. Most training programs and colleges prefer students who have varied backgrounds and who have joined in after-school activities, volunteered in the community, or worked at part-time jobs.

Decisions Affecting Your Experience

Like many students, you may have a part-time or summer job or are seriously thinking about finding one. Statistics show that part-time jobs help students develop characteristics that employers value. The characteristics include responsibility, organization, and time management.

Working also provides benefits that teens value, such as money and increased independence. However, make sure that a part-time job does not interfere with your schoolwork or your career goals.

Illustration 9-3: Madison Brown's High School Credits Tracker

High School Credits Tracker

Black = Ink (Use for completed courses)

Name: __Madison Brown__

Blue = Pencil (Use for courses not yet completed)

Required Subjects	Required Credits*	Credits Planned								Totals
		Sem. 1	Sem. 2	Sem. 3	Sem. 4	Sem. 5	Sem. 6	Sem. 7	Sem. 8	
English	8	Eng ▢	Eng ▢	Eng 1▢	Eng 1▢	Eng 11	Eng 11	Eng 12	Eng 12	8
Math	8	Alg 1	Alg 1	Geom	Geom	Algebra 2	Algebra 2	Calculus	Calculus	8
Science	8	Earth Science	Earth Science	Biol	Biol	Chem	Chem	Physics	Physics	8
History	4	US	US			AP[1] US	AP[1] US			4
Economics	1						Econ			1
American Government	2							AP[1] AG	AP[1] AG	2
Fine Arts	4	Orch	Orch	Performing Arts	Performing Arts					4
Health	1					Health				1
Physical E▢ucation	2			PE	PE					2
Electives–Language	8	Chinese 1	Chinese 1	Chinese 2	Chinese 2	Amer Sign Lang 1	ASL 1	ASL 2	ASL 2	8
Total Credits Planned	48	6	6	6	6	6	6	▢	▢	48
										44

*Each semester of a class is worth one (1) credit

[1]Advanced Placement Class

Will a job fit into your high school life? Why or why not?

Madison Brown appeared to have a problem. She desperately wanted a summer job to earn some spending money. However, she is on the school track team and runs club track in the summer. In addition, she will have expenses after high school graduation, no matter the amount of her scholarship. Madison needs to start saving some money for college expenses.

Madison's schedule of classes and athletics leaves little time for a part-time job. She reviewed her schedule with her family and school counselor. They decided that she could work between eight and ten hours a week.

Madison had not really started looking for a part-time job when her track coach mentioned that he needed an assistant to work with the younger runners, keep records, and take care of some of the equipment. Would Madison be interested?

Working with her coach not only would help Madison earn money, but she also would have personal coaching help. After hearing the offer, Madison realized there was no problem. The job would provide the work experience most related to Madison's athletics, the source of her college financial aid.

Part-time and summer jobs can provide valuable experience that directly supports your career goals. You have spent much time and energy describing your personal goals and developing your career plan. Doesn't it make sense to choose jobs that further your career plans or help you meet your goals?

Consider

Why is it your responsibility—not your counselor's—to follow up on your career preparation timeline?

Getting Ready

All education and training programs have an admission process. Your research and planning will prepare you to meet admission requirements when the time comes. Completing and tracking your application will be the final steps toward entering the career preparation program of your choice.

Many schools and training programs allow you to complete and send your application online. Keep in mind that even schools that encourage online application submission may require hard copies of other application materials. Check with your career preparation providers to find out how they prefer to receive applications.

Apply for Admission

Complete your application documents truthfully and neatly. Answer all questions. Dishonesty is an automatic disqualifier. Career preparation providers may not discover dishonest information on applications right away. However, if they do discover dishonesty, they will probably withdraw any acceptances or financial aid offers.

Incomplete applications will delay your acceptance. In addition, you will not receive any financial aid offers until you submit a complete application packet. Make sure your application packet is neat. Check your spelling. Applications that are not neat enough for admission counselors to read are incomplete.

Submit your application packet and the required fees in time to meet submission deadlines. A late application will most likely disqualify you for admittance or for financial aid. Most admission departments have a policy of offering the most favorable financial aid options to students who submit timely applications, or even at the earliest date.

In addition to neatness, completeness, and accuracy, admission counselors judge applications on the quality of the answers. You may find it helpful to complete a copy of the application as practice. Then you can review the practice application with your counselor before filling out the final application.

Many schools allow you to submit an application online and take the option of paying your admission fees online also. Additionally, nearly 500 colleges and universities, both private and public, use the **Common Application**. This web site allows you to track the application process for each school, your recommendation letters, and fee payment. Artist and athletic applications, plus early decision, may be submitted through this web site.

Track Your Applications

Keep copies of each application packet in your files. Applications contain many parts and involve the participation of several people. Each school has a particular timeframe for its application process. Additionally, athletics has a very different timeframe, as do many scholarship deadlines. You will find that you need to refer to your application packets often.

Your responsibility during the admission process includes following up to make sure that the other people involved meet the application deadlines. If you submit an application through the Common Application web site, tracking the process will be easier.

The keys to a successful application process are as follows:

- Plan when you will begin the application process based on each application's due date.

- Give teachers and counselors all of the information they need to support your application. Include a copy of your activities and accomplishments and a list of application deadlines.

Web Connections

If you are planning to attend a college after high school, you will need to be familiar with the multi-step college application process. Access the Web Connections link for Chapter 9. Investigate the web sites provided. Each of the sites includes timeline lists for each year of high school and often middle grades as well.

Complete a timeline for your current school year. What do you need to prepare for next year?

www.cengage.com/school/iyc

- Choose your recommendations based on each career preparation provider's needs. You do not need to use the same references for each school. However, you must always use the same counselor. Allow plenty of time for teachers and counselors to do their part.

- Use an application checklist, such as the one provided for the *Web Connection*, to track the progress of each application.

- Check to make sure that teachers, counselors, and other references are able to meet application deadlines.

The File

The application is not a single form, but a collection of key pieces of information. Colleges can ask for anything—from samples of high school writing to letters from families. Here are the most common application pieces.

- High school transcript, which is your academic record.

- Test scores, such as ACT and/or SAT scores. Advanced placement scores and other exams may be included.

- Letters of recommendation. Generally two or three from your guidance counselor, teachers, and possibly your family.

- Essay. The topic may be straightforward or very abstract.

- Interview. Private schools more often have mandatory interviews, as do some scholarships and athletic funding.

- Application. (Of course.)

Admission Timeline Exceptions

If you find a college that you are sure is right for you, consider applying early. Early decision and early action plans allow you to apply early, usually in November. You will get an admission decision from the college well before the usual spring notification date. By December or January, you will know whether your first-choice college accepted you.

You should understand the differences between early decision and early action plans before sending in your applications. Keep in mind that the rules may vary somewhat by college. Check with your counselor to make sure you understand your rights and obligations. Below are some important facts about the types of early-application plans.

Early decision plans are binding. That is, when you apply, you are agreeing to attend the college if it accepts you and offers an adequate financial aid package. Although you can apply to only one college for early decision, you may apply to other colleges through the regular admission process. If your first-choice college accepts you early, you must withdraw all other college applications.

Goodluz/Shutterstock.com

Athletic letters of commitment are similar to early decision admittance. The college generally notifies athletes by December of their senior year.

Early action plans are similar to early decision plans, but are not binding. If you have been accepted, you can choose to commit to the college immediately, or wait until the spring. Under these plans, you may also apply early action to other colleges. Usually, you have until the late spring to let the college know your decision.

Sometimes students who apply under these early decision or early action plans have a better chance of acceptance than they would through the regular admission process. These plans are also good for colleges because they receive commitments early in the admissions processs from students who really want to go to the college.

The Total Package

Grades, studies, presentations and papers, activities, sports, and jobs are important. On top of that, you have the application process—whether it is working with a military recruiter, an employer, an apprenticeship council, or a college. However, each of these career preparation providers will be looking at you— the total package.

Time Management

Like many of today's students, you may be juggling family, school, work, social, athletic, and community commitments. Busy teens may leave the house to attend team practice at 6 a.m. or earlier, rush to work a part-time job after school, return home, eat dinner, and then do homework until nearly midnight. WebMD reports that teens need an average of nine hours sleep a night. Most of you are lucky to get that much sleep on the weekends!

As you begin putting your career plan into practice, look at the Weekly Time Planner you prepared in Activity 6.3. (It should be in your Career Portfolio.) Then review the time management tips in Chapter 6. Before starting new activities, consider how they will affect your schedule. Keep your planner current and record each time commitment.

Being organized will help you use your available time more productively. When do you feel most productive? Are you a lark or an owl? For example, you may need less time in the evening for study if you work on your homework during the day between other commitments. Also, consider different approaches. If you work during the evening but do not have early morning obligations, try switching your homework period from evening to morning.

Remember, you will need some downtime to recharge. Try planning breaks into your day. If your schedule is so busy that you have no time to relax, rethink your commitments.

Career FACT

The five most common mistakes that first-year students can make are:

1. Cutting class. Do the math—you are losing tuition money.

2. Oversurfing. Schedule your Facebook and even CNN time after you finish studying.

3. Overloading. Taking on as many courses or hours as possible does not impress the college or employers. Quality versus quantity.

4. Procrastination. Planning and time management are important.

5. Doing everything yourself. Talk to those in charge when you have a question. Office hours are there for a reason.

—*The Secrets of College Success* by Jacobs and Hyman

Social Media

Most everyone knows about high school students who have made inappropriate social media posts or tweets. Foul language and photos of partying and underage drinking are, sadly, not uncommon. Some students go so far as to brag about bad behavior, such as cyberbullying or cheating on tests. However, anyone who desires admission to a college, select military group, or apprenticeship program should have no inappropriate posts. Even deleted posts are still in cyberspace, possibly forever. This applies to cell phone texts as well.

Admission directors and scholarship committees, plus employers and recruiters, have possibly Googled you or searched your Twitter, Facebook, or MySpace accounts. Even if you have all of your privacy settings turned on, others might be able to see your account through your friends' accounts. Those people writing your recommendations may see your inappropriate postings.

Having a social media account may not affect your future, but think before posting. Would you want your family, your favorite teacher, your minister, or the admissions representative to see everything you post? Why study so hard and get fantastic ACT scores, if you blow it with what you posted online or sent as a text?

ACTIVITY 9.3

Leadership

Learning from Others

Interview a recent graduate from your high school who is pursuing a career path similar to your career choice. Discover how the person chose his or her career preparation provider. Use the following questions as the basis for your interview.

- What career path did you choose? Why?
- What education or training option did you choose?
- What type of career preparation provider did you use?
- How did you choose your career preparation provider?
- How did you determine your provider's reputation? Its accreditation?
- Are you getting, or did you get, the education/ training needed for your career path?

- Did you have any type of financial aid for your education/training? If so, what type of aid was it, and how did you get it?
- Did you visit your career preparation provider before applying? If not, why not?

Portfolio

- If you could repeat the selection process, would you use the same career preparation provider? If not, what would you do differently?
- What advice would you give a student about selecting a career preparation provider?

Write a summary of your interview results. Include what you discovered about selecting a career preparation provider. Share your results with the class.

Chapter Summary

9.1 Career Preparation Path

- Listing the options and requirements of the career path choices is the first step.

- Realizing the requirements of the career path based on one's *P*A*T*H to Success*, education/training needs, and experience and skills is important.

9.2 Education/Training Path

- Research the reputation, program offerings, and campus culture of all prospective career preparation providers.

- Understanding financial aid is necessary when planning one's education/training path.

- Determining the entrance requirements for each provider is crucial for planning.

9.3 Career Plan Implementation

- Create and finalize a high school schedule that matches both the admission requirements of potential schools, as well as one's own needs for a future career path.

- One must successfully manage the admissions process and timeline for the career preparation provider.

- The total package includes managing time wisely and avoiding social media embarrassments.

Chapter Assessment

Vocabulary Builder

Match each statement with the term that best defines it.

a. accreditation
b. campus culture
c. career preparation provider
d. Common Application
e. co-signer
f. early action
g. early decision
h. EFC
i. FAFSA
j. grant
k. need-based
l. SAR
m. scholarship
n. student loan
o. work-study program

1. Financial aid that depends solely on your family's income
2. Any program, school, or business that offers education/training
3. Forms required for education/training financial aid
4. The amount FAFSA says you and your family should contribute towards your education/training
5. The FAFSA process
6. Financial aid money you do not have to repay, usually awarded on achievement
7. Money provided by government, schools, or private donors that you do not need to repay
8. Provides money, paying students for qualified campus jobs
9. Money that a student borrows and must repay
10. College submission web site used by hundreds of colleges
11. Measurement process to ensure schools have basic quality
12. Characteristics that give each training program its unique personality
13. Person responsible for paying back a loan if you do not
14. An early college application method that is binding
15. An early college application method that is not binding

Review What You Have Learned

16. Why do you need to know your career path's entry-level requirements?
17. What is next after you identify the requirements of the career path?
18. What aspects of career preparation providers should you consider?
19. Why know your education/training entrance requirements now?
20. Why is knowing the types of financial aid important?
21. What steps should you take to implement your career plan?
22. What are the major steps in managing the admissions process?

Case Challenges

Each case study begins a career path. How might the journey continue?

23. Owen graduated from his high school with a focus on information technology. A discount department store hired him as a salesperson. Owen quickly learned about his department's merchandise. He received many compliments from customers and led his department in sales. Soon the manager promoted Owen to assistant department manager. Because of the promotion, Owen decided to make retailing his career

with his next step as department manager. Owen knew he did not yet have the knowledge in sales techniques, inventory management, and supervision that managers needed.

24. Last year, Charlotte worked part-time in a machine shop while taking manufacturing technology courses at the career center. After earning her high school diploma, a union apprenticeship program admitted her. During the day, she worked full-time in the machine shop. Nights, she took classes sponsored by the union. She dreamed of working directly with engineers, building prototype machines for the auto industry.

Make Academic Connections

Portfolio

25. **MATH** High school dropouts have median weekly earnings of $444. Below is a list of median weekly earnings for different levels of career preparation. For each level, calculate the percentage of salary increase compared to high school dropouts.

Career Preparation	Median Weekly Earnings	Percentage of Increase
High School Graduate	$626	
Some Education/Training	712	
Associate Degree	767	
Bachelor's Degree	1,038	
Master's Degree	1,272	

Discuss the results. Is it true that education pays?

26. **LANGUAGE ARTS** Assume the role of a recruiter for a career preparation provider. Use your results from Activity 9.2 to create a presentation to "sell" your provider when choosing your specific career path. Your teacher will give you specific instructions about the length of your "sales pitch."

Workplace Connection

27. Interview three people currently working in your chosen career path. Ask them where they received their basic career preparation and why. Then create a table listing the person's name, career, career preparation provider, and years of experience in the career. What conclusions do you draw from your data? Discuss the results in career cluster groups or as a class.

Blogging: My Education/Training Path from First Choice to Plan B

Blog

Use the information from your investigation of career preparation providers in Chapters 8 and 9. Describe the education/training path you selected as your first choice. Include your choice of career preparation provider.

But what happens if your first choice does not work out? Describe your Plan B—both education/training path and career preparation provider.

Portfolio

Capstone Project: Part 3

In Part 1, you began your research. In Part 2, you wrote your proposal, which your teacher approved. Part 3 of the Capstone Project is the completion of your research paper.

The requirements of the paper are:

- Subject: *Why I Chose _____ for My Career*
- Audience: Family and class
- Purpose: To explain your career path decision to your family, but still be interesting to students
- Minimum of 5 pages, plus reference sheet
- Minimum 3 references and 1 interview

Your teacher may change the requirements for your specific class.

The steps in the writing process are:

_____ *Use Plan (Map and Storyboard)*

_____ *Create*

_____ *Edit*

_____ *Peer Review*

_____ *Edit*

_____ *Teacher Review*

_____ *Edit*

_____ *Finish – Teacher approved*

_____ *Bring saved paper (on flash drive) to your teacher*

Before moving to the next step of the process, have your teacher initial the completed step. Use the form found at www.cengage.com/school/iyc, Chapter 9.

Career Readiness

PART 4

Digital Vision/Getty Images

Blend Images/Getty Images

What Do You Know

1. How have your career interests changed over the years?

2. Do you have plans for volunteering in the community or completing internships in career areas that interest you?

Jo always dreamed of being a police officer. Her two cousins, Jackson and Keith, are both police officers and Uncle Barron is a chief of police in a neighboring town. Jo watches every police show on TV and looks forward to an exciting career that will allow her to help others in the community.

Some people tried to convince Jo that being a police officer was just for men and it was too dangerous for women. Others told her that the hours she would work would vary and she would have to work at night, all for low pay. She began to wonder if this was a job she would like and one that would provide a good income.

Working with her teachers, counselor, and family, Jo began to think more carefully about her career goals and investigate other careers related to public safety. She began to volunteer at the neighborhood community center, which provides a safe haven to teenagers after school and offers classes on personal safety. She also completed a summer internship at the local police department. With these experiences, Jo's interests began to expand. She began to think about how she could help people outside of her community.

Today Jo has finished a degree in security administration and is working for homeland security. There are many positions in homeland security that do not require a bachelor's degree, but now she can work at a higher level to support her passion to help protect others. Jo never thought she would work outside her community, but as she learned more about public safety careers, she has achieved more than she ever dreamed.

Planning a Career in . . . Law, Public Safety, Corrections, and Security

Take your passion for law and public safety and build it into a profession. Law, Public Safety, Corrections, and Security is one of the 16 career clusters.

Many professions associated with this career cluster are available to you through the achievement of certifications or degrees through technical colleges or universities. Security and Protective Services is one pathway in this career cluster.

Employment Outlook

- Numerous openings in the field because of a desire to increase corporate, industrial, and homeland security.
- Additional growth in security guards and gaming surveillance with more states legalizing gambling.

Career Possibilities

- Certified Security Officer
- Loss Prevention Specialist
- Security Director
- Armored Car Guard
- Info. Systems Security

Needed Skills

- Problem solving skills.
- Speaking skills.
- Critical thinking.
- Certification or degree in the area.

What's It Like to Work in Security and Protective Services?

Those who enjoy working in the area of security ensure the safety of others and protect information, products, buildings, and military areas. No matter where you work, security and protective services are important.

This is a career in which you may undergo training, earn certificates, and become an expert in specific areas of security. You may become a Certified Protection Officer (CPO) or Personal Protection Specialist (PPS) or work in a variety of areas.

Every day will be an adventure. You must have the stamina and agility to deal with a variety of situations. The ability to speak a foreign language will be beneficial to you and the agency. You may work shifts that begin early in the morning or end late at night. You may also work weekends and holidays.

The work may be physically and mentally demanding. Other requirements may include being at least 20 years of age and passing a background check. However, the satisfaction you get from protecting others is rewarding and makes Security and Protective Services a great career choice.

4x6/iStockphoto.com

What about You?

Do you like helping others? Can you think critically and solve problems? Do you have stamina? Security and Protective Services has many areas in which you can work.

Personal Career Goals and the Job Market

Goals

- Recognize personal job search goals.
- Identify ways to research the job market.
- Investigate the job market and careers.

Terms

- job market, p. 228
- employment professionals, p. 229
- hidden job market, p. 229
- Occupational Outlook Handbook (OOH), p. 229
- O*Net OnLine, p. 230

Real Life Focus

Did you ever think about how many jobs exist today that didn't exist ten years ago? Here are a few:

- Social Media Manager
- Search Engine Optimization Specialist
- Online Advertising Manager
- Green Funeral Directors
- Patient Advocates
- Interior Redesigner
- Senior Move Management

As you investigate careers you are interested in and develop your career and job search goals, remember that there will be careers in your future that do not exist today. Ten years ago, someone who wanted to work with the elderly might not have foreseen a career helping older adults downsize, relocate, or modify their homes, like senior move managers do. Do you want to do something that doesn't exist today? Investigate the careers that exist now, but know you will have more choices in the future.

Your Personal Goals

As you develop your personal career goals, you also need to establish personal goals for your job search. Your job search will be affected by the type of job you want to obtain. For example, if you simply need a job in the summer to make some extra money, you would not apply for a position that requires you to work year round and is advertised as a full-time position. Right now, your personal job search goals may fall into the following categories.

- *Meeting your budget.* You may be saving for your future education or to start your own business. You may be saving for a car, a trip, or drum lessons. Regardless of your reason for searching for a job, you should have a plan for how you are going to save and/or spend the money. Your personal goal should be to find a job that provides you with sufficient income to meet your needs and stay within your budget.

■ *Supporting your P*A*T*H to Success.* Reflect back on your career plan and career clusters that pique your interest and think about your *P*A*T*H to Success*: Passion, Attitude, Talents, and Heart. When you follow your *P*A*T*H to Success*, the career you obtain will not seem like work. You will enjoy going to work and achieve a sense of accomplishment. Supporting your *P*A*T*H to Success* should be one of your personal goals as you search a career that will give you experience, improve your skills, use your talents, and allow you to move forward in your career choice or within a desired career cluster.

> *Ranier has a career goal to be employed in the health industry. More specifically, he is interested in becoming an athletic trainer. He has researched the career, understands the necessary career preparation, and is excited about his future. He has three personal goals as he searches for a part-time job this summer: (1) to work 20 hours per week, (2) to gain experience in an athletic environment, and (3) to save money for his education.*

> *Ranier searched the Internet, newspaper, and other job advertisement areas for jobs in athletics. He also asked family and friends, "Do you know of any jobs in athletics?" He discovered he was asking too broad of a question when they began to tell him about jobs as an umpire, life guard, and other similar jobs. He refined his search and his question to include athletic training and found a job at the local YMCA as a Summer Camp Assistant. His job involved working in the weight room, outdoor training environment, and pool area.*

> *The camp was for children who were recuperating from injuries. Therefore, the job provided Ranier with experience in working with others, instruction in basic physical therapy, and an understanding of some components involved in athletic training.*

Reviewing your career goals can help you determine your personal goals for your job search. You may have more goals than meeting your budget and supporting your *P*A*T*H to Success*, but these are two important goals to consider. Once you clarify your job search goals, your job search will become more targeted and go more quickly as you will not waste time pursuing jobs that do not help you move toward your career goals.

Also, review your financial goals as discussed in Chapter 7. As a teenager, you face many challenges in making decisions and reacting to life situations. This is an important time in your life to determine financial goals, the necessary education to achieve those goals, and a career to make your financial aspirations a reality. You should consider your current and future financial goals. Start planning now for your future career and financial stability. And, remember that money isn't everything, but working within your *P*A*T*H* will result in being happy within your career.

Job Market Research

Searching the job market is more than surfing the Internet. It is necessary to research and analyze the job market to find an appropriate job. The **job market** is the total number of vacant jobs available to people looking for employment.

As you learned in Chapter 3, attending career fairs and other events in which companies are looking for employees is one way to begin your job search and learn more about the job market. Researching the job market in this way gives you an idea of how many jobs are available in your career area. More in-depth research can help you understand the industry and employers better. You can also further investigate specific companies that have jobs matching your skills and interests. Knowing about the industry, companies of interest, and which job qualifications match your skills will give you a competitive edge when you apply for a job.

You can research the job market in a variety of ways. Typically, individuals think of the Internet as the main way to begin their search, but there are other avenues. The following provides an overview of resources such as libraries, professional organizations, specific companies, employment professionals, television and radio, and career centers.

■ Libraries house many newspapers, journals, business directories, and other material to provide you with information about employment possibilities and the job market. Other materials libraries typically house include the Occupational Outlook Handbook, books pertaining to developing your job search, and career clusters. The media specialist at your school or a librarian at the public library can help you find a variety of types of information to meet your needs. Additional information to search for includes working conditions, salaries, and educational requirements for career clusters or careers of interest.

■ Professional organizations often provide information about employment through newsletters or their web sites. They may also offer student memberships at a reduced rate. Through your membership, you may be eligible to receive scholarships, internships, particular business information, and breaking news in the industry. Membership in a professional organization may help you gain essential information related to the job market.

■ Companies of specific interest may post information on their web sites. Look for their Human Resources page for specific job information. You may also call the Human Resources Department and ask where specific information is located or how to best apply: in person, by mail, or online.

- **Employment professionals** include recruiters, headhunters, search consultants, and employment agencies who are in the business of helping people find jobs. A headhunter may work for businesses or individuals for a fee to help them secure employees or employment. Many times headhunters help search for employees in specialized fields. People looking for very specific types of jobs sometimes use employment professionals to help them find jobs, but there are other reasons to use employment professionals. Such reasons include time constraints, help in negotiation, and finding jobs in the hidden job market. The **hidden job market** is a term used to describe jobs that are not advertised through traditional means or posted online.

- Television and radio newscasts also provide job market and employment information. Local news broadcasts often provide information about the job market in your specific community, while national news programs are more likely to discuss trends affecting the entire country.

- Local college placement offices or career centers also provide information to assist with a job search. They may also provide services for resume and interview skill development.

Whether you read or listen to information about the job market, you must analyze what you see and hear to make sure it is relevant to your personal and financial goals. If you do not analyze the information, you may be wasting your time simply going through information that does not meet your needs.

Consider

With all of these ways to research the job market, how do you decide which way suits your needs and how do you analyze the information?

Occupational Outlook Handbook and O*Net OnLine

With an abundance of information, you need additional resources to help you analyze information and find specifics about careers that interest you. Two specific resources include the Occupational Outlook Handbook and O*Net. The **Occupational Outlook Handbook (OOH)**, provided by the Bureau of Labor Statistics, provides information such as projections for the job market, employment change, and additional information about the labor force. It also provides information about training and education needed for specific jobs in addition to earnings, expected job prospects, what workers do on the job, and working conditions.

On the OOH web site, you can find out about hundreds of careers and occupations. You can view an alphabetical list of occupations with one click of your mouse. The OOH also provides an overview of employment projections for a ten-year period. If you are searching specific occupations, you can first choose from several categories such as management, professional, service, sales, administrative, or farming. This helps you begin to narrow your search.

For example, if you want to research specific information on a job dealing with food preparation and serving, you would first look in the service category. Several subcategories will be available. Once you select one, specific jobs such as chefs, food preparation, food and beverage serving, and related jobs will be available. Once you select the specific job, you can then find all of the following information about that job.

- Nature of the Work
- Training, Other Qualifications, and Advancement
- Employment
- Job Outlook
- Projections
- Earnings
- Wages
- Related Occupations
- Sources for Additional Information

Additional significant points are also provided. For example significant points about chefs, head cooks, and preparation and serving supervisors include the fact that most workers in these occupations have prior experience in the food industry, have some postsecondary training, and are facing keen competition in the field.

O*Net OnLine is an online tool containing information on hundreds of standardized and occupation-specific descriptions to assist with career exploration and job analysis. O*Net was developed through the U.S. Department of Labor/Employment and Training Administration and a grant through the North Carolina Employment Security Commission. It was developed with the belief that each occupation requires a combination of knowledge, skills, and abilities using a variety of activities and tasks.

O*Net provides descriptors diagrammed in a model that provides (1) job-oriented descriptors such as occupational requirements, workforce characteristics, and occupation-specific information and (2) worker-oriented descriptors such as worker characteristics, worker requirements, and experience requirements. Therefore, it provides detailed descriptions of occupations and allows you to search in a variety of ways.

When researching the job market or a career, you can search O*Net by career cluster, industry, job zone, outlook, green economy sector, job family, and STEM (Science, Technology, Engineering, and Math) discipline. The job zone is divided into five categories representing the amount of preparation needed: little or no, some, medium, considerable, or extensive. The occupation's outlook is divided into three categories: rapid growth, numerous job openings, and new and emerging. The advanced search

East/Shutterstock.com

Why is it important to find as much information as possible about jobs of interest?

feature allows you to search by abilities, interests, knowledge, skills, work activities, work context, and work values. The tools on O*Net help you search for additional information to assist you in analyzing the job market and a variety of occupations.

It is common to hear people say, "The more information the better." However, this is only true if you can analyze the information to make sure it meets your needs and matches your goals. This is an important step as you search for a job. You should experiment with a variety of tools and use the ones that help you the most.

ACTIVITY 10.1

Leadership

Investigating Your Career

Do you know everything that may be involved in any occupation or career choice? How much do you know about various careers? Do some research to find more information about a career of your interest.

Work in teams and use the OOH and O*Net OnLine to answer the following questions about one career of your team's choice.

1. What is the career choice?
2. With which career cluster does this career align?
3. What tasks are involved in this career?
4. What skills are necessary for this career?
5. What earnings can you expect for this career?
6. What is the nature of the work of this career?

7. What training and/or education is necessary for this career?
8. What is the job outlook for this career?

Portfolio

Now, as a team, think about and answer the following questions.

1. What courses could you take to help you prepare for this career?
2. What part-time jobs or volunteer positions might you consider to help you learn more or develop key skills pertinent to this career?

Save the results of your research in your Career Portfolio.

Robert Kneschke/Shutterstock.com

The Job Search and Possible Pitfalls

Goals

- Explain how to develop a search routine.
- Develop a network with others.
- Investigate how to use technology to enhance your job search.
- Examine possible pitfalls to your job search.

Terms

- task timeline chart, p. 233
- search routine, p. 233
- networking, p. 235
- Monster.com, p. 237
- CareerBuilder, p. 237
- Twitter, p. 237
- Indeed, p. 237
- LinkedIn, p. 238
- Facebook, p. 238

Real Life Focus

Various studies show that teens spend at least 20 hours per week using technology. If you are going to use technology, learn to use it to your advantage and develop a method to enhance your job search. Think about using technology to

- Create a timeline for conducting a job search.
- Track which companies you have researched.
- Log the skills, salary, education, etc. needed for a particular job.
- Search information about various careers.

Once you begin your search, it's important to develop a routine, organize your findings, and keep track of what you have done. This will help save you time because you won't waste time researching the same information over and over again.

Managing Your Time

Managing your time is particularly important when you are searching for a job. Without good time management skills, your search may become chaotic and you will not use your time wisely. Managing your time helps you reach your goals more efficiently and you can spend time doing other things. Managing your time also helps you stay on task. Time is a critical and limited resource; use it wisely. We discussed time management skills in Chapter 6. You may want to review Lesson 6.3 before you begin your job search.

Another thing you can do to stay on task is to develop a job search timeline. As you learned in Chapter 6, a timeline is typically divided into parts or steps. It ends with the completion of a goal, and there may be a few shorter-term goals within the timeline. When you begin to think about your timeline, you must analyze the various tasks, estimate how long each will take, and determine the order of the tasks. Many times, the most difficult part of developing a timeline is to estimate how long each task will take. So be prepared if the tasks take longer than you may have estimated.

You may need to adjust your timeline after the first few days for tasks that take more or less time than expected.

It may be beneficial to create a task timeline chart. A **task timeline chart** is a personalized schedule of which job search tasks need to be completed, when they need to be completed, and how long they will take to complete. See the example below.

	Monday	Tuesday	Wednesday	Thursday	Friday
Task 1: Searching	Library Job Search (2 hrs.)			O*Net Search (1 hrs.)	
Task 2: Contacting		Use the newspaper to review job advertisements	Contact Companies of Interest (3 hrs.)		Follow Up With Previous Calls (1 hr.)
Task 3: Additional Searches	Business Web Site Searches (1 hr.)				OOH Search (1 hr.)
Task 4: Additional Contacts			Contact More Companies of Interest (2 hrs.)		
Task 5: Review Findings			Review all job search leads (2 hrs.)		

Preparing a task timeline helps you organize your thoughts, prepare for your search and develop a search routine. A **search routine** is a regular, unvarying procedure you use to search for jobs. To develop your search routine, it may be helpful to break your tasks down into subtasks such as the example below.

	Monday	Tuesday
Task 1	Library Job Search	
Task 1.1	Newspapers	
Task 1.2	Business Directories	
Task 2		Contact Companies of Interest
Task 2.1		Contact those who provide online method of contact
Task 2.2		Call those who do not provide a method of online contact

An effective search routine uses several different strategies. If you limit yourself to just one or two strategies, such as searching only the Internet and asking friends about job openings, you will miss many potential jobs that can help you reach your career goals. Your search routine should include:

■ Choosing a target job/career area

■ Determining your search tactics

■ Examining how to use a variety of tools to enhance your search

■ Planning your search

■ Searching for jobs

■ Following up on job searches

Therefore, planning your time and developing a search routine can help you use your job search hours more productive. Make your task timeline so that it shows exactly when and for how long you will work on a specific search activity. During the school year, your search routine should be limited to after school and weekends.

Demetrius realized he needed to begin his search now for a job this summer. He had a job lead through his neighbor, but Demetrius knew he couldn't count on that lead alone to get a job. He needed to plan for his job search. He knew he would have to complete his homework and chores at home before he could search for a job. He also knew he would have baseball practice three days a week, so he decided to search for a job the other two days per week. Demetrius developed the following schedule for Tuesdays and Fridays for the next few weeks.

7:30 – 8:00 a.m.: Check out books about effective job searches and business directory from the school library

8:00 a.m. – 3:00 p.m.: School

3:30 – 6:00 p.m.: Homework

6:30 – 7:30 p.m.: Dinner

7:30 – 9:00 p.m.: Review (1) job search books and business directory; (2) newspaper want ads; and (3) Internet for jobs

After following this schedule for three weeks, Demetrius had information on several jobs and set up another schedule to begin contacting companies and applying for jobs. He was successful in finding a job close to home that paid well and provided work all summer.

Consider

Why do people have to do several job searches in their lifetime? How many job searches do you think one person does in his or her lifetime?

Using Traditional Sources to Assist in Your Search

There are a variety of sources to assist in your job search. Some of the more traditional sources include the following.

Networking

The most important thing to remember is that your face-to-face interactions are essential to your success. One of the most effective job search tools is networking. **Networking** is building relationships as you spread the news of your job search among the people you know—and the people they know—and asking for their help. Many of these relationships will last beyond the current job search. And remember that networking goes both ways. You may be asked later to help someone else.

kali9/iStockphoto.com

Who are some people you should include in your network?

Networking is not simply asking people for a job, it is acquiring leads or becoming aware of possible leads. Networking takes time and perseverance and can be done anywhere. It can be done at school, within professional organizations you have joined, at church, or in the stands of a football game. Your network may consist of friends, family, teachers, school counselors, previous employers, and other people you know. Once you have established your network, using it is like using the Internet. On the Internet, you can enter keywords into a search engine and links appear to help you find pertinent information about jobs that meet your goals. People in your network are like those links. They can take you to more information about specific jobs. Different studies indicate that 70–80 percent of jobs are found through networking.

You have probably heard the saying, "It's not what you know, it's who you know." In reality, "who you know" may give you great leads on jobs and help you get into the hidden job market. But jobs are secured mainly based on your skills, experience, and attitude.

Networking not only benefits you, but the employer. Network referrals make the employer's job easier. Employers may get referrals from other employers, employees, and business professional organizations. It has been estimated that approximately 80 percent of the jobs are in the hidden job market. Networking helps employers save time and money. They may not need to pay to advertise the position for long (if at all) and may not need to spend as much time sorting through large numbers of resumes. However, just because someone recommends you does not mean you will automatically get the job. You will need to apply, interview, and have the right *P*A*T*H*.

To build your network, start by:

- joining professional organizations.

- volunteering and/or participating in job shadowing and service-learning projects.

- making a list of everyone you know.

- making sure you have a well-thought-out job search plan.

After you have completed these steps, you can request help from the people you listed. Talk to them about the kind of job you are looking for and how it will help you reach your career goal. Ask if they have any advice for you or any leads to help you in your search. Also, ask them if they know of anyone else who may be able to help you. This is an excellent way to expand your network. Make sure you follow up on any leads you have received. This helps continue the good relationships you have built.

Other Traditional Sources

Several other traditional sources can also help you with your job search. A few are described below.

- *Newspaper want ads.* Newspaper want ads include jobs in the surrounding area. The ads are typically categorized under a "Jobs and Employment" section. Specific categories may include Accounting and Bookkeeping Jobs, Construction Work, IT Jobs, Labor Jobs, Medical Jobs, Office Jobs, and Other Jobs. This makes it easier for you to locate a job in a particular career cluster.

- *Department of Labor offices.* Each state has a Department of Labor that provides assistance in obtaining jobs. There may be a local office in your area. You can find more information online or in the government pages of your telephone directory.

- *Contacting individual businesses.* Going to businesses and asking if they are hiring is a great first step. If they are not hiring at the moment, ask if you can complete an application to leave for future positions that may become available. This gives businesses an opportunity to establish a first impression of you. Dress appropriately and be professional in your communication.

Using Technology to Assist in Your Search

Traditional methods can be used in conjunction with technology to enhance your search. Several web sites can help make your search successful. The following are just a few examples:

- **Monster.com** Monster.com is one of the largest search engines that allow you to search by job title, skills, keywords, and/or location. It has millions of job postings.

- **CareerBuilder** CareerBuilder is also one of the largest online employment web sites. New jobs are listed daily, and you can ask for email alerts to be sent to you when a job that meets your goals becomes available.

- **Twitter** As you learned in Chapter 2, Twitter is a microblog that many people use to post short messages. However, people and businesses are using it as a job searching tool as well. Twitter has a search component in which you can enter information such as "jobs in IT" and click to find matches.

- **Indeed** Indeed is another search engine that allows you to search several job sites, newspapers, professional associations, and company career pages all at once with minimal clicks of the mouse. As with other job search engines, you can upload your resume so that others can review your qualifications.

Web Connections

Web sites offer information and advice about searching for a job.

Click on the Web Connections link for Chapter 10. Search at least two of the sites listed as well as *Career Transitions*. As you are reviewing sites, write down ideas that may help be more effective when searching for a job. Share your ideas with the class.

www.cengage.com/school/iyc

There are many benefits to using such web sites in your job search. For example, they provide a convenient and fast way to conduct a job search. You can learn about job openings with a click of the mouse. They also provide a way to email or post your resume and cover letter so others can view your qualifications. You can also correspond with individuals via email, company blogs, or other communication methods.

An online job search is also quite expansive. You can search vast resources in a just a few minutes. The jobs listed may be local, statewide, nationwide, or even worldwide. You may find jobs that you would have never known about otherwise. You can also focus and narrow your search to specific jobs. The sites are typically current as well. Jobs can be filled and very shortly disappear from the list of available jobs. This is not so with jobs printed in newspapers or other venues.

Some search engines and web sites may ask for contact information, for you to create an account, and possibly charge you a fee to apply for a job. You may be required to pay a membership fee in order to use all the features of the web site. When using technology to enhance your

How will you use technology to enhance your search?

kpatyhka/Shutterstock.com

job search, make sure you are using the right technology for the right job. Also, stay focused to accomplish your search goals and help you find a job just right for you. Avoid things that distract you from your search routine and task timeline.

Using Technology to Build Your Network

As you begin to enter the workforce and widen your network, you should begin to ask people in your network if they are on LinkedIn, Facebook, or other social networks. You may also ask if their company has a business blog or professional chat areas to discuss business ideas and also network with others.

LinkedIn is a business-related, professional social networking site with millions of members. It connects professionals to one another and allows them to exchange knowledge and ideas. LinkedIn also provides opportunities to network with professionals around the world. It is available in a variety of languages to allow for networking across cultures as well. When you create your LinkedIn profile, you may include as much or as little information as you want. LinkedIn also helps you to stay informed about your contacts and the industry.

Facebook is usually thought of as a social networking site, but many businesses are using it as a marketing tool and a method for finding employees. Facebook is open to anyone who confirms they are aged 13 years or older. It is accessed by millions of users every day.

If you use online social networks as part of your job search, think of them as professional sites and be careful what you post on your pages. Employers check these social networks prior to hiring individuals and also check them after employment. What you post on your pages could help employers make the decision to hire or not hire you or even fire you.

Businesses also use blogs to communicate with customers, employees, and potential employees. Through a business blog, a company can share knowledge and expertise as well as provide general information to the public. A blog is an inexpensive way to gain knowledge about a variety of topics and share expertise with others. Businesses also use blogs to market themselves and get the company's name out on the Internet. The most simple blog component includes a section for Frequently Asked Questions (FAQs) and is a great place to go to learn about the business, discover new information, and make contacts.

Possible Pitfalls

Pitfalls are unapparent sources of trouble or danger. They are detrimental to your success. Don't let yourself fall into these job search pitfalls. Stay positive and motivated in your search. Don't be the person who

- has not defined his or her job search goals.

- is not making a serious commitment.

- doesn't make a timeline, develop a search routine, and manage the search.

- procrastinates or makes excuses.

- has a negative attitude.

Be serious about your job search and be loyal to your task timeline. There are other people and resources available to help you find a job, but you must instigate the search and be dedicated to the routine. Think of the job search routine as a job itself. Prove yourself by your dedication.

Have a clear plan for your search and set aside the appropriate time to complete your search. Keep in mind that at this point you are beginning your search for a job, but soon you'll need to begin to think about developing your cover letter to apply for the job and preparing for your interview. The face-to-face components involved in getting the job are as important as finding the job.

ACTIVITY 10.2

Portfolio

Developing Your Timeline

In this activity, you will develop a timeline for searching for a job to help you establish a search routine.

1. At the top of the timeline, list the job for which you are searching. Be as specific as you can by including the location, number of hours, etc.

   Assuming you will be searching for a job next week, develop a timeline of your choice that includes the following:

   - List 8–10 tasks to complete.
   - List the time allotment and day assigned to each task.
   - List 4–5 online resources you believe will assist in your search.
   - List 4–5 other resources you believe will assist in your search.

2. Answer the following questions. How does developing this task timeline
   - help you begin your job search?
   - help you establish a search routine?
   - help you stay on task?

3. Be prepared to share your timeline and the answers to your questions with the class.

4. Within the next week, complete the tasks on the timeline and write a one-page summary on your findings.

Goals

- Review and reflect on your job search goals.
- Narrow the focus of your search.

Term

- diversify, p. 241

Real Life Focus

Narrowing the focus for your job search is like narrowing the focus of an essay you are writing. If you are asked to write a 200-word essay about Hospitality and Tourism careers, there's too much information in general to limit your writing to 200 words. You must develop a focus, theme, or main point, but you can't be too narrow or you won't have 200 words to write.

If you are interested in the Hospitality and Tourism career cluster, how do you narrow your interests and search to find a job that meets your needs?

Spend time exploring the pathways and possible careers in the cluster to help you narrow your focus.

Review of Goals and Search Routine

If you always did one thing the same way and it was always wrong, would you try something else? Of course you would. It is always important to review what you have done to make sure it's working for you. First, look at your task timeline. Are you on track and staying true to your commitment to searching for a job to meet your needs? Did you waste too much time surfing the net instead of effectively using technology to enhance your job search?

If you are not on track and have not used your task timeline effectively, your first step is to get back on track. Make sure you are tracking your progress. The task timeline can help you stay on task, but you may also keep a daily job search journal. Writing down your specific steps during the job search can help you recall and properly follow-up later during the job search.

If you successfully completed your timeline and you found jobs to apply for, did they meet your needs? Will they help meet your budget and do they support your *P*A*T*H to Success*? Keep in mind that one of your personal goals is to find jobs that will give you experience, improve your skills, use your talents, and allow you to move forward toward your career.

As you develop your search routine and you complete your timeline, it is important to track your activities. Keep a detailed record of your job search so you can follow up with leads and applications and be ready for interviews. Your records will also help you remember to make phone calls, send thank-you notes, and organize the information you have received. You can track your activities on paper or electronically.

Keeping track of your activities on paper is easy, inexpensive, and always available to you. You may choose to use a notebook, a three-ring binder, or notecards to record your activities. No matter what method you prefer, make sure you keep track of the following information.

■ Company name and information

■ Contact person, title, and information

■ Job title

■ Where you located the job advertisement and information

■ Information you provided

■ Any information you received

■ Due dates for any commitments you made

■ Due dates for further information you should be receiving

If you decide to track your activities online or through your smartphone, that's possible too. Online planners and toolkits allow you to keep contact information, dates, notes, and reminders. An electronic calendar alone may have all of these components. However, other online tools, such as JibberJobber, allow you not only to keep this content online, but connect the information to other online tools or sites such as Microsoft Outlook or LinkedIn to ensure you're connecting with others as needed.

Keeping track of your activities can help you review your timeline and goals and see if your search routine is working for you. One thing to consider as you continue your job search is to determine whether you need to diversify. To **diversify** means to become more varied or vary your range of skills. If you are not finding jobs that meet your particular skills, see if you can apply your skills to other jobs. Your skills don't have to always be used for exactly what you have been using them for. There are other things you can do with your skills. Diversifying your skill set will give you added flexibility. Be creative and you may develop a path to interesting possibilities.

What are some things you do to make sure you're on track?

littleny/Shutterstock.com

Narrowing the Focus

As you outline your goals, develop your timeline, and begin your search for a job, consider narrowing the focus. If you begin with a broad job search, you may be overwhelmed with job positions that do not meet your needs and level of skills. There are various ways you can narrow the focus before you begin the job search or while the job search is in progress.

Draw on previous job shadowing and service learning experiences (see Chapter 3) to help you narrow your focus. Anytime you have an opportunity to try different components of a job or test your skills in specific areas through these means, you are gaining experience. This experience can help you determine if this type of employment would meet your needs and if you like that type of work. This is valuable information.

Through volunteering, job shadowing, and service-learning projects, you are also developing items to put on your resume. Many times young people don't believe they have anything to put on a resume, but they do. Take advantage of opportunities such as these to narrow the focus on a future career and build your resume.

To further assist you in narrowing your focus for the job search, make a list of your answers to the following questions.

- What are things I like to do?

- Do I have skills in the things I like to do?

- What are some things that I liked to do and I have been paid to do?

- Do my skills and experience match the job I'm searching for?

- Does the job I'm searching for match my career goals?

Focus on your goals, transferrable skills, and the job market. Taking the time to narrow your focus saves you time in the long run as you are not wasting time with job searches that do not meet your needs. Prioritize

Real People / Real Careers

Brady Jacobs / *Firefighter/EMT (Emergency Medical Technician)*

Brady Jacobs decided to become a firefighter at age 13 when he began living with his father, who is the chief of a township's fire and emergency services. "I wanted to help people," declares Brady. "I saw that firefighters make quick decisions and save lives. That is an amazing opportunity."

Brady decided to enroll in the Firefighting program at the nearby career and technical school while finishing his last two years in high school. He completed the state's certification for EMT and Firefighting and became a National Registered EMT and Firefighter. Finishing the program in high school saved him thousands of dollars and earned him college credits. His constant study and review, plus the "ride-alongs" with EMS units and fire stations in the community, prepared him for the demanding industry and government standards.

Currently Brady is working fulltime as a firefighter/EMT. However, he is planning for the future. The college credits he earned in high school will apply toward a nursing degree at a nearby community college, after which he will transfer to the university to complete his R.N. in Emergency Medicine. In ten years, Brady would like to become a physician's assistant, which he considers the top of his profession.

Brady Jacobs' career preparation and career decision were perfect choices for him. As he explains, "When I was handed my diploma, I was handed my career. It was amazing—I did not just have a job; I had a career!"

For more information about:
* EMT careers
* firefighting

Access **www.cengage.com/school/iyc** and click on the appropriate links in Chapter 10.

Source: *Personal Interviews*, September 2010 and July 2011

what is important to you, analyze your experience and skills, and consider how all of these align with your goals. Thinking on a positive note, you might write what you consider to be the perfect job description. Through this exercise, you'll gain perspective on what you want, clearly define the job, and develop keywords to use in your searches to help you narrow your focus.

As you are involved in job shadowing and service learning projects, you continue to develop your network. You are meeting new people in a professional environment and working in a variety of situations. These people can later serve as references for you and/or be a part of your network to help you find full-time employment later. Make sure you always act in a professional manner. As you develop your network and interact with professionals, ask them questions about different positions within their businesses. What do people do in those positions? What skills are needed for the jobs? You can then learn more about a variety of jobs and see if your skills and interests match those jobs. This can help you narrow your focus to those particular jobs that do.

Consider

What might happen if you never reviewed your goals or job search routine?

ACTIVITY 10.3

Portfolio

Learning from Others

As you learn more about various jobs, it's important to narrow your job search focus.

Interview two people about how they got their current jobs. Change their names in your notes to protect their privacy. Ask the following questions:

- What job search strategies did you use to find your job?
- How long did it take to get your job?

- How many applications did you complete?
- How many interviews did you go through?
- How did you track your job search activities?
- What job search advice could you give me?

Ask any other questions pertinent to topics discussed in this chapter. Write a one-page report describing your findings. Be prepared to report your information to the class.

PhotoAlto Agency RF/Jupiter Images

Chapter Summary

10.1 Personal Career Goals and the Job Market

- As one develops personal goals, one also needs to establish personal goals for the job search. Personal job search goals may include meeting a budget and supporting the *P*A*T*H to Success.*

- Libraries, newspapers, business directories, professional organizations, company web sites, and employment professionals can all be used in a job market search.

- The OOH and O*Net provides specific job market information about hundreds of jobs and careers.

10.2 The Job Search and Possible Pitfalls

- Developing a search routine is important to the search. A task timeline can help the job-seeker stay on track.

- Networking is one of the most effective job-search tools.

- Using technology should not be the only way to complete a job search, but it can help enhance the search if used properly. Monster.com, CareerBuilder, Indeed, and Twitter are a few online resources that may help.

- Job search pitfalls are detrimental to one's success. Job-seekers must stay positive, motivated, and on track.

10.3 Narrowing the Focus

- As one develops a search routine and completes a timeline, it is important to track one's activities. Keeping a detailed record of the job search will help job-seekers follow up with leads and applications and be ready for interviews.

- When searching for a job, it's important to narrow one's focus. Various ways to help you narrow the focus include volunteering, job shadowing, service-learning projects, and gaining invaluable experience through other means.

- Networking with others can lead to job search success and can help the job-seeker narrow the focus of his or her search.

Chapter Assessment

Vocabulary Builder

Match each statement with the term that best defines it

1. A regular, unvarying procedure you use to search for jobs

2. To become more varied or vary your range of skills

3. A social networking site that many businesses use as a marketing tool and a method for finding employees

4. A search engine that allows you to search several sites, newspapers, professional associations, and company career pages

5. Provided by the Bureau of Labor Statistics, this gives information such as projections for the job market, employment change, and the labor force

6. One of the largest employment web sites and search engines to search by job title, skills, keywords, and/or location

7. Building relationships as you spread the news of your job search among the people you know—and people they know—and asking for their help

8. A tool containing information on hundreds of standardized and occupation-specific descriptions to assist with career exploration and job analysis

9. A microblog that many people use to post personal information, but it can be used as a job-search tool as well

10. A business-related, professional social networking site

11. An employment web site on which new jobs are listed daily and which provides email alerts

12. Recruiters, headhunters, search consultants, and employment agencies

13. Jobs that are not advertised through traditional means or posted online

14. The total number of vacant jobs available to people looking for employment

15. A personalized schedule of job search tasks that need to be completed, when they need to be completed, and how long they will take to complete

a. CareerBuilder
b. diversify
c. employment professionals
d. Facebook
e. hidden job market
f. Indeed
g. job market
h. LinkedIn
i. Monster.com
j. networking
k. Occupational Outlook Handbook
l. O*Net OnLine
m. search routine
n. task timeline chart
o. Twitter

Review What You Have Learned

16. Your personal job search goals may fall into what two categories?

17. What resources can help you with your job market research?

18. How can the OOH and O*Net OnLine help in your job search and analyzing the job market?

19. Why should you develop a search routine?

20. How can technology help you enhance your job search?

21. What are some job search pitfalls?

22. Why is it important to review your goals and search routine?

23. How do you narrow the focus of your job search?

24. Why is networking with others important?

25. How can you develop your network?

Case Challenges

After reading both case studies, analyze each situation. Have the students successfully prepared for their job search? If yes, explain why. If not, suggest activities they can do to be more prepared.

26. Edward is searching for a summer job in a restaurant. He has no experience in cooking, but has bussed tables before. He is searching the Internet for jobs and is finding many. Some of the jobs are close to the town he lives in, but others are far away. Some of the jobs are for cooks; others are for servers and those who bus tables. His plan is to print out every job announcement he finds and spend time Saturday sorting them into piles of jobs he can do and jobs he cannot do.

27. Elise developed a task timeline to help her establish her job search routine. Her target job is to become a pet sitter or dog walker. Some items she has included in her task timeline for her job search include asking neighbors and putting up signs in the neighborhood. She is going to start asking neighbors this week and wants to begin working next week.

Make Academic Connections

28. **LANGUAGE ARTS**   Using the OOH and O*Net, research one particular job. Write a one-page report about it, including the following information: Career Cluster, Job Market Projections, Needed Education, Working Conditions, and Knowledge/Skills/Abilities. Use these items as headings within your report.

29. **MATH**   Below is a list of three jobs and the salaries for each job. You are interested in all three jobs, but want to make the most money you can. Based on the fact that you will work 20 hours per week and 5 days per week, which job would pay the best per week?
    - **Job 1:** $8.00 per hour.
    - **Job 2:** $5.00 per hour plus tips. Estimated tips are $20.00 per day.
    - **Job 3:** $7.00 per hour plus bonus pay. Estimate the bonus pay as 10% of your weekly salary.

Workplace Connection

Learning about yourself, knowing your job search and career goals, and achieving your goals is important. One of the first steps is thinking about jobs you would like to pursue. Complete the following statements.

Portfolio

30. When I think about future jobs I may hold or my future career,
- in 5 years I hope to . . .
- in 10 years I hope to . . .
- in 20 years I hope to . . .
- in 30 years I hope to . . .

31. When I think about future jobs I may hold or my future career,
- volunteer activities I may get involved with include . . .
- jobs I could get now include . . .
- my main goal right now should be . . .

Blogging

As you continue to blog or journal about your career plan process, reflect upon your initial career goals and what you have learned in this chapter. Blog about how your career goals have changed or how they have remained the same. Explain why you believe your career goals have changed or remained the same. Access www.cengage.com/school/iyc and click on the appropriate links in Chapter 10.

Blog

Applying for a Job

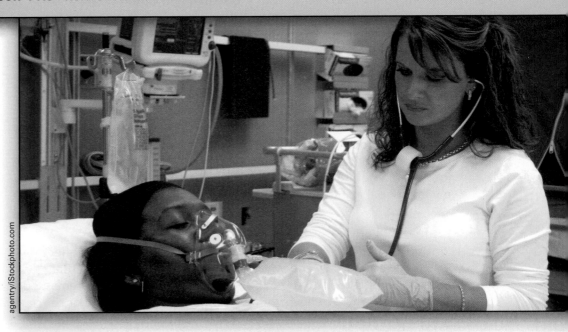

agentry/iStockphoto.com

What Do You Know

1. Which of your interests and skills relate to your career goals?

2. Who can help you investigate scholarships that may help you reach your career goals?

Margie loved to learn and always wanted to go to college, but she knew her family didn't have enough money to pay for her schooling. She never really thought about what she wanted to be when she grew up, but she liked taking care of others. She was sad that she could not go to college and continue her learning.

One day Margie's school counselor, Mr. Jansen, told her about scholarships that paid for students' college education. A few scholarships interested Margie. One scholarship was for students interested in becoming a veterinarian, one for students who wanted to teach in low-income areas, and another for students who wanted to go into nursing. Margie had the desire to take care of others and thought nursing would be a good fit.

Mr. Jansen helped Margie apply for the scholarship. Some requirements were a minimum family income, courses taken in Health Science, a minimum GPA of 3.25, and an essay about why she wanted to become a nurse. Margie's family met the minimum family income, she had taken courses in Health Science, and she studied hard to get her GPA up to 3.25. Margie wrote her essay about why she wanted to become a nurse and gave a copy to Mr. Jansen and her English teacher to review. With their help, Margie was awarded a scholarship to pursue a degree in nursing.

Margie's family is very proud of her, and she is happy in her career. Sometimes you may know what you like doing or what you are good at, but don't know which degree will enhance your skills. It may happen that a scholarship can help you reach your career goals. Talk to school counselors and teachers for more information.

Planning a Career in . . . Health Science

Take your passion for helping others and use it in a career in Health Science. Health Science is one of the 16 career clusters. If you are interested in planning, managing, and providing therapeutic services, diagnostic services, health information, support services, and biotechnology research and development, this is the profession for you.

This profession is considered a service occupation. Professions within this career cluster include Counseling & Mental Health Services, Family & Community Services, Personal Care Services, and Consumer Services. Within these professions there are various certifications and degrees that can be achieved. Not all areas require a college degree.

Employment Outlook

- Numerous job openings are expected with faster than average growth.
- Many jobs can be expected because people are living longer and the Baby Boomers are aging.

Career Possibilities

- Medical Counselor
- Chiropractor
- Dental Assistant
- Nursing Assistant
- Pediatrician

Needed Skills

- Active listening.
- Development of written documentation.
- Adapt language for audience, purpose, and situation.
- Certification or degree in the specific field.

What's It Like to Work in Health Science?

Those who enjoy caring for others can find a job in the field of Health Science. There are high replacement needs for nursing and psychiatric aides, but the pay may be low and the physical and emotional demands may be high. More opportunities will be available in this field with a college degree.

You may begin many careers in Health Science right out of high school. However, you will probably need training and certificates to do the specific job you would like to do. Some positions require a college degree.

Every day will be different because you are working with people. You need to be able to think on your feet and alter your communication to the situation and person. You may work shifts that begin early in the morning or end late at night. You may also work weekends and holidays.

The work will be physically and mentally demanding. However, the satisfaction you get from helping others is rewarding and makes Health Science a great career choice.

What about You?

Do you like helping others? Can you think on your feet and change your communication to match the situation? Can you work various hours, handle the physical and mental strain, and maintain your stamina? Health Science has many areas in which you can work.

aceshot1/Shutterstock.com

Goals

- Identify components of a personal fact sheet and resume.
- Describe the different types of resumes.
- Explain the differences between traditional versus electronic resumes.

Terms

- personal fact sheet, p. 250
- resume, p. 251
- chronological resume, p. 254
- functional resume, p. 256
- combination resume, p. 256
- traditional resume, p. 258
- electronic resume, p. 258

Real Life Focus

Laura looked in the local newspaper want ads and found several jobs that match her skills and times she can work. She has been going to the different companies and applying in person. Each time she begins to complete the job application, she can't remember some particular bit of information: a phone number, the specific years she worked elsewhere, a previous position title, and so forth.

Laura would benefit from having that information written down in some fashion. Her friend, Lupe, told her that she takes a personal fact sheet with her when she applies for jobs. Laura is now investigating what should be included in her personal fact sheet.

What information do you think you'll need to complete a job application? Investigate the components of job applications and create your personal fact sheet today.

Using a Personal Fact Sheet

A **personal fact sheet** is written document that summarizes basic information about you, your education, experience, skills, and other pertinent data. When you apply for a job and to colleges, additional information will be requested. You will need to have specific background and personal information when you

mrloz/iStockphoto.com

- complete applications.
- write your resume.
- write cover letters.
- prepare for interviews.
- complete forms after you get a job.

The amount of information in your personal fact sheet will depend on your work experience, skills, and involvement in activities. When writing the information about your work experience, make sure you include complete names and addresses of your previous employers in addition to their phone numbers. This same information should be included about your school in addition to dates attended and your grade point average.

Keep a copy of your personal fact sheet with you during your job search and during others times you may be applying to schools or for scholarships. Having a complete and up-to-date personal fact sheet will save you time and will help prevent you from leaving information blank on an application or providing incorrect information. Review Illustration 11-1 to see Camilla Sanchez's personal fact sheet.

Components of a Resume

Using the personal fact sheet, you can develop a good resume. A **resume** is a written record of your experience and qualifications related to a specific job or career. The purpose of a resume is two fold: (1) to represent you well on paper and (2) to persuade a potential employer to offer you an interview. Ultimately, the purpose is to get a job. Your resume should answer the following questions for the employer.

- Who is the applicant?
- How would the applicant's *P*A*T*H* help the company succeed?
- Why should I hire the applicant?

Developing your resume to represent your experience and skills honestly is critical to your success. When you provide your resume to potential employers, they will check with previous employers to verify your employment and work behavior. If a company discovers that an applicant has lied on his or her resume or other application information, the application will be rejected. When a company discovers lies on the employment documents after the hire, the employee is typically fired immediately. Protect yourself by being honest and ethical.

Casey wanted a job at Jimbo's Motorcycle Racing Center. Casey owns a motorcycle and has done mountain cycling twice. He enjoys working on his motorcycle, but has never held a job doing motorcycle repair nor has he ever raced a motorcycle. However, he is confident in his ability to do motorcycle repair.

When he created his resume, he indicated that he had skill in motorcycle repair and listed his uncle as his employer. He did repair his uncle's motorcycle once. He also indicated that he had been involved mountain motorcycle racing and listed his best friend as his employer. When Jimbo reviewed Casey's resume, he called Casey's uncle and friend to ask about Casey's work experience. Jimbo found out the truth. Jimbo was then skeptical about everything else on Casey's resume and concluded that he was unethical. He threw away Casey's resume and did not call him for a job interview.

On average, employers take only ten seconds to glance over a resume and develop a first impression of an applicant. Employers are not interested in how a job will benefit you, but how your *P*A*T*H* will benefit the company. So tailoring your resume to the needs of your audience

Illustration 11-1: Camilla Sanchez's Personal Fact Sheet

PERSONAL FACT SHEET

Camilla Marie Sanchez 383 Moss Creek Drive Orlando, FL 32801	Phone: 407-555-9981 E-mail: cmsanchez@mail.com SS#: 222-33-4444

Educational Background and School Information

Manville School 456 Wildcat Boulevard Orlando, FL 32802 GPA: 3.25	Phone: 407.558.9344 FAX: 407.558.9366 Dates Attended: August 2011 – Present Honors Classes: Algebra

Certifications/Diplomas/Degrees

Microsoft Office Specialist (MOS) Certification

Internships/Volunteer Work/Service-Learning Projects

American Society for the Prevention of Cruelty of Animals (ASPCA) *Duties:* Calling potential donors	Supervisor: Ms. Nancy Califf June – July 2015 June – July 2016
Peer Mediator, Manville School Orlando, FL 32802 *Duties:* Assisted students in developing conflict management skills	Supervisor: Mr. Caleb Norton 456 Wildcat Blvd., Orlando, FL 32802 Phone: 407-555-3331 January 15, 2016 – May 15, 2016

Skills

Fluent Spanish Microsoft Word and Excel	Key 60 words per minute Exceptional teamwork skills

Honors and Awards

Principal Merit Award	Girl's State

Professional Organizations/Clubs

Future Business Leaders of America (FBLA)	Spanish Club

Previous Employment

Babysitter *Duties:* Prepared meals, designed educational learning activities, and bathed children	Employer: Mr. and Mrs. Samuel Christian 385 Western Place, Orlando, FL 32805 Phone:407-555-4550 February 22, 2016 – Present
Administrative Assistant *Duties:* Filed paperwork, keyed letters, and answered phone	Employer: Mr. Nathan Nichols Nichols Real Estate Company 65 Northview Avenue, Orlando, FL 32804 Phone: 407-555-3889 May 20, 2015 – August 1, 2015

Reference Other Than Previous Employers

Ms. Lila McNeese Teacher Manville School Orlando, FL 32802	Mr. Zachary Collins Principal Manville School Orlando, FL 32802

(the employer) and writing with a "you attitude" will help you develop a successful resume. The "you attitude" refers to something being written so that the readers see a benefit for themselves. A successful resume leads to job interviews and possible employment.

A resume has several components, which are discussed further in this section. Additional components may be added if you have special skills or talents, such as speaking a foreign language. Work to effectively design your resume to meet the requirements of the job and the company's needs.

Personal Information This information, located at the top of the resume, includes your legal name, complete address, telephone number(s), and email address. When posting an electronic resume on the Internet, include only your name and email address.

Job Objective Your job objective should accurately identify the job you want. A job objective may not be included if the job you are applying for is very specialized or your resume will be submitted electronically and already linked to a specific job. The job objective should be placed directly below your personal information. Write a clear, specific job objective using the "you attitude" to address the company's needs.

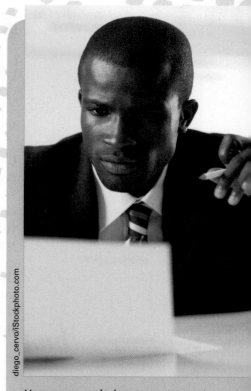

How can you design your resume to meet the needs of the employer?

Weak: Job to allow me to use my skills to further my career.

Specific: Nursing assistant with the Johnson City Hospital.

Strong: Sales representative position requiring excellent communication and customer service skills.

Education and Related Course Work If your education relates directly to the job you are applying for, place the information under the job objective. If your work experience is more important and better represents your qualifications for the job, place your education section near the end of the resume. Your education section will include schools you have attended, degrees or diplomas, and additional course work or certifications.

Related Experience This section may include past employment information and volunteer work, internships, service-learning projects, and other experience related to the particular job. This is a place to highlight all of your experience. Provide details of your experience, including dates employed, job title, and job responsibilities. Use the present tense to write about current experience and past tense to write about previous experience.

Workplace Skills Workplace skills include such things as technology skills, foreign language proficiency, skills with special tools or equipment, notable communication skills, and time management skills. Be specific and honest as your employer may ask you to demonstrate the listed skills. Exemplary skills may put you a step above the other applicants.

Honors and Activities In this section, list honors, activities, and membership in professional organizations that pertain to the job or employer. These honors and activities may show responsibility, productivity, and a connection to the career field. Hobbies are typically not listed unless you hold a leadership position in a professional organization associated with the hobby or the hobby is related to the position.

Consider

As you begin to gather information for the personal fact sheet, how will this information help you create a resume?

Types of Resumes

Organizing your information on a resume and ensuring there are no typographical or grammatical errors is essential. Employers expect to see resumes organized in one of three ways: chronological, functional, or combination. Each resume organizational style helps the employer focus on different aspects of your qualifications. It is important to choose the resume type based on the information you want to highlight.

Chronological. A **chronological resume** type presents your information by date in reverse time, or chronological order. Therefore, the most current information is listed first. If you lack experience directly related to the job or if you have gaps in your work experience, this would not be the most appropriate type of resume. Consider that a chronological resume is

■ effective in showing a record of education, improvement in skills, and continued experience.

■ typically used when applying for jobs in conservative career fields such as banking and government.

Teddy found an opening for a part-time position as a sales representative. He has good communication and leadership skills, has experience in customer service, has notable technology skills, and has held part-time jobs consistently while in high school. He is trying to organize his resume, but is not exactly sure how to proceed.

Teddy asked his uncle for advice. His uncle has worked in the customer service industry and showed Teddy the resume of the last person he hired. The resume was organized in chronological order and highlighted the person's continued experience. Teddy designed his resume in the same way. Illustration 11-2 shows Teddy's chronological resume.

Konstantin Sutyagin/Shutterstock.com

Illustration 11-2: Teddy Lamarsh's Chronological Resume

Teddy Lamarsh

1920 Riley Avenue
Nashville, TN 37201

615-555-3445
lamarsht@tn.net.com

OBJECTIVE: Sales representative position requiring excellent communication and customer service skills.

EXPERIENCE

Zantone News Corporation   **Nashville, TN**
Delivery Person   **September 2015 – Present**
- Deliver newspapers
- Communicate with customers
- Accept payment for newspaper delivery

Live and Learn Leadership Camp   **Murfreesboro, TN**
Camp Counselor   **June 2015 – July 2015**
- Gave orientation to all attendees
- Developed leadership training modules
- Assisted attendees in developing leadership skills
- Served as a team leader for those learning leadership skills

VOLUNTEER WORK

Caring Hands Association   **Nashville, TN**
Volunteer   **June 2014**
- Made phone calls to possible donors
- Organized food pantry

HIGHLIGHTS OF QUALIFICATIONS
Good communication, teamwork and customer service skills

WORKPLACE SKILLS
Fluent Spanish   Key 60 words per minute
Microsoft Word and Excel   Exceptional teamwork skills

HONORS AND AWARDS
Caring Hands Volunteer of the Month   June 2014

PROFESSIONAL ORGANIZATIONS AND CLUBS
Student Mentor Association   Christian Athletes Club

EDUCATION
Archer School   August 2015 – Present
Panther Paw Parkway
Elderberg, TN 37220
- Earned Students Mentor Certification   January 2016

Functional. The **functional resume** matches your capabilities to the job tasks. Therefore, your abilities are emphasized rather than your work history and experience. Consider that a functional resume is especially effective

■ when you are making a career change as it downplays gaps in your education and/or work experience.

■ if you can show measurable accomplishments to prove your ability in each skill area.

Employers will be cautious or tentative in granting you an interview if your accomplishments do not outweigh your gaps in experience.

> *Anh was familiar only with chronological resumes and organized her resume in the same format. She was planning on applying for a job as a daycare assistant at Grow With Us childcare facility. When Anh showed her resume to her school counselor, he noticed that most of her experience has been in the food industry with only some experience as a summer camp counselor. He asked Anh about her gap in employment and asked why she wanted a job in childcare. Anh explained that one summer she worked at a camp for children with special needs. She enjoyed the work and wanted to pursue a career in childcare.*

> *Anh's counselor explained that her previous jobs had responsibilities that will benefit her as she works in childcare, such as customer service, childcare development, and food preparation. The job at Grow With Us childcare facility includes feeding children lunch, working with children with different abilities, and greeting parents as they bring their children to the facility each morning. So Anh's abilities needed to be highlighted more than her past employment. Anh created a functional resume to highlight that information. Illustration 11-3 shows Anh's functional resume.*

Combination. A **combination resume** is designed to use features of both functional and chronological formats. Immediately after your job objective, you should include brief information about how your skills directly match the job requirements. Then include your work experience in reverse chronological order, as in a chronological resume. When using a combination resume, consider that this format is the best to use when

■ you want to emphasize immediately how your skills match the position requirements.

■ you have good skills but limited on-the-job experience.

An example of a combination resume can be found on the web site for this book.

Illustration 11-3: Anh Ngo's Functional Resume

Anh Ngo

1107 Knights Court
Indianapolis, IN 46128

317-555-5746
ango@cable.in.net

OBJECTIVE: Daycare Assistant at Grow With Us Childcare

SUMMARY OF QUALIFICATIONS
- Fluent in Spanish
- Hardworking, enthusiastic, and dependable
- Patient with young children
- Works will independently or as a part of a team

JOB RELATED SKILLS:
Childcare Development

4-H Summer Camp
- Four-year-old children
  - Assisted with alphabet recognition
  - Assisted with English language development
  - Assisted with learning Spanish
  - Prepared healthy meals

Camp Ability
- Eight-year-old with special needs
  - Assisted with motor development
  - Assisted with learning disability
  - Organized field trips

Customer Service

Delish Deli
- Greet and seat customers
- Answer the telephone
- Process payment for meals
- Develop relationships with repeat customers

EXPERIENCE
Delish Deli, Indianapolis, IN	September 2015 – January 2016
4-H Summer Camp, Bloomington, IN	June 2014
Camp Ability, Terre Haute, IN	July 2014

EDUCATION
Jackson County School	8th grade
385 School Road	
Indianapolis, IN 46126	

Traditional versus Electronic Resumes

Traditionally, applicants sent employers well-designed resumes printed on quality paper. A **traditional resume** is a printed resume you provide to the employer through the mail or in person. A cover letter should accompany the resume. You will learn more about cover letters later in this chapter. Many companies still request a traditional resume, but they may require an online application in which you can submit your resume electronically. An **electronic resume** is designed to be transmitted over the Internet and stored and accessed on a computer. Follow the employer's instructions for submitting the proper type of resume. However, when you go for the interview, make sure you take a traditional resume with you so the employer can review your well-designed resume.

These guidelines will help you prepare a professional-looking and easy-to-read traditional resume.

- *Keep the resume to one page.* After you have substantial experience over several years, a two-page resume may be developed.

- *Use light-colored, high-quality paper.* You should typically use white or beige resume quality paper. If you are applying for a creative position in an artistic field, however, you may use other colors.

- *Use a standard business font.* Use a clear, easy-to-read font, such as 12-point Times Roman.

- *Use simple elements.* Using bulleted lists and boldface text can draw the employer's attention to specific information. However, overusing these techniques lessens their power. Do not italicize words; they can be difficult to read. Do not include your picture to protect your personal safety and make sure the employer remains objective.

- *Use appropriate white space.* *White space* is the unprinted area of the page. It makes your resume visually appealing. Typically you should use one-inch margins (top, bottom, left, and right) along with appropriate spacing before and after headings.

When you submit an electronic resume over the Internet, your resume is stored in a database and then searched for specific keywords to see if you are a qualified applicant. The human resources department or other hiring personnel develop a list of keywords that match those of an available job. If the keywords are found in several resumes, the software prepares a report and the hiring personnel can then review the specific resumes that match the job's keywords. Therefore, it is essential that you prepare your resume with keywords used in the job advertisement.

Since your electronic resume is being reviewed by computer software, the attractiveness of the resume is not as important as it is for traditional resumes. The electronic resume must be easy for computers to read. They should be designed without special formatting such as underlining, italics, boldface text, tables, and columns.

Image Source/Jupiter Images

Word processing programs insert special formatting codes into documents. Follow the steps below to remove the codes with a text-editing program.

- Open your traditional resume using word processing software. Resave the file with a new name such as *EResume.*

- Remove any special formatting such as columns, underlining, boldface text, italics, tables, and so forth.

- Resave the file with the new name (*EResume*) as a plain text or ASCII. txt file.

- Close the file and exit the word processing program.

- Click the Start button to find and start the text-editing program. This program is typically found in the Accessories link. NotePad and WordPad are examples of text-editing programs.

- Open the *EResume* file.

- Make sure that only your name is on the first line of your electronic resume. This assists in an easy search for your name. If you have your name and email address on the first line, the employer would have to enter your name and email address to search for your specific resume.

- Start each main line at the left margin and do not use the tab key.

- Limit the length of each line to a maximum of six inches. Otherwise an employer's email program may wrap the lines of your resume and it will be more difficult to read.

- Resave your electronic resume and make sure it is being saved as a plain text file or an ASCII.txt file.

Unlike your traditional resume, your electronic resume may be longer than one page. This is not a problem because the computer can process the information quickly. When you create an electronic resume, also remember to use keywords common to your career cluster as well as keywords used in the job description. Use keywords within your resume and, if requested, at the top or bottom of your electronic resume.

An example of Teddy Lamarch's electronic resume can be found on the web site for this book.

Your e-resume will be suitable for resumes that may be scanned. If you are asked to attach your resume to an email, attach both a traditional and an electronic resume and note that in your email. If you apply for a job through an online application, make sure you complete each section with the appropriate information and submit the application.

Be honest and ethical in providing your information and make sure your resume is free from grammatical and spelling errors. Include the appropriate information and be specific in describing your duties and responsibilities. As you develop your resume and describe your duties, the following guidelines will be helpful.

Do

■ Do use brief phrases instead of complete, descriptive sentences. Use simple, direct language to make your information easy to read and understand.

- *Weak*: I watched two pre-school children during the summer months. I made sure they were fed and did appropriate activities.
- *Strong*: Cared for two pre-school children, ages three and four, during June and July. Prepared meals for the children and led them in appropriate activities.

■ Do use action verbs to help employers focus on your accomplishments.

- *Weak*: My duties included feeding the children and doing appropriate activities with them.
- *Strong*: Fed the children and led them in appropriate activities.

■ Do use specific examples and numbers to show measurable accomplishments. Instead of simply saying you accomplished something, be specific in how long you worked to accomplish the task, what goal you achieved, and so forth.

- *Weak*: I helped the children learn to recognize letters and learn some sign language.
- *Strong*: Helped the children learn to recognize all 26 printed letters by sight. Also taught the children 50 words in sign language.

■ Do use correct grammar, spelling, and keywords. Don't rely totally on the spellcheck to catch all of your errors. Use the spellcheck feature, but also proofread your resume carefully. Make sure to use keywords used in the career cluster of interest and those used in the job description.

Do not

■ Do not use the word *Resume* in the title area of the resume. Employers will recognize it as a resume based on its format.

■ Do not state "References available on request." Employers assume you will provide references when necessary.

■ Do not use the words *I*, *me*, and *my*. Of course your resume is about you, but using phrases within your resume without these words makes your phrases sound more active.

- *Weak*: I cared for two pre-school children during the summer.
- *Strong*: Cared for two pre-school children, ages three and four, during June and July.

ACTIVITY 11.1

Portfolio

Investigating Your Career

Write a traditional resume using the format (chronological, functional, or combination) that best aligns with your job goals. Restructure your resume as an electronic resume and save it as a plain text or ASCII.txt file. You can create it online via **Career Transitions.**

Job Applications and Pre-employment Tests

Goals

- Identify the components of a job application.
- Describe the differences in applying face-to-face versus applying online.
- Examine various pre-employment tests.

Term

- pre-employment tests, p. 263

Real Life Focus

Did you know that you may be required to take a test before an employer will hire you? Employers may require a variety of tests. Tests may include

- Physical tests
- Drug tests
- Skills test
- Personality tests

and many more. Prior to the interview, it is appropriate to ask if there are any pre-employment tests required for the position.

Components of a Job Application

When you fill out a job application, remember to refer to your personal fact sheet for the specific information you will need to complete the application. You may be required to complete and submit only an application, or an employer may ask you for your resume as well as the application. Employers review applications to compare applicants' qualifications. Make sure you complete the application thoroughly and provide all of the information requested.

Job applications are designed so that all applicants provide the same information. This makes is easy for employers to compare the information and quickly determine which applicants meet the qualifications and job requirements. Job applications also provide employers a place to ask for your permission for drug tests and background checks. The application will clearly state that your signature gives the employer special permission to give you such tests and that you agree to take the tests.

The job application may be in printed format and you can pick it up at the employer's location. Some employers require you to complete the application on-site. Be prepared (with your personal fact sheet) to complete the application, make sure you read the questions carefully, write legibly, and complete the entire application. If you have the option, you might choose to take the application home. This may be a better choice as you can take your time to study and answer the questions. However, the application may also be available online. If this is the case, complete the application according to the online instructions and submit it when you are finished.

Follow the steps below to complete a job application.

■ If you have the option of taking the application home to complete it, make a copy of the application. Use the copy as a practice application. Then, if you make a mistake, it won't matter because it is on the copy. Once you have filled out the copy, transfer the information to the actual application.

■ Read the entire application before completing it. There may be sections that seem confusing. Make sure you understand what information should be included in each section.

■ Follow the instructions carefully and exactly. Many employers use the application to measure the applicant's ability to follow directions. Therefore, the application is actually used as a screening tool.

■ Answer every question. If a question does not apply to you, write *NA*. NA stands for Not Applicable. This lets the employer know that you did not just overlook the question, but that the question does not apply to you. For example, you may be asked to list any maiden names or names you may have used in the past. This question may not apply to you.

■ Make sure you write legibly. Your answers should be easy to read. Print neatly using blue or black ink or key the answers. When completing online applications, use spacing and returns to separate your answers for easy reading.

■ Answer questions, particularly those about your skills, with accurate, descriptive, and measurable statements. For example, instead of noting that you speak foreign languages, note that you speak Spanish fluently and speak conversational French.

■ Be honest, accurate, and thorough.

Why is it important to fill out a job application carefully and exactly?

Consider

What does a job application tell the employer about you? What's the best piece of advice you would give a friend before he or she goes to an employer to complete a job application?

Applying for a Job Face-to-Face versus Online

There are different things to think about when applying for a job face-to-face versus applying for a job online. Of course, with both you want to make sure you complete the job application thoroughly and truthfully. You want to make sure the information is easy to read and free from spelling and grammatical errors. And you want to show that you can follow directions. The job application may be the first thing the employer sees to begin to understand who you are and what your qualifications may be.

When you apply for a job online, complete all sections of the application, follow directions, and submit it according to the instructions. If you do not receive an automatic reply that your application was received, it is appropriate to email the designated person to ensure that your application was received. At that time, you may also attach your resume for review. Remember that your application, resume, and email should all represent you in a professional manner. Your email should address the person, refer to the job, note that an attachment (your resume) is provided for review, and ask if there is any additional information you need to provide. You should end your email with a thank you, your contact information, and your name. Do not use emoticons, slang, or texting language in your email.

When you apply for a job face-to-face, dress in a professional manner and make sure you take your personal fact sheet and resume with you. More than likely, an administrative assistant will provide you with the job application. He or she will also take you to an area where you can complete the application. Be polite to this person as he or she may report (about your demeanor, professionalism, and appearance) to the person with whom you will be interviewing.

Come to the employer prepared to complete the job application. Bring your personal fact sheet, resume, black pen *and* blue pen (some employers require a specific color of ink for the applications), and anything else that would help you complete your application. Read the entire application before filling it out. If you have questions about the job application, ask the person who gave you the application for clarification.

Pre-employment Tests

Employers may require potential employees to take pre-employment tests. **Pre-employment tests** are screening tools that help employers determine if applicants have the knowledge, skills, and personality to perform job duties successfully. These tests help the employer determine if you are right for the job. You learned about some of these tests in Chapter 3.

Pre-employment tests must meet specific legal requirements. They may not cause undue hardship to people with disabilities, they may not be discriminatory against groups specifically protected by civil rights laws, and they must assess qualities directly related to job performance.

A variety of pre-employment tests may be given at different times during the hiring process. For example, physical exams, skill, ability and integrity tests may be given before job interviews. Without the proper skill, ability, or ethics, a job interview would be a waste of time for the employer and applicant. Therefore, unqualified applicants can be eliminated early in the selection process.

After an interview, a more qualified applicant may be asked to complete a personality test to determine whether his or her personality matches the job characteristics. Another test qualified applicants may be asked to take is a drug test. After employment, companies may require periodic drug tests along with other tests to determine if the new employee needs additional training.

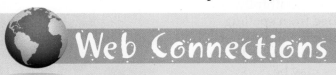

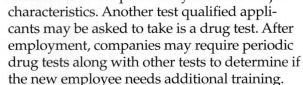

Web sites offer additional information about pre-employment testing.

Click on the Web Connections link for Chapter 11. Search at least two of the sites listed. As you are reviewing sites, write down ideas that may help you be more prepared for pre-employment tests. Share your ideas with the class.

www.cengage.com/school/iyc

Skills tests measure how well you can perform certain functions related to the job and how much you know about the environment of a particular job. For example, if you applied for an administrative assistant position, you may be required to take a keyboarding speed skills test and an incorporated test about business letter formats. With these types of tests, employers can quickly determine which applicants have the skills and knowledge to effectively do the job.

Personality tests are used to determine how you respond to authority, what motivates you, and how well you work with others. Matching applicants' personality to the job characteristics helps employers choose a more successful candidate. For example, a person who enjoys work in nature and being outdoors would not be a good match for the job requirements for an accountant.

Ability tests are used by employers to determine if an applicant has the basic capabilities necessary for almost any job. These ability tests typically include reading and math. Employers may also have specific ability tests for specialty jobs.

Integrity tests are used to determine your level of honesty. These tests can be as simple as true/false or multiple choice tests or as complicated as a lie detector test. Integrity tests typically include scenarios in which you would respond with what you believe to be the best answer. The following is an example of a question you may find on an integrity test.

> *You work part-time as a clerk at a pharmacy. You are also learning how to take inventory of prescription drugs, so that when you become a full-time employee you will be able to perform this task. Benny is the co-worker who is training you. He and his family are struggling financially. His mother was in a bad car accident and they do not have health insurance. He shared with you that his mom is almost out of her pain medication and she is afraid that she cannot afford more. As Benny is training you, you notice he takes some prescription drugs and puts them in his pocket. What do you do?*
>
> • *Tell him to put the prescription drugs back.*
>
> • *Report him to your supervisor.*
>
> • *Tell him to put the prescription drugs back and report him to your supervisor.*
>
> • *Say nothing.*

With integrity test questions such as this, employers can determine whether you would sympathize with Benny or whether you would report him for taking the drugs. These are the types of questions you can expect on integrity tests.

Drug tests are designed to let employers know if a person is taking illegal drugs. Drug use can impair a person's judgment and abilities and prevent him or her from doing the job or doing the job safely. Employers may be legally liable if employees under the influence of drugs injure others or damage property. When an employer asks you to take a drug test, you have the right to refuse. However, the employer has the right not to hire you if you refuse to take the drug test.

Before you take a drug test, tell your employer of any prescription medications or vitamins you are taking. These may impact the results of the test. If your drug test indicates drugs in your system and you are not using any illegal drugs, ask for a retest or a more sophisticated test.

ACTIVITY 11.2

Leadership

Develop a Pre-employment Test

Work in teams to write a pre-employment test. Assume you work for the Simply Edible Catering Company. You are designing an employment test for those who will book catering jobs, deliver food to customers, and receive payment for catering jobs.

Once your team has completed the pre-employment test, join another team and compare your test with theirs. Work with the other team to develop a single pre-employment test combining the necessary components from both pre-employment tests.

Be prepared to share your final pre-employment test with the class.

Portfolio

Goals

- Discuss the procedure for selecting references.
- Identify the components of a cover letter.
- Write a cover letter.

Terms

- references, p. 266
- cover letter p. 269

Real Life Focus

A cover letter is your written introduction. This letter gives the employer the first impression of you—on paper. Remember, you never get a second chance to make a first impression.

Nigel had typographical and grammatical errors in his cover letter. The employer read one sentence and threw away his letter. The employer never even looked at Nigel's resume.

When Bernice wrote her cover letter, she connected her qualifications to the job requirements, highlighted her skills that pertained to the job, and noted how hiring her would benefit the employer. Her resume was included. It was easy to see she was the right person for the job. She was granted an interview and is on her way to joining the company.

Spend time reviewing the components of a good cover letter. Word your cover letter carefully to develop one that represents you well.

Selecting References

References are typically people you know who are not related to you who will give you a positive recommendation for a job. Employers expect you to supply a list of references when applying for a job. This list should include the following for each reference: complete name, job title, complete address, phone number(s), and email address. Illustration 11-4 shows a portion of a reference sheet.

Employers ask for your references so that they can verify your employment and ask about your work habits, abilities, and skills. This helps employers determine if you are a good fit for their position. So you should choose your references carefully. Ask if they are willing to serve as a reference for you, tell them about the position you have applied for, and ask if they can give you a good recommendation. Keep them informed of your job search, scheduled interviews, and companies where you have applied so they know when and from whom to expect notification to provide a recommendation for you. When you are hired, write your references a thank-you note to show you appreciate their help and to let them know that you have secured a job.

Illustration 11-4: Partial List of Camilla Sanchez's References

Camilla Sanchez
383 Moss Creek Drive
Phone: 407-555-9981
Orlando, FL 32801
E-mail: cmsanchez@mail.com

REFERENCES

Mr. and Mrs. Samuel Christian
385 Western Place
Orlando, FL 32805
Phone:407-555-4550
E-mail: samterrychristian@worldnet.com

Mr. Nathan Nichols
Nichols Real Estate Company
65 Northview Avenue
Orlando, FL 32804
Phone: 407-555-3889
E-mail: nicholsrealestate@nngs.net

Your references should not be related to you. They may be previous employers, your teachers, the school counselor, coaches, ministers, and other people who can speak to your work ethic, personality, skills, and abilities. Look for people who can write and speak well and who

- would be willing to spend time writing recommendation letters and talking to prospective employers.

- can attest to your qualities, skills, and abilities that will make you a good employee.

- have worked with you on a job or on a project.

- know you well.

Your references may need to write letters, complete online reference information, or speak to potential employers. All of these things must be done by certain deadlines. Your references should know your career goals and qualifications and be willing to put forth the effort involved in serving as a reference. Do not assume that someone will be a reference for you—always ask first. Also, make sure that the person will give you a *good* reference. If a potential reference has some issues with your work, the person may actually hurt your chances to secure a job. Finally, if someone declines to serve as your reference, thank him/her sincerely for talking with you.

Securing a reference can be done simply by casually talking with the individual or more formally by writing a request for a reference letter. No

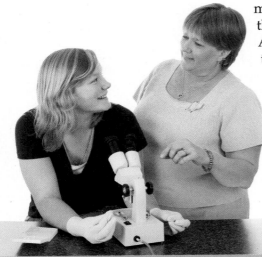
Lisa F. Young/Shutterstock.com

matter how you ask someone to be your reference, make sure the person understands what he or she will be asked to do. Also, provide references with as much information as possible to help make their job easier. Give your references your up-to-date resume, career goals, and a list of the types of positions you are applying for. If possible, also give your references the names of the companies to which you are applying.

Stay in contact with your references. If you get an interview, if your plans change, or if you secure a job, notify your references. If you receive an interview and if you think their recommendation helped you get that interview, sincerely thank them for taking the time to help you. As your job search ends and you secure a job, write thank-you letters to your references. Thank them for their time, energy, and support as you made progress in reaching your career goals. You can find an example of a thank-you letter to a reference on the web site for this book.

Who would be a good person for you to ask as a reference?

Real People / Real Careers

Deborah Whittaker / *LPN (Licensed Practical Nurse)*

Healthcare was always Deborah Whittaker's passion. She finished her high school education in a career and technical program, Diversified Health Occupations. Soon after she started working in a nursing home, Deborah married and had a child who became chronically ill. During her many hours at Children's Hospital, Deborah knew she could meet his and other's needs.

After her son got older, Deborah restarted her education in an adult workforce development program and earned her LPN license. She chose to become an LPN because she wanted to further her education in healthcare. In addition, she wanted to have the confidence to take better care of her son.

Deborah currently works in a long-term care facility as a charge nurse. The environment focuses on residents' long-term needs. They are often elderly, but may be chronically ill younger patients. To Deborah, "The residents feel our facility is their home. We are there to make sure all their needs are met with dignity and respect. Sometimes, we are the only friendly faces they see. To take care of them is very rewarding."

Learning never stops in healthcare. Deborah must take 24 hours of education each year to keep her license current. Classes include CPR for healthcare professionals, treatment of wounds, and working with patients who have certain diseases.

Deborah advocates, "The healthcare field is very fulfilling. You have so many choices to help those who are in need of a smile, a warm touch, and the knowledge to make each day worth living."

For more information about:

* nursing careers

* healthcare careers

Access **www.cengage.com/school/iyc** and click on the appropriate links in Chapter 11.

Source: *Personal Interview,* August 2011

Photo courtesy of Deborah Whittaker

Components of a Cover Letter

Your cover letter is your written introduction to an employer. A **cover letter** will accompany your resume and help you show employers how your knowledge, skills, and abilities connect to the job requirements. A cover letter must be free from spelling and grammatical errors and be properly formatted. These types of errors will immediately eliminate you from the possibility of a job interview. On the other hand, a good cover letter can convince an employer to read your resume and persuade the employer to give you an interview.

Your cover letter should consist of an introduction, body and conclusion; connect your skills and abilities to the employer's needs; be written in a standard, business format; and be error-free.

Think of your cover letter as a way to get "in the door" of the business and get an interview. Also, think of your cover letter as the first impression the employer will get about you. Your cover letter is a way of expressing your interest in a position, presenting your skills and qualifications, and asking for an interview. These are the key components of a cover letter. As with your resume, keep the cover letter to one page.

Introduction. Open your cover letter by expressing your interest in the position and explaining why you are interested. The introductory paragraph in your cover letter should explain the purpose of your letter—to apply for a job. Be specific about which position you are applying for, note that you are interested in the position, and point out that your qualifications match the job requirements and the employers' needs. Be specific in why you are interested in the company and how your interest fits the company's needs.

Body. Use the body of your cover letter to present your knowledge, skills, abilities, and measurable accomplishments. Explain what you bring to the company and give the employer good reasons to hire you. Convince the employer, in an organized fashion, that because of these things, you can benefit the company. Support this claim by noting information from your resume and relating your characteristics to the specific job requirements. If the position requires good communication skills or motivating others, explain how these were qualities necessary for your previous work and how you used them successfully. Show the employer that you are confident and capable without bragging. Highlight your qualities that match the job requirements and help the employer answer this question: Why should I hire you?

Conclusion. The conclusion paragraph should be where you request an interview. Indicate when and how you will follow up with the employer. For example, indicate that you will follow up in one week by phone. When you indicate that you will follow up, then do so. Be persistent, but not bothersome. For example, do not call every day or email twice a day to see if you can get an interview, as this would annoy the employer.

What can you write in your cover letter to make you stand out to the employer?

In the conclusion, make sure you indicate how the employer can contact you. Give the employer more than one contact option (for example, a phone number *and* an email address). End the letter with a complimentary close that includes your keyed name, your signature, and the word *Enclosure* (as your resume will be enclosed). If you are emailing the letter or applying online and attaching your resume, use the word *Attachment* instead of *Enclosure*.

Consider

What might happen if you wrote a great cover letter, said you would follow up, and never did?

Formatting the Cover Letter

There are various types of business letter formats, but the easiest and quickest business letter format is a block style, open punctuation letter. A *block style* letter is formatted with all text aligned at the left margin. If you key the *block style* letter with *open punctuation*, no punctuation is used after the salutation and the complimentary close. With block style and open punctuation, you will save time as you do not need to indent the date or paragraphs and you will use fewer keystrokes.

It is a good idea to develop a letterhead for the letter that contains the same information at the top of your resume. After the letterhead information, key the date and press Enter four times (quadspace) before including the inside address. The *inside address* is the address to whom the letter is begin sent. A double space below the inside address, include the *salutation*, which is the greeting to the person to which the letter is being written. The salutation should include the person's title (such as Mr., Ms., or Dr.) and the person's last name. You may key the word *Dear* before this information or just include the title and the person's last name. For example, *Dear Mr. Laboe* and *Mr. Laboe* are both correct salutations. Do not use *To Whom it May Concern* or *Dear Sir* or *Dear Madam*.

The *complimentary close*, the closing information for the letter, includes the word *Sincerely*, a quadspace, your keyed name, and your signature above your keyed name. Also key the word *Enclosure* a double space below your keyed name so that the receiver will be reminded something (your resume) is enclosed. (If you apply online or attach the cover letter and resume to an email, key the word *Attachment* a double space below your keyed name.)

Work hard to match your qualifications to the job requirements and make sure your letter is error-free. Think about your *P*A*T*H* and how these qualities can be integrated into your cover letter. Your cover letter, along with your resume, is all you have between you, a job interview, and securing a job. Illustration 11-5 shows an example of Teddy Lamarsh's cover letter.

Illustration 11-5: Teddy Lamarsh's Cover Letter

Teddy Lamarsh

1920 Riley Avenue
Nashville, TN 37201

615-555-3445
lamarsht@tn.net.com

November 1, 2016

Mr. Jack Miller
Communications Manager
Nashville Newsline
588 Carmike Avenue
Nashville, TN 37204

Dear Mr. Miller

The sales representative position advertised in *Nashville Today* on October 31 listed specific qualifications that match my skills. My experience, skills, and reputation of providing excellent customer service will help me excel in the sales representative position.

As you can see from my resume, I have also been involved in leadership training. Through my involvement in the development of training modules and helping others learn how to be effective leaders, my leadership skills have developed as well. My communication skills have also improved through my work at the leadership camp and as a mentor to others. My ability to work as a team member and be an effective team leader will also be helpful as a sales representative.

May we set up an interview to discuss my qualifications and the sales representative position in more detail? If we can meet next week, I will be in your area on Thursday, November 10. I will call your administrative assistant before then to see if I may set up an appointment. You may reach me at 615-555-3445 or by email at lamarsht@tn.net.com. Thank you.

Sincerely

Teddy Lamarsh

Teddy Lamarsh

Enclosure

ACTIVITY 11.3

Learning from Others

Search the newspaper, library, Internet and other sources for a job that you are qualified for and that looks interesting. Write a cover letter for that job. Then ask a family member, school counselor, or another adult to review your cover letter and give you suggestions on making it better. Make the suggested changes and give your letter to your teacher for his/her review.

Chapter Summary

11.1 Personal Fact Sheet and Resumes

- Create a personal fact sheet with complete information to summarize education, experience, skills, and other pertinent data. Use a personal fact sheet when completing applications, creating resumes, writing cover letters, and preparing for interviews.

- A resume must represent a person's experience and skills honestly to help them be successful. Resumes should answer the following questions: Who is the applicant? How would the applicant's P*A*T*H help the company succeed? Why should I hire the applicant?

- There are three basic types of resumes: chronological, functional, and combination. Individuals should choose the appropriate type of resume based on their experience, qualifications, and job requirements.

- Both traditional and electronic resumes are in demand by employers. Job applicants need to know how to prepare both types of resumes.

11.2 Job Applications and Pre-employment Tests

- Job applications are designed so that all applicants provide the same information. Employers can then compare several applicants' information and determine which meet the qualifications and job requirements.

- When applying for a job online, individuals should make sure they include all information and submit according to the instructions. When applying face-to-face, individuals should be dressed in a professional manner, be polite and professional, and ask questions for clarification if necessary.

- Employers can require applicants to complete any number of pre-employment tests. A few include skills, personality, ability, integrity, and drug tests. These tests may be given before or after an interview. It is appropriate for applicants to ask if pre-employment tests will be given and to ask for details about the tests.

11.3 References and Cover Letters

- References are people who are not related to the job applicant who are familiar with the applicant's abilities and goals. Good references should be willing to take the time needed to write recommendation letters and speak to prospective employers about the applicant's qualities, skills, and abilities.

- A cover letter is a written introduction of the applicant. It will accompany the resume and help the employer connect the applicant's knowledge, skills, and abilities to the job requirements.

- There are various types of business letters, but the easiest and quickest type is a block style, open punctuation letter. This type of letter is formatted with all text aligned at the left margin and no punctuation after the salutation and the complimentary close.

Chapter Assessment

Vocabulary Builder

Match each statement with the term that best defines it

1. A printed resume you provide to the employer through the mail or in person
2. A written document that summarizes basic information about you and your education, experience, skills, and other pertinent data
3. A resume that matches your capabilities to the job
4. A record of your experience and qualifications related to a specific job or career
5. A letter that introduces you to employers
6. A resume that presents your information by date in reverse order
7. People you know who are not related to you who will give you a positive recommendation
8. A resume that combines functional and chronological formats
9. Screening tools that help employers determine if applicants have the knowledge and skills to perform job duties successfully
10. A resume designed to be transmitted over the Internet and stored and accessed on a computer

a. chronological resume
b. combination resume
c. cover letter
d. electronic resume
e. functional resume
f. personal fact sheet
g. pre-employment test
h. references
i. resume
j. traditional resume

Review What You Have Learned

11. Why should you create a personal fact sheet?
12. What type of resume is best to represent your knowledge, skills, abilities, education, and experience?
13. What are the main differences between a traditional resume and an electronic resume?
14. What are the most important things to remember when completing a job application?
15. What are two differences between applying for a job online and applying face-to-face?
16. Why do employers give pre-employment tests?
17. How do you select references?
18. What are the key components to a cover letter?
19. What is the quickest and easiest business letter format?

Case Challenges

After reading both case studies, analyze each situation. Are the applicants ethical? Explain your answers.

20. Louisa has worked for a law firm in the summer months. She does minimum research, files paperwork, answers the phone, and greets clients. She is interested in applying for another job in the legal field to earn more money to help her pay for an associate degree to become a paralegal. She is a

member of the Association for Paralegals and Legal Assistants, but has never attended a meeting or become actively involved with the organization. The job application asks for particular information relating to her experience. Louisa completed the application with the following information: excellent researcher, familiar with legal terms, excellent communication skills, detail oriented, and involved in legal professional organizations.

21. Marvin had an interview as a pet sitter for his cousin's friends, Ethel and Maquel Hawthorne. He does not personally know the Hawthornes. Marvin was fired from his last two jobs for not showing up on time and not completing his assigned duties. He knows he did wrong and he is ready to do this job. The Hawthornes asked him about his previous jobs and asked why he left those jobs. Marvin answered, "The job ended."

Make Academic Connections

22. **LANGUAGE ARTS**   Work with a family member to help him/her create a new resume or update an existing one. Choose the appropriate format. Then assume he or she is applying for a job or a promotion at their current job. Write a cover letter to accompany the resume.

23. **BUSINESS**   Interview someone who has been involved in hiring employees and ask the top three things he/she looks for in a good resume. Then ask for three things that may prevent him/her from hiring an applicant. Also ask if the firm uses any pre-employment tests. If so, ask what type of pre-employment tests are used. Be prepared to share your findings in class.

Workplace Connection

24. It's never too early to begin to develop your list of references. Complete the following.
    - List five people you believe could serve as a reference for you. They may not be your personal friends or relatives.
    - List each person's full name, complete mailing address, email address, and phone number.
    - Take the list to each person and ask if the information is correct and if you can use him/her as a good reference.

25. It is important to know which jobs meet your skills, ability, and needs. Think about what you like to do, what you are good at doing, your career goals, and your financial goals. Taking all of this into consideration, write a job advertisement that would be the perfect job for you. Be realistic and include all pertinent information in the job advertisement.

Blogging: My Job Objective

As you continue to blog or journal about your career plan, consider your job objective. Think about what you learned about resumes and cover letters in this chapter. Write your job objective. Discuss how it has changed or has not changed due to what you learned in this chapter. Access www.cengage.com/school/iyc and click on the appropriate links in Chapter 11.

Interviewing for a Job

AISPIX/Shutterstock.com

What Do You Know

1. How can you show your best qualities in an interview?

2. How can you prepare yourself for an important interview?

For as long as she can remember, Caroline has loved to write. She kept a journal as a child, and her interest in writing grew over the years. After obtaining a degree in Journalism with a minor in English, she has five years of experience working for various newspapers. But tomorrow she is going on an interview to become editor of *The Sandville Times* newspaper. She is confident, yet nervous about the interview. Her resume and cover letter explained her experience and skills well and helped her get her interview.

She has practiced her answers to questions she has been asked on previous interviews, knows her strengths and weaknesses, and understands how to address other questions about the newspaper business. However, she has had some conflict issues with employees before when she was a supervisor at her last job. She is worried that the interviewer may ask her to describe a time when she was involved in such a situation. She continued to think about other times when she worked well with all employees while in a supervisory role.

The next day, Caroline dressed professionally for the interview. The interviewer had on a suit and tie, which made Caroline feel better that she was appropriately dressed. The interview went well. She answered the questions about her experience, skills, strengths, and weaknesses. When asked about dealing with conflict, she stressed the positive experiences in her supervisory roles, but indicated she also had difficult experiences and she realizes that is a part of the job. The interviewer indicated he would call by the end of the week to tell her if she got the job. She left with a good feeling and knows that even if she doesn't get this job, she will be better prepared for the next interview.

Planning a Career in . . . Arts, Audio Visual Technology, & Communications

Take your passion for Arts, Audio Visual Technology, & Communications and build it into a career. Arts, Audio Visual Technology, & Communications is one of the 16 career clusters.

Many professions associated with this career cluster are available to you through the achievement of certifications or degrees through community colleges or universities. Journalism is one pathway in this career cluster.

Employment Outlook

- Many people are attracted to writing and editing jobs, so there is a lot of competition for these jobs.

- Because of the increase in online publications, writers and editors with the technology skills needed for these jobs will be in demand.

- Jobs in this area are often located in the larger cities such as Los Angeles and New York.

Career Possibilities

- Journalist
- Musician
- Actor
- Video Producer
- Graphics Technologist

Needed Skills

- Creativity.
- Critical thinking.
- Technology skills.
- Certification or degree in the area.

What's It Like to Work in Arts, Audio Visual Technology, & Communications?

People who enjoy working in the area of Arts, Audio Visual Technology, & Communications might work in television or radio, perform on stage, write, or work in computer graphics. There is a wide variety of job types in this area. No matter where you work, jobs in this area are important and provide needed services for our society.

Every day could be an adventure. You must have the ability to deal with a variety of situations and people. Depending on which specific job you have in this area, you may work a regular Monday-Friday schedule or you may be required to work weekends and holidays.

The work is demanding and fulfilling. Other requirements may include your passing a background check.

What about You?

Are you creative? Do you enjoy being on stage? Are you a good writer? Can you think critically and solve problems? Are you interested in computers? Are you willing to work hard? Do you have a good work ethic? If you can answer *yes* to most of these questions, a career in Arts, Audio Visual Technology, & Communications might be right for you.

The Interview Process and Preparation

Goals

- Explain the purpose of interviews.
- Identify the different types of interviews.
- Describe how to prepare for an interview.

Terms

- job interview, p. 278
- unstructured interview, p. 279
- structured interview, p. 279
- screening interview, p. 279
- performance interview, p. 279
- group interview, p. 279
- behavioral interview, p. 280
- dining interview, p. 280
- telephone interview, p. 280
- virtual interview, p. 280

Real Life Focus

Have you ever thought about what it would be like to have an interview over dinner? Think about that! You are answering interview questions and trying to do your best in the interview while having dinner.

Carlos was placed in this exact situation after an initial telephone interview. He was very nervous about the interview because he had never been on a dining interview. As he entered the restaurant, he realized that everyone who was going to interview him was already seated at the table. As he approached the table, he noticed that not all of the male interviewers were wearing a coat and tie. He also realized that he wasn't sure what silverware to use or which glass was his. He was now wishing that he had listened to his aunt Dodie when she offered to teach him proper etiquette.

Would you know what to do? How would you prepare for a dining interview? How would you dress for a dining interview?

Purpose of and Types of Interviews

A **job interview** is a conversation between a job applicant and one or more people in a company or organization to discuss the applicant's qualifications for a specific job. The *interviewer*, the person interviewing you, wants to determine your skills and abilities to decide if you will be a good fit for the company. The interviewer will also assess your attitude and appearance. The employer wants to ensure that you have the skills needed for the position, the work ethic necessary to carry out the job, and that your personality is a good fit for the environment you would be working in.

You, as the applicant, should also have goals for the interview. Not only are you being interviewed for the job, you are also interviewing the potential employer to see if you can answer *yes* to the following question: Do you want this job at this company? You can use the interview to find out specific job qualifications and details about the company. You want to match your skills and abilities to the necessary qualifications of the job. But you also want to make sure that *you* are a good fit for the job. Would you enjoy working with this company? Does the company share your values? Throughout the interview, you should provide information in a professional way and convince the interviewer that you are the best applicant for the job.

Marshal's friend told him about a job at a local chemical company. The job was advertised as a floor supervisor. Marshal was not familiar with the company; however, he had supervisory experience and he really needed a job. He applied for the job and when he arrived for the interview, he noticed a strong odor. He wasn't sure what the odor was, but it was very unpleasant.

The interviewer asked Marshal questions about his skills and experience. He also asked questions about how he would deal with certain situations that might come up as a supervisor. The interviewer asked Marshal if he had any questions. Marshal's first question was, "What was the odor I smelled when I first entered the building?" This question surprised the interviewer. He told Marshal the company makes cleaning supplies and the odor was a combination of all the cleaners. Before he left, Marshal also asked the interviewer about pay and working hours.

Types of Interviews

There are two basic types of interviews. An **unstructured interview** is usually somewhat informal. Since the interview does not have a set format, the interviewer often asks questions based on the responses given by the person being interviewed. This makes it much more personal and conversational. This type of interview is also called a *nondirective interview*.

By contrast, a **structured interview** is one that is more formal. For this interview, everyone being interviewed for the job is asked the exact same questions. The questions are determined before the interview begins. Though this type of interview is less conversational, it is often considered more fair and reliable for making job offer decisions. A structured interview is also called a *directive interview*. A structured interview may include one or more of the following styles:

YinYang/iStockphoto.com

Which type of interview would be the most difficult for you? Why?

■ A **screening interview** is a preliminary interview that an employer uses to determine whether you have the basic qualifications and personality for the position. Screening interviews usually are conducted on the telephone or at a job fair.

■ In a **performance interview**, the interviewer asks you to demonstrate a specific skill needed for the job. For example, you may have to complete a task on the computer to show how well you use a specific type of software. An applicant for a welding job may have to demonstrate knowledge of welding on various metals.

■ In a **group interview**, the applicant is interviewed by more than one interviewer at the same time. This allows the employer to have different people's opinions of the person being interviewed.

- A **behavioral interview** is designed to determine how the person being interviewed has behaved in certain situations in past jobs. This gives the employer the opportunity to understand what you have done, not just what you think you would do in a particular situation.

- A **dining interview** is one that takes place during a meal. Even though the interview typically takes place at dinner, it can be at any meal. The interviewer is not only interested in learning information from the interviewee that would be obtained in a more traditional interview, but also how the person behaves in a social situation. Understanding proper dining etiquette is extremely important in this type of interview.

- A **telephone interview** is one that is conducted over the telephone. This type of interview is usually used as a screening interview. However, for some positions and in certain situations, the telephone interview may be the full interview.

- A **virtual interview** is a new form of interview that sometimes replaces the telephone interview for initial screening of candidates. The virtual interview may be conducted in one of two ways. The person being interviewed might be asked to use the Internet for a voice-only interview or use a webcam to allow for both voice and video. In another type of virtual interview, the interviewee creates a video recording of his or her answers to specific interview questions.

You have worked hard to search for a job that meets your career goals and have identified jobs you want to pursue. You have sent out your resume with your cover letters that specified you would follow-up with the employer by a certain date. When you provide the employer with a specific follow-up date, make sure you meet that deadline. Completing all of these tasks has helped you land an interview. That's great! Now it's time to think about what you should do *before* the interview.

Olivia sent her resume to Shaneel's Pottery Studio to apply for a summer internship. She indicated in her cover letter that she would follow-up on September 14 if she had not heard back from the artist, Lena Shaneel, by then. Olivia did not hear back from Lena, so she called the studio, as noted in her cover letter.

Ms. Shaneel answered the phone. Olivia introduced herself over the phone and noted that she previously sent her resume for Ms. Shaneel to review. Ms. Shaneel informed Olivia that she had reviewed her resume. Olivia asked if there would be interviews for the internship position available and expressed an interest in an interview. "Yes," Ms. Shaneel replied, "we are interviewing applicants for the internship position next week."

Olivia told Ms. Shaneel about the art classes she has taken in high school and how much she enjoys working with pottery. She also explained how her career goal is to start her own pottery studio after she finishes an associate degree in art at the community college. She emphasized her business classes in high school such as accounting, insurance, and entrepreneurship so that she

Career FACT Some reasons you might not get the job include: (1) arriving late, (2) dressing inappropriately, (3) not doing a good job of presenting your strengths, (4) not answering questions completely, and (5) not being yourself.

can learn important aspects of running a business, but also explained that she wants hands-on experience with experts in the field.

Ms. Shaneel asked Olivia if she would accept a non-paid internship this summer. Olivia explained her career and financial goals and noted that she is trying to save money now so that she does not have to take out student loans when she goes to the community college. She said she would prefer a paid internship for these reasons. Ms. Shaneel looked at Olivia's resume again while they were on the phone and was impressed with Olivia's professionalism and how she expressed her career and financial goals clearly.

Ms. Shaneel set up an appointment with Olivia for an interview for a paid internship. Olivia thanked Ms. Shaneel for her time and the opportunity for an interview. Later, Ms. Shaneel wrote on Olivia's resume: "Good communication skills and professional. Well-thought-out career goals. Enthusiastic. Interview Monday at 9:00 a.m." Olivia is on her way to a successful interview.

Preparing for the Interview

When you agree to an interview, you can begin to prepare for it. When you have an interview with a specific company, follow these steps.

1. Review the research you have done on the company.
2. Prepare your portfolio.
3. Know your resume.
4. Prepare answers to interview questions to connect your skills and abilities to job qualifications.
5. Review last-minute details.

Review Research on the Company

As you are completing your job search, keeping track of your efforts and following up on job leads, you should be researching specific compaines that have jobs that will help you meet your career goals. Learn everything you can about the company before the interview. The information you find during your research will help you create a good impression in the interview. The interviewer will recognize that you did your homework and know about the company.

As you conduct your research, you will find useful information about the company that you can use during the interview and also to help you determine if you really want to work for this company. This will help you establish a relationship with the interviewer, who will believe you when you say you want to work for this company.

Make sure you carefully analyze the company information you research. It is important to determine if the company's values match your personal values. Remember that even though you are being interviewed, during the interview it is your opportunity to ask questions about the company as well. Your satisfaction with the job and the company will help you move toward your career goal. This may depend on how comfortable you are with the company's policies and culture.

Prepare Your Portfolio

When you are getting ready for an interview, it's important to make sure you have all of the documents you need. You should organize your portfolio to make sure you have the materials you need for that specific job. Your interview portfolio—a small briefcase or professional folder—should include the following.

■ *Resume and reference list*. Take several copies of your resume and your list of references with you to the interview. Although you have already sent a resume to the company, there may be several people involved in the interview process. Give a copy of your resume to each interviewer you meet. Give your reference list only to those who ask for it.

■ *Personal fact sheet*. Take your personal fact sheet with you when you go to the interview. You may have to complete an application or other employment forms while at the company. Your personal fact sheet has all the information you will need.

■ *Samples of work*. Bring copies of samples of your work that are relevant to the specific job for which you are applying. Be prepared to present these samples during the interview and to discuss them with the interviewer. If asked, leave copies of your samples with the interviewer.

■ *Legal pad or notebook*. Take a legal pad or notebook with you to take notes during the interview. Do not let your note-taking interfere with the interview process, but simply jot down important names or specific details about the job. Specifically, write down the names and titles (or get business cards) from persons involved in the interview so that you can send thank-you notes after the interview.

What will be in your portfolio?

Stuart Miles/Shutterstock.com

Know Your Resume

Interviewers often ask questions pertaining to activities or experiences listed on your resume. For example, if you worked as a soccer coach for young children, the interviewer may ask you to describe your responsibilities, how you interacted with the children and parents, and how you organized events. The interviewer will listen for skills you may transfer to this job. Are you organized? Did you solve problems? Did you use good interaction skills? Practice talking about how the experience listed on your resume applies to this specific job to help the interviewer see that your qualifications match the job requirements.

Practice for the Interview

Research, preparation, and practice are essential components to a successful interview. Review the list of common interview questions provided later in this chapter and think about questions specific to the job or company that you may have for the interviewer. Prepare your answers and practice those answers. It is helpful to have others practice with you so that they can ask you the questions and you can practice your answers aloud. This helps you feel more comfortable and gives you an opportunity to get feedback from others and edit your answers before going to the interview. Through your answers, you should be able to demonstrate that you are interested in the position; provide information pertaining to your skills and abilities; explain how you are qualified for the position; and help the interviewer see how the company can benefit from hiring you.

Make your final practice interview a dress rehearsal. Ask an adult who has work experience to role-play the interviewer. Provide this person with the questions you expect to be asked, but also allow him or her to ask other questions so that you can practice answering questions for which you did not prepare. Dress in your professional attire and practice entering the room with your portfolio, shaking hands, and sitting with good posture.

This practice will allow you to feel more comfortable and determine how you will use your portfolio and your answers to provide specific examples of your accomplishments. Ask your practice interviewer to give you constructive criticism on your clothing choices, appearance, attitude, and answers. You may want to complete this practice interview more than once until you feel that you are more confident in your appearance and answers.

Employers typically do not discuss salary or pay with you until they have provided a job offer. However, eventually you must decide the amount of money you will accept. Before you interview, research the standard pay range for that type of work. Honestly judge your experience and skill level and decide the lowest amount of pay you will accept. Consider your financial goals and your budget. An important consideration is the fringe benefits a company may provide. If asked what salary or wage you expect before a job offer is made, try to avoid naming an exact dollar amount. You could say, for example, that you are willing to negotiate a wage that falls within the normal pay range for that job. Some interviewers will then ask what you think the normal pay range is. Since you have researched that information, you will know what to say.

Review Last-minute Details

When you are scheduled for an interview, make sure you write down the specific details. These details may include the following.

■ Date and time of the interview

■ Address and directions to the interview

■ Name and title of the interviewer

■ Official title of the prospective job

■ Information about specific forms you should bring

■ Any other pertinent information

Review the research you have completed on the company and the job advertisement. Verify that you have all necessary components in your portfolio. Review the directions to the interview site and determine what time you should leave for the interview. Leave for the interview earlier than necessary in case of unexpected delays. It may be helpful to drive from your home to the interview location the day before the interview to help you judge the best time to leave. Being on time for the interview is essential.

Consider

With so many things to do before an interview, how will you organize to make sure you have thought of everything you need to do?

Preparing for Interview Questions

You must carefully prepare for successful interviews. They do not just happen by accident. Make sure you know your skills and abilities well and have prepared appropriate answers to common interview questions. It is important to plan your answers to common and illegal interview questions and develop a list of questions to ask the interviewer.

Plan Answers to Common Questions

Each interview will be somewhat different; however, you can expect some of the same questions to be asked at every interview. Knowing these questions in advance can help you prepare your answers. Employers commonly ask you about your strengths and weaknesses. Be truthful and frame your answers in a positive way. For example, a strength can also be a weakness. If your strength is that you are an organized person, explain how it is your strength, but sometimes you spend too much time organizing. Explain what you are doing to improve upon that weakness, such as setting time limits for organization time.

Illustration 12-1 lists common questions asked by most interviewers. Some questions relate to an interview for a specific job, while others are general interview questions. Think about your answers for each question. Know what you want to say, but do not memorize your answers as it will seem too rehearsed. You want to appear natural and self-confident during the interview.

filipk/iStockphoto.com

Plan Answers to Illegal Questions

Employers cannot legally ask you about your race, ethnicity, national origin, religion, age, membership in certain organizations, marital status, or physical condition. The wording of a question can determine whether the question is illegal. For example, an interviewer cannot ask the question "Do you have any disabilities?" Asking, "Do you have any physical conditions that might limit your ability to do this job?" is a legal question to ask.

> Jin-Sang has applied for a job as a front desk attendant at a small local hotel. In his interview, the owner said that some employees must work during holidays. He asks Jin-Sang whether he celebrates Christmas. Jin-Sang understands the interviewer wants to know whether he can work on Christmas Day, but he is uncomfortable discussing his religious beliefs. He also knows the question is illegal, but may be an unintentional mistake. He decides to give the owner the benefit of the doubt. Jin-Sang does not say whether he celebrates Christmas. Instead, he answers that he would be available to work on holidays.

Employers are required to understand the law and not ask illegal questions during an interview. However, you should be prepared just in case it happens. If you are uncomfortable, ask the interviewer how the question pertains to the job. If you do not get a reasonable explanation, you can say that you prefer not to answer the question. You also may decide that you do not want to work for a company whose interviewer asks an illegal question. You are interviewing the company as well as being interviewed. You should always make sure the company's values match your personal values.

Illustration 12-1: Common Interview Questions

1. How would you describe yourself?
2. What are your strengths and weaknesses?
3. Why are you interested in this position?
4. Where do you see yourself in five years?
5. How would you describe the perfect job, working environment, or supervisor?
6. How have you resolved a conflict in the workplace?
7. Do you work better in a team environment or on an individual basis?
8. What courses, extracurricular activities, or professional organizations have helped prepare you for this job?
9. Why should I hire you?
10. Why are you leaving your current position?

Plan Questions to Ask

Interviews help employers decide whether you are a match for a job and help you decide whether the company and the job are a match for you. The job should satisfy your needs and career goals. After your company and career research, prepare three to four questions you would like to ask the interviewer to help you clarify specifics about the job and company. Asking intelligent and relevant questions will help the interviewer understand you are serious about the job, organized, and well-prepared.

When the interviewer explains the position and the job duties, your questions may be answered. Prepare questions that concentrate on the job requirements, your qualifications, the company's goals, or opportunities for career development and advancement within the company. Questions about wages or benefits should not be asked at this time unless the interviewer brings up those subjects. Illustration 12-2 lists some questions you might ask at the end of the interview.

Illustration 12-2: Questions to Ask at the End of the Interview

1. What is the most important quality the person filling this job should have?
2. What is a typical day for a person in this position?
3. How does this position fit with the rest of the organization?
4. When will you be making a decision and an offer to fill this position?
5. Why do you like working for this company?
6. Do you provide educational support for further training for growth within the organization?
7. What would you expect from me during the first two months of this position?
8. How do you evaluate employee performance?
9. When do you think you will be making a job offer to the selected candidate?

ACTIVITY 12.1

Answering Interview Questions

Choose three common interview questions and write your answers to these questions. Role play as if you were in an interview by pairing up with another student and complete a role play. One person should play the part of the interviewer. Practice answering questions as he or she asks you the questions one at a time. Ask your partner to give you constructive feedback and edit your answers. Do the role play again using your edited answers. Then, switch and become the interviewer for the other student. Provide your partner with constructive criticism and allow him or her to practice a second time.

track5/iStockphoto.com

The Interview

Goals

- Discuss image as it pertains to interviewing.
- Explain the components of the interview.
- Examine nontraditional interviews.

Term

- body language, p. 290

Real Life Focus

Ciara knows her resume well and recognizes her skills, strengths, and weaknesses. She has practiced her answers to common interview questions and is prepared for her interview. She has also prepared three questions to ask the interviewers about the job and company. She has asked two people in her network to help her practice her interview. They have helped her develop appropriate answers and have reassured her that she is prepared. However, Ciara is still very nervous about the interview.

A friend told Ciara to try the following relaxation techniques. She is doing these each night before she goes to bed and plans on doing them before the interview.

1. Take deep breaths and think about something calm and relaxing.

2. Picture herself answering the interview questions and being successful in doing so.

3. Envision the interviewers smiling, shaking her hand, and offering her the job.

What techniques have you used to help you relax whenever you were nervous?

You may be nervous and anxious before your job interview. This is normal! Each interview will become easier because you will have a better idea of what to expect. The best way to reduce nervousness is to be well-prepared.

You have the basic qualifications for the job. Otherwise, the employer would not have selected you from the many applicants and asked you to come in for an interview. Be prepared to provide accurate information to help the employer know why you are the best person for the job. Make sure you arrive ahead of time, project a positive image, listen attentively, and try to relax.

Image and Arrival

Arriving 15–20 minutes before your scheduled interview time is a wise choice. Arriving early will allow you to make sure you find the right office and/or person, make sure your portfolio is organized, and become familiar

Web Connections

Web sites offer information and advice about interviewing.

Click on the Web Connections link for Chapter 12. Search at least two of the sites listed. As you are reviewing sites, write down ideas that may help you be more effective when interviewing for a job. Share your ideas with the class.

www.cengage.com/school/iyc

with your surroundings before the interview. Collect your thoughts, review your prepared answers to common interview questions, and think about your questions for the interviewer. This is also an appropriate time to make sure you are projecting a positive image.

Projecting a positive image includes your attitude, your appearance, your posture, your language, and your nonverbal cues. Make sure all of these convey a positive image of courtesy, enthusiasm, and self-confidence. No matter what you say or do, your positive image should reinforce your behavior. Through your positive image you are also demonstrating skills that may be necessary for the job. For example, when you are courteous and respectful to others during the interview, these are key transferable skills for every job. As you model these behaviors, the interviewer better understands your attitude and professionalism.

Projecting your professional image begins the minute you step in the door and before you even meet the interviewer. Many times the interviewer will ask the administrative assistant at the front desk how you behaved. Was the applicant polite? Did the applicant act nervous while he or she waited? If asked to complete any forms, was the applicant prepared with a pen or pencil? The administrative assistant's impression of you is also very important. This person may pass pertinent information on to the interviewer.

Your Attitude

Your attitude is portrayed through your words and actions—what you say and what you do. A positive attitude can set you apart from other qualified applicants. When you develop a positive attitude, you also build your self-confidence. You should be confident, but not cocky, during the interview process. There is a fine line between the two. You attitude will help you emphasize your best qualities and skills and your interest in the company. The following demonstrate a positive attitude and self-confidence.

- Good posture when walking, sitting, and standing
- A smile and firm handshake when you meet others
- Enthusiasm and energy
- Honesty and sincerity
- Friendliness, courteous behavior, and being respectful to others

Your Appearance

Your appearance and attire will either help or hurt your professional image. A pleasant appearance and professional attire will enhance your professional image. On the other hand, an unpleasant appearance and untidy attire will damage your professional image. It's important to note that not every job has the same requirements for appearance and attire.

For example, financial institutions may require employees to dress more conservatively than a manufacturer. Other industries may provide a uniform for you to wear. However, no matter what dress is required, it is up to you to convey a positive professional image through your appearance and other means.

Remember that you are a representative of the company. Companies typically expect their employees to look clean, appropriately dressed, and focused on the task at hand. You can represent all of these key components during the interview process. The following tips may be helpful as you develop your professional appearance for the interview.

- *Clean*. You should be freshly bathed and groomed for the interview. Use an effective deodorant, but avoid heavy perfumes or cologne. Make sure you have fresh breath and that your fingernails are clean and trimmed. Wear clean clothes and polished shoes. Follow basic grooming guidelines.

- *Appropriately dressed*. You want to err on the side of conservative dress. Your hair should be groomed in a professional-looking style and your clothes appropriate for the position. For example, if you are interviewing for a fast-food server position, you do not wear a business suit. However, a suit or more professional attire would be appropriate if you are applying for an office position. No matter what position you are applying for, your clothes should be clean and pressed, fit properly, and help you portray that professional image. Wear few or no accessories. Women should wear appropriate makeup and simple jewelry. Men should limit their jewelry to a conservative ring. Remove any unusual pierced jewelry and cover tattoos. An interview is not the time to make a fashion statement, but a time to be dressed professionally.

- *Focused on the task at hand*. Being organized and answering questions asked are two ways of staying focused. Interviewers do not have time to listen to many personal stories from job applicants. Staying focused also involves portraying a calm appearance. Avoid fidgeting, chewing gum, tapping a pen or pencil on the table, or other nervous habits. Maintain eye contact with the interviewer, answer the questions asked, and stay focused on getting the job.

Your Verbal Language

Your verbal language is your spoken language—what you say. What you say and how you say it reflects on your professional image. Poor grammar, poor word choice, and inappropriate vocabulary will harm your professional image and leave a lasting impression. Do not use slang or fillers such as *um*, *like*, or *you know*. The most effective verbal language is simple and direct. Speak confidently and transmit the information clearly. When you are asked an interview question, it is appropriate to pause briefly to gather your thoughts and develop your answer. Speaking too quickly may result in an answer that is not complete or well-developed. Your verbal language should have a pleasant tone and also show courtesy and respect for others. A simple thank-you can go a long way.

Your Nonverbal Language

Your nonverbal language is your body language. **Body language** includes mannerisms, gestures, and facial expressions. Your body language either reinforces or undermines your professional image. Your body language often sends more accurate messages of your feelings than your verbal communication. There is positive and negative body language. Positive body language includes good posture, appropriate eye contact, a pleasant expression, and a firm handshake. Negative body language includes rolling your eyes, slouching, looking around the room not paying attention, frowning, and crossing your arms. When you demonstrate positive body language, you are more engaged in the interview and the interviewer will develop a more positive image about you. When you demonstrate negative body language, an interviewer may think you are disengaged, not interested in the job, or unable to stay on task.

Consider

What do you need to work on to develop your professional image? What will you do to improve upon this component of your professional image?

Components of the Interview

When preparing for an interview, consider these three components: the opening of the interview, the questioning process, and the closing of the interview. The opening is basically the greeting of the interviewer. The questioning process is the part you have probably prepared for the most—the questions. The closing is how you leave the interview.

Opening the Interview

Before going to the interview, make sure you know the name of the interviewer and how to pronounce his or her name correctly. As you greet the interviewer, use his or her last name preceded by *Mr.*, *Ms.*, or *Dr.* Do not use the interviewer's first name. This is a more formal approach. The interviewer will let you know if you can use his or her first name. Introduce yourself with your first and last name.

The interviewer will set the tone for the interview at the beginning of the interview. Follow the interviewer's cues and adjust to the formality of the interview. For example, if the interviewer extends a hand, shake it firmly. Wait to be asked to be seated and allow the interviewer to begin the conversation. Remember that your positive professional image and body language will help set the tone for the interview.

The Questioning Process

This should be the part for which you are best prepared—the questions. You know your resume, skills, and abilities and you have developed appropriate answers to potential questions. Review your answers before the interview. Try to relax and act naturally as you take time to clearly and concisely answer each question. Most interviewers understand that you may be nervous and will try to make you feel comfortable. However, the interviewer's purpose is to hire the best candidate for the job. Expect the interviewer to evaluate you based on your answers, behavior, and professional image throughout the interview.

Listen carefully to each question, think about your answer, and answer honestly, concisely, and directly. Through this process, remember to highlight your strengths and accomplishments. Give concrete examples and use the samples of your work in your portfolio to reinforce the presentation of your skills, abilities, and experience.

Don't forget to use your research and knowledge of the company to show your interest in the job. Make sure the interviewer understands how your qualifications meet the requirements of the job. Be positive in your responses, and do not make negative comments about a situation at a former job or bad situation with a supervisor. Employers value people who bring a positive can-do attitude to the workplace.

How do your interests relate to your future career?

Closing the Interview

An interviewer will typically end the interview by asking if you have any questions. This is your opportunity to get answers to all of your questions. The interviewer may then make a closing statement such as, "Thank you for coming in. We will contact you soon." At this time, if you want the job restate that you are interested in the position and you believe you can do the job well. Ask what the next step is and when you will be notified about a hiring decision. Smile, shake hands, and thank the interviewer. Continue to keep your professional image and positive body language as you leave the office and building. If you pass the administrative assistant on the way out, thank him or her again.

Tips for Nontraditional Interviews

Interviewing can be especially stressful in a nontraditional setting. Dining interviews, telephone interviews, and virtual interviews all have unique characteristics.

Dining Interview When preparing for a dining interview, review effective dining etiquette techniques. For example, when you have more than one fork at a place setting, you simply begin from the outside and work your way in, course by course. The small fork on the outside is for the salad and the larger fork for the main course. There will be several glasses and small plates on your table. Your bread plate is on the left and your glass on the right. If you have not dined at a formal type of restaurant, it would be to your benefit to do so prior to the dining interview. This would be good practice for you.

When involved in a dining interview, men should wear their jackets while dining and women should place their purses on the floor in a location that will not hinder the movement of others (i.e., under their chair). Stand behind your chair, and wait until others have been seated before you enter your chair from the right hand side. Place your napkin folded in half in your lap. If you leave the table, place your napkin in your chair. When you are finished eating, you may leave your napkin on the table.

Be prepared to participate in small talk with other people at the table. Small talk typically revolves around books you have read, movies you have seen, or your hobbies. However, know that you will be judged on those items as well. Try to relate your conversation to the job and your skills and abilities. As with any type of interview, be prepared!

Telephone Interview When being interviewed over the telephone, many times you will be on a speaker phone so that everyone in the room can hear you. As you begin to speak, ask if everyone can hear you before you continue. Do not speak too quickly, and make sure you maintain a pleasant tone. Many believe that you should dress as though you were interviewing in person. The professional attire helps you feel as though you are in a traditional interview and help you maintain your professional image. This not an informal process just because you are not being interviewed face-to-face. Therefore, the same techniques for a successful interview apply.

Take the time to find a location in which you will not be interrupted. Mobile phones are known to lose service at times. Therefore, if possible, use a landline for the telephone interview. Do not try to multitask while you are involved in a telephone interview. For example, do not check your email or favorite social networking site while interviewing. Do not participate in a telephone interview while driving a car. All of these lead to distractions that will prevent you from interviewing at your best.

Virtual Interview When being interviewed virtually, there will be some type of Internet-based program involved. Make sure you connect to the Internet site early and test your technology. A microphone and/or Web camera will be used for the virtual interview and it is crucial that your technology works. If possible, practice using the technology prior to the interview. Dress in professional attire and speak clearly to answer all questions asked.

Learn From Others

Contact an individual from a local business who regularly conducts job interviews. Ask him or her the following questions and record the responses.

- What styles of interviews do you use most often?
- What styles of interviews do you use least often?
- How do you decide which applicants to interview?
- What do you look for in applicants?
- How do you interview for honesty, dependability, and teamwork skills?

- What do you consider the most important interview question?
- What is the most important quality you look for in an applicant?
- What are some things that will make you not hire an applicant?

Keep the responses in your portfolio for future reference.

After the Interview

Goals

- Discuss how to evaluate performance after the interview.
- Describe follow-up procedures after the interview.
- Explain steps to consider after the interview.

Term

- evaluate, p. 294

Real Life Focus

Have you ever watched a reality television show where people sing, dance, or perform in auditions and are evaluated by judges? Many times, the people auditioning think they are fantastic and very talented, but it is obvious to us that they are not so fantastic. In fact, many do not seem to be talented at all. It is hard sometimes to evaluate our own performance.

The same is true when we interview. There may be situations where we think we have interviewed well, but in fact we have not done such a great job during the interview. So how can you evaluate your own performance realistically?

Ask yourself these questions after each interview: How do you think the interview went? What did you do well? What could you have done better?

Evaluate Your Performance

As soon as possible after your interview, evaluate your performance in the interview. In this instance, **evaluate** means to assess yourself to determine the quality of your performance. How do you think the interview went? What did you do well? What could you have done better? Since this will probably not be your last interview, what you learn from evaluating your performance in this interview will help you to do better in future interviews.

Completing a written evaluation of your interview performance will help you to have a better understanding of how you did in the interview. Start your evaluation by making a list of positives (things you did well) and a list of negatives (things that you think you could have improved). Review the things you did well, and make sure you understand why these things were good and how to carry these over into your next interview. Next, take each item on your negatives list and make notes on how to improve each area. For each of these areas, get advice from those people who might be able to help you improve (parents, teachers, guidance counselors, etc.).

pjcross/Shutterstock.com

What can you do to evaluate your performance after an interview?

Follow Up After the Interview

As a follow-up to your interview, you should write a thank-you letter or email to the person who interviewed you. If you had a group interview, write a thank-you to each interviewer. You can make each letter different by referring to a specific question or point made by that interviewer. Since the interviewer may be interviewing people for more than one job, always refer to the specific job that you interviewed for. Thank the interviewer for his or her time and for giving you the opportunity to interview with the company. This will leave a positive and lasting impression on the interviewer.

After evaluating your interview performance, you may find that you need to clarify some information for the interviewer. This letter or email is an opportunity to do that. Also, since you do not know how many people may have interviewed for the position since your interview, this additional contact will also put your name in front of the interviewer one more time.

Even if you decide that you are no longer interested in the position, you should write a letter thanking the interviewer for his or her time. Advise the interviewer that you no longer wish to be considered for the position. However, if you think you might want to be considered for future jobs with the company, state this in your letter. No matter what the reason, make certain your letter is positive and complimentary.

Real People / Real Careers

Jacquelyn Bollmer Freiermuth / *Graphic Designer*

If Jackie Freiermuth's mother had a crystal ball and could predict her daughter's career, she probably would have been very close. Drawing, coloring, and creating crafts were Jackie's favorite childhood activities. Instead of dolls, Jackie preferred to spend hours at her child-sized desk drawing and coloring. At the top of her wish list were always sharpened crayons and markers with the newest colors.

Though Jackie did well in her middle school and high school classes, she excelled in her art courses—her favorite classes. Her passion led her to choose Graphic Design as her major in college. Jackie knew that her career had to involve art, but she still needed to find a job. Design allowed her to work with art every day without becoming a starving artist.

Jackie Freiermuth is a designer for an advertising firm. She creates concept advertising campaigns; that is, advertisements that provide images and perceptions about an item, a brand, or a company. As Jackie explains, "I chose graphic design because I like the challenge of communication. In graphic design you are using icons, graphics, text, and headlines to communicate with others through visuals and words."

Looking into her future, Jackie sees herself becoming an Art Director within a design company. Even better, she would like to have her own freelance business that would allow her the freedom to work independently.

For more information about:

* graphic design careers

* careers for art majors

Access **www.cengage.com/school/iyc** and click on the appropriate links in Chapter 12.

Source: *Personal Interview,* September 2011

Photo courtesy of Matthew C. Jordan

Consider

What might happen if you did not evaluate your performance in your last interview? Think of two or three reasons that make it important to send a thank-you letter or email to the interviewer after the interview.

Considering the Next Steps

What if your interview went poorly and you did not get the job? The most important thing to remember is that everyone has experienced a bad interview. Try to think about jobs just as you think about people. Sometimes they are a good fit and they become your friends, and sometimes they are not. Well, sometimes the job is a good fit and you get the job, and sometimes you do not. Remember, if the job is not a good fit for your skills or your personality, you do not want it anyway. Working in a job that is not a good fit is a recipe for unhappiness.

So, what do you do now? First, review your written evaluation of the interview. Consider all the things you did well and make sure you understand why they went well. Did they go well because you were well prepared or did they go well simply by mistake? If it was by mistake, consider these components of the interview and make sure you're prepared next time. For the parts of the interview that did not go well, consider them in-depth. Do you need to do more research about the company? Do you need to practice your interviewing skills? Just remember to use your written evaluation to determine where you need to improve. This will guide you as to what you need to do to be ready for your next interview.

ACTIVITY 12.3

Leadership

Thank-You Letter

Review the information in this lesson about writing a thank-you letter after the interview. Assume you had a successful interview this week for a position as a web page designer at the Visual Studio Company. Francis Marcum was the manager who interviewed you and you would love to have the job. Work in teams to list important points to include in the thank-you letter, discuss the letter format, and write the letter. When you are finished, exchange your letter with another group and proofread each other's letter. Make appropriate edits to your letter before submitting it to your teacher.

Portfolio

RapidEye/iStockphoto.com

Chapter Summary

12.1 The Interview Process and Preparation

- The interviewer's goal during a job interview is to determine the applicant's skills and abilities and to determine if he or she will be a good fit for the company. The applicant should be active during the interview process and learn about the company to determine if this is a company where he or she wants to work. There are two basic types of interviews: unstructured and structured. Structured interviews include screening, group, behavioral, dining, telephone, and virtual interviews.

- Before each interview, applicants should research the company, prepare their portfolio and review their resume, practice answers to common interview questions, and review last-minute details.

- Applicants should be aware of common interview questions and how to answer them. They should also plan how to deal with illegal interview questions, and determine three or four questions to ask the interviewer.

12.2 The Interview

- It is important to arrive approximately 15–20 minutes early to an interview. This provides time to find the right location, review the portfolio, and become familiar with the environment. Applicants should also be aware of their professional image, which includes their attitude, appearance, verbal language, and nonverbal language.

- The three main components of an interview include opening the interview, the questioning process, and the closing.

- Nontraditional interviews include dining, telephone, and virtual interviews. Extra preparation may be needed for these types of interviews.

12.3 After the Interview

- Evaluating your performance after your interview is an important component of any interview. This evaluation should be a true learning experience. Make sure you evaluate the areas of the interview where you did well and those areas where you did not do well.

- Make sure to follow up after an interview with a thank-you letter or email. If you had a group interview, write a thank-you to each interviewer. Several people may have been interviewed, so make sure to refer to the specific job that you interviewed for.

- If the interview does not go well and you do not get the job, remember that everyone has experienced a bad interview and you are not alone. The job may not have been a good fit for your skills and abilities. Review your interview evaluation and make any necessary changes before the next interview.

Chapter Assessment

Vocabulary Builder

Match each statement with the term that best defines it.

a. behavioral interview

b. body language

c. dining interview

d. evaluate

e. group interview

f. job interview

g. performance interview

h. screening interview

i. structured interview

j. telephone interview

k. unstructured interview

l. virtual interview

1. Mannerisms, gestures, and facial expressions

2. An interview with more than one interviewer

3. An interview designed to determine how the applicant has behaved in situations in the past

4. An interview in which the applicant must demonstrate a specific skill

5. An interview conducted over the phone

6. An interview that takes place over a meal

7. A conversation between a job applicant and one or more people in a company or organization to discuss the applicant's qualifications for a specific job

8. An interview that has little structure and is more informal

9. A preliminary interview that the employer uses to determine if the applicant has the basic skills and personality for the job

10. To assess yourself to determine the quality of your performance

11. A more formal interview

12. A type of interview that is often conducted online via the Internet

Review What You Have Learned

13. What should be your goal during an interview?

14. Name the different types of structured interviews.

15. Why is it important to plan for illegal questions?

16. Why is it important to arrive early for an interview?

17. Which of the three interview components do you think is most important?

18. How would you prepare for the opening and closing of an interview?

19. Why is it important to evaluate your performance in an interview?

20. What are three reasons for following up after an interview?

21. What should you do if your interview does not go well?

Case Challenges

After reading both case studies, analyze each situation. Have the students successfully prepared for their job interview? If yes, explain why. If not, suggest activities they can do to be more prepared.

22. Christopher has prepared answers for common interview questions and has purchased new clothes for his interview at Mt. Olive's State Park. He has researched the park and visits it regularly. He is familiar with many

trails and waterfalls in the park. He feels prepared for the interview, but he keeps thinking he is forgetting something. However, he is going on the interview tomorrow.

23. Clarice is convinced that she is prepared for her interview with the Treeline Lawn Service tomorrow. The only thing she knows about the job is that she will get to work outside and she want to improve her tan. She also knows it pays $12.50 per hour and she is saving for a car. She had her hair cut yesterday and bought a new hat. She is ready to go to work and feels ready for the interview.

Make Academic Connections

24. **LANGUAGE ARTS**   Members of your network helped you get an interview with Aims Van Lines. You went on an interview yesterday, but after the interview you are not particularly interested in the position anymore. However, you may want to work in another capacity with this company in the future. With this in mind, write a thank-you letter for the interview.

25. **BUSINESS**   You work for Gainesville Amusement Park and have interviewed several people to work at the front gate greeting customers, taking tickets, and handling any issues that may come up. You want to evaluate everyone fairly and consistently. Develop an evaluation sheet you could use to assess the applicants.

Workplace Connection

26. It is important to know what to do at an interview. Review the information in this chapter and other sources in the media center or online and complete the following.

- List five things you should do during an interview.
- List five things you should *not* do during an interview.

27. Know what to expect in an interview. Assume you are going to interview two people for a job as a courtesy clerk at a grocery store. Besides the common interview questions, develop 3 to 5 questions you would ask the applicants during the interview process to judge their ethics, ability to work with others, and work ethic.

Blogging: Interview Questions

As you continue to blog or journal, reflect upon the common interview questions in this chapter. Choose one question and write your answer. Discuss how hard or easy it was to write your answer and whether you believe this type of answer will help you during an interview.

Capstone Project: Part 4

Part 4 of the **Capstone Project** is creating a visual for your presentation. You have two choices for your type of visual. Whichever you choose depends on your expertise.

- **Slide presentation.** Create a slideshow. You may use PowerPoint or another web site found at <u>www.cengage.com/school/iyc</u>, Chapter 12. Your slideshow must be 8 to 10 slides and may include video clips, audio clips, and hyperlinks.

- **Video.** The video must be three minutes long.

Whether you present a slideshow or a video, the presentation will tell the story of your project. Your instructor will provide you with specific content guidelines.

The visual is an addition or extension of your project. It does not speak for you. Instead, the visual emphasizes the research and information. Ideally, you will have fewer than 15 words per slide.

Some tips for your visual are:

- Focus on your topic throughout. Use clear, simple visuals to make the slide's content clearer.

- Let the picture or graphic tell the story. Use as little text as possible.

- Use legible and professional font styles. A good title size is 44 points. A **bold** font (28 to 34 points) is best for subtitles.

- Backgrounds should never distract from the presentation. A background that is not distracting and a soothing color, like blue, appears professional.

- Proof read *everything*, including visuals and numbers.

The steps in the visual process are:

_____ *Use Guidelines for Visuals*

_____ *Create*

_____ *Edit*

_____ *Peer Review*

_____ *Edit*

_____ *Teacher Review*

_____ *Edit*

_____ *Finish – Teacher approved*

_____ *Bring saved visual on a flash drive to your teacher*

Tools for the Future

kali9/iStockphoto.com

CHAPTER 13

Succeeding in a Career

© Danita Delimont/Alamy

What Do You Know

1. How might your career choice influence other parts of your life?

2. What qualities do you have that employers might need?

Aidan loved fish—and science. As he was growing up, his family had many aquariums. He took his passion to heart by majoring in natural science with a concentration in biology. After all, he had raised fish for 15 years with his father. To help with his college expenses, Aidan formed a small company that cleaned fish tanks in offices and homes. During the summer, he also managed a pet store's fish department.

From one of his college professors, Aidan discovered Freshwater Farms. After graduation, he started working there fulltime as a breeder. The fish farm had three divisions: a fish market, breeding for stocking ponds and lakes, and waterscape design and maintenance. Raising fish came naturally to Aidan. The owner, Mr. Smith, hired Aidan in the hatchery, which supplied both fish for the market and stock for ponds. Aidan's education and love of fish were the reasons he was hired.

Rather than work only with the fish, Aidan found himself interacting with customers. Freshwater Farms had over 25 varieties of fish. Aidan worked with each customer to find the type of fish suited for each. Also, if a customer had a problem with fish disease or plant maintenance, Aidan worked with the customer to solve the problem. Observing him closely, Mr. Smith soon realized that Aidan was an excellent employee to work with customers. Aidan is on the career track to become the department manager.

Planning a Career in . . . Agriculture

Agriculture, Food & Natural Resources

When you think of an Agriculture career, you may naturally picture a farmer on a tractor in a field. However, the majority of Agriculture careers do not involve growing crops or raising livestock.

The diversity in this career cluster spans the production, processing, marketing, distribution, financing, and development of agricultural products and resources. Agricultural products include food, fiber (such as wool), wood products, natural resources, horticulture, and other plant and animal resources.

Employment Outlook

- Nearly 40 percent are self-employed.
- The merger of ranches and farms has caused a decline in employment.
- Faster than average growth for food science production and science because of biotechnology and environmental influences.

Career Possibilities

- Recycling Supervisor
- Nutritionist
- Animal Caretaker
- Golf Course Manager
- Forest Ranger

Needed Skills

- Knowledge of health and safety.
- Ability to apply scientific inquiry.
- Understanding of organizational systems.
- Certifications for various tools, machinery, and technology.

What's It Like to Work in Agriculture?

If you choose a career in Agriculture, you will have many options. You may work in a laboratory designing ways to create more nutritious food. You may work to eliminate environmental hazards. Your workplace may be a zoo or a national park. You may work with people and their animals or work alone landscaping. From machines to plants, from soil to rock, the variety of Agriculture careers is endless.

Employment in some Agriculture careers is declining. As more companies purchase small farms to create shopping malls and housing developments, fewer people are raising crops and livestock.

Entry-level Agriculture careers often mean working at a low pay scale for long hours. Some entry-level positions are seasonal. However, following an Agriculture career track will offer you a variety of opportunities to succeed in both your career and your income.

Those in Agriculture careers often have a deep passion for their profession. Are you one of them?

What about You?

Do you enjoy the outdoors? Are science courses interesting to you? Are you concerned about the environment? If you answered *yes* to some of those questions, then consider a career in one of the aspects of the Agriculture career cluster.

liquidlibrary/Jupiter Images

What Employers Want

Goals
- List the qualities needed for 21st-century employees.
- Explain how teams function in the workplace.
- Describe how to manage conflict within a team.

Terms
- competencies, p. 304
- collaborate, p. 307
- empowerment, p. 308
- conflict resolution, p. 309
- mediator, p. 309

Portfolio

Real Life Focus

Are you ready to be a member of a workplace team? Mark each statement if it *always* applies to you, *never* applies to you, or *sometimes* applies to you.

1. I like solving problems with a group.
2. In a group, I often let others talk before I express my opinion.
3. I am a good listener. I listen to others before I give my opinion.
4. I see myself as a leader.
5. If I disagree, I consider the other side before I answer.
6. I enjoy hearing others' opinions and questioning them on issues.
7. For me to be part of the group, the group must set specific goals.
8. When I set goals, I usually complete them.
9. I often referee in arguments among friends and family.

Score **10 points** for *always*, **5 points** for *sometimes*, and **0 points** for *never*.

80–90	I am a good leader and team member.
60–70	I am a good team member, but need more leadership skills.
0–50	I need to work on my team skills.

Employers need intelligent employees who can learn their responsibilities and deal with the demands of their jobs. Education, business, and government organizations work together to identify certain workplace skills and abilities necessary for all employees. The results are the *21st-Century Learning Skills*. These characteristics are necessary to keep the United States competitive in the global market.

Important Qualities for Employees

Competencies are the skills and personal qualities you need to have a fulfilling career. If you are weak in any of the categories listed below, work on the skill and even try to master it before entering the work world.

Core Subjects and 21st-Century Themes

Every employer wants employees with at least minimum basic skills. After all, reading, writing, and math are important for *every* career. The core subjects are your academic courses in school and include:

- Language arts, especially reading

- Mathematics

- Economics

- Science

- Social studies, including geography, history, and government

- Also suggested are world languages and fine arts

These subjects have important foundation skills. However, 21st-century careers require more than pure academics. Also necessary are:

- Global awareness—Being aware of different cultures and nations.

- Financial, economic, business, and entrepreneurial literacy—Explaining the role of economics in society. Determining personal financial choices and goals.

- Civic literacy—Understanding government at all levels.

- Health literacy—Learning basic health and safety information. Setting personal health goals.

- Environmental literacy—Analyzing environmental issues and society's impact on it.

Workplace Competencies

Now that you have the basic knowledge of the core subjects and 21st-century themes, there are specific workplace competencies for a 21st-century workplace. The workplace competencies are:

Learning and Innovation Skills Sometimes called the 4Cs, these skills will prepare you for life and work as the 21st-century workplace becomes more and more complex. Focusing on creativity, critical thinking, communication, and collaboration is essential to prepare employees for the future. Knowing these skills will make you an employee who is prepared for 21st-century life and the workplace.

Information, Media, and Technology Skills People in the 21st-century live in a technology-filled environment. Employees must know how to access and analyze the great amount of information that is available. Technology tools change rapidly, so to be effective in the 21st-century, employees must have critical thinking skills relating to information, media, and technology.

Why is attendance so important for an employee?

i_frontier/iStockphoto.com

Life and Career Skills Today's life and work environments require far more than thinking skills and knowledge of basic subjects. You must develop adequate life and career skills. Throughout this textbook, you have been developing these skills. They include:

■ Adapting to change

■ Working independently

■ Interacting with others

■ Managing projects

■ Guiding others

Becoming skilled in the workplace competencies will definitely give you the edge over the ordinary employee. Challenge yourself. Try different projects and activities that will give you experiences with these skills.

A Good Employee

The 21st-Century Learning Skills are very important. However, a good employee will definitely follow these guidelines. They are a *must* in every workplace.

■ *Employees must observe work hours.* You are expected to arrive at work *every day* and *on time*. Oversleeping is not an acceptable reason for being late. You should come to work even when you do not feel your best or you have a personal problem. Remember, one of the top two reasons employers fire employees is for attendance problems.

■ *Employees must have basic reading and math skills.* Without these skills, performing your work well will be difficult.

■ *Employees must be willing and able to learn.* If you have little or no experience working in a particular career, you must be willing to listen to your supervisor and your coworkers. You can learn from them.

- *Employees must be able to get along with their coworkers and supervisors.* Your supervisors and fellow workers expect you to communicate with them respectfully and pleasantly, as you expect of them. Most careers involve working with others on a daily basis. Not getting along with your coworkers is the other top reason employers fire employees.

- *Employees must be able to pass a drug test.* Over 60 percent of workplaces drug-test as part of the hiring process. Some companies will randomly test current employees. If you are a substance abuser, you are an unreliable employee. Ultimately, being an abuser may cost you your job. Of accidents that take place at work, 65 percent are drug- or alcohol-related.

Workplace Teams

In the workplace, a team is a group of employees working together to reach a specific goal. Companies find that teams often accomplish tasks and solve problems more efficiently than individuals working alone. Being able to work effectively as part of a team is an essential skill for employees in most organizations.

In school and at work, you will be asked to **collaborate**, or work with others, to complete assignments. You may collaborate on a short-term basis, such as completing a project with fellow students. You also may be a member of a long-term, more permanent team. In either situation, you must be able to work with your classmates and coworkers in order to be successful. In fact, a major reason people are fired in the United States today is that they cannot get along with their coworkers.

In the workplace, your supervisor may create a team to complete a task or to do an ongoing job. Temporary teams may be together for only a short time. For example, a team created to plan and coordinate an event will remain together only until the event follow-up details end. Permanent teams, such as factory teams, may work together for several years. Those teams are invaluable to an employer because team members can fill in for one another for an absence. When an individual member leaves a permanent team, the employer selects another employee as a replacement.

Benefits of Teamwork

Teamwork benefits both the workplace and the team members. For example, no one member of a baseball team can win a championship for its school. Team members must work together to win games. Companies that use teams to develop, produce, and market their products require fewer people to help make decisions. As a result, they often are more efficient in getting their products to market.

Teams also encourage members to take pride in their efforts and to think creatively. Team members who are proud of what they do tend to make fewer errors. For a company, fewer errors means saving money. In the workplace, team members who are happy with their jobs stay with the company longer. The result is lower employee turnover.

> *"Toyota wants to not only get bigger, but also get better at the same time," stated the company's senior managing director. The occasion? A ribbon-cutting ceremony for a new Toyota training center in Kentucky.*

Toyota will use the center to train workers from all over North America to do things the same way—the Toyota way. Workers learn identical hand movements for quality consistency. The trained employees will join their teams at the home plants to provide team training the Toyota way.

Toyota wants to be the biggest automaker in the world. Because employees are using their skills in a standard way, Toyota hopes the teams will build cars that customers will buy in larger numbers.

Team members also benefit from working together as a group. One reward is the sense of empowerment that comes from working on a successful team. **Empowerment** is the ability to manage and control your own work and feel satisfied about that work. If your team is successful, the team success reflects well on each team member. Your supervisor's appreciation of your contributions as a team member may result in your being promoted.

Problem Solving

The team is ready to begin its work after the goals are set. However, sometimes they need to find solutions to specific problems so they can work together.

The process of problem solving has six key steps. By skipping any problem-solving step, a team has less change of reaching the best solution.

Step 1: Define the Problem The team must understand the problem. For example, suppose you are on a workplace team at a clothing store. The store sales are down from last year. Step 1 will determine the cause of the decrease in sales. The problem could be economic troubles, outdated merchandise, poor customer service, road construction in front of the store, or another reason. Your team must define the problem by researching the differences between last year's sales and this year's sales.

Step 2: Set the Criteria The team should determine what it wants as the solution. The criteria are the conditions for solving the problem. Your workplace team should deal with the real problem for the clothing store, not just the symptoms. A good solution will increase sales. An even better solution would be to provide marketing to continue the sales increase. For example, if the real problem is poor customer service, slashing prices during a sale will not solve the problem.

Step 3: Explore Alternative Solutions Instead of settling quickly on the most obvious solution, the team should identify several possible alternatives. For the clothing store, the alternatives could include cutting prices to attract more shoppers, updating displays to increase appeal, or training salespeople to provide better customer service.

Step 4: Evaluate Alternative Solutions At this stage, the team uses the criteria it set in Step 2 to study the various solutions it identified in Step 3. Part of the evaluation process for the clothing store is to decide how much each proposed solution will cost and amount of profit each solution will generate.

Andresr/Shutterstock.com

Having more clothing sales is a quick fix that will bring in more customers. But it is only temporary solution. However, improving customer service is a long-term solution that does not cut into the profits.

Step 5: Choose the Best Option and Implement It After discussing the alternatives, the team chooses the best solution based on its analysis in Step 4. The solution is then put into action. The best option for the clothing store may be to lower prices, or it may be to improve customer service. The option chosen should solve the store's problem and produce steady results over time.

Step 6: Review the Effects of the Solution In some cases, the problem solving ends after the team proposes a solution. Sometimes, however, a team needs to evaluate the results of its decision. The team may need to determine whether the solution is successful or whether to consider another alternative. The clothing store team should review the store's profits to see if they increased over last year's. If sales do not increase, the team should consider an alternative solution.

consider

What method did you last use to solve a problem? How successful were you? How could using the six steps have helped you?

Managing Conflict

Problem solving is a structured way of making decisions. However, teams cannot always solve every problem. Sometimes disagreements arise that must be resolved. **Conflict resolution** is a way of settling problems productively. Conflict resolution techniques can help you work out disagreements and prevent them from interfering with your work. Conflict resolution has a sequence of six key steps:

1. You may need to ask a mediator to help resolve the disagreement. A **mediator** is a neutral person who is not directly involved in the disagreement. The mediator gives advice when needed and acts as a referee. Choose a private meeting place for the discussion.

2. Put yourself in the other person's position. Listen carefully as the other person speaks directly to you. Then repeat what you think the other person just said. That review helps avoid any miscommunication.

3. Ask the other person to consider your position and listen to you as you speak directly to him or her. The other person should repeat what you just said.

4. Look at the problem objectively and discuss the conflict. Encourage the others present to do the same. Discuss solutions that will work for both sides. This discussion makes everyone aware of the differences of opinion.

5. Speak respectfully to create a climate of trust.

6. Reach a solution that allows everyone to agree on something that he or she wants. Your team may not agree on the entire solution, but it will agree on parts of the solution.

Conflicts may happen because of poor communication that is accidental. For example, you may hear a comment incorrectly. Before getting frustrated or angry, repeat the comment to make sure you heard it correctly. Another common communication problem is with interpreting directions. Some people need visual clues such as a map or a drawing. Other people do better with written directions. To avoid a communication problem, provide both visual and written instructions.

When conflicts between team members cannot be resolved, the team's success may be in jeopardy. When the team fails to perform for any reason, the careers of those team members may suffer. Every member of a team must work hard to help the team resolve differences and focus on the team goals.

Leadership

ACTIVITY 13.1

Resolving Workplace Problems

In small groups, consider each situation. What should each employee do? Reach a group consensus. Choose a leader, a recorder, and a reporter.

1. Working in the mall office is a great job for Mae. She meets many people when she answers questions about the mall and sells snacks and souvenirs. The office is in a separate building since not all of the stores in the mall are under one roof. During the summer, Mae is very busy. In the winter, though, she has only a few customers during the week but has hectic weekends. During the winter weekdays, her supervisor, Mr. Shirokawa, allows her to use her laptop as long as she takes care of the customers first. On weekends, Mae continues to use her laptop so she can IM her friends. She knows she can do her work and talk to her friends at the same time. Besides, Mae is sure she will spot Mr. Shirokawa before he sees her using her laptop.

2. Clinton's supervisor, Ms. Ramones, asked him to go to the post office to mail pizza coupons for the restaurant. The coupons needed to be mailed two weeks before the holiday weekend. To be ready for the coupon promotion, Ms. Ramones needed to order extra supplies in advance. Clinton left the coupons in his friend's car. When he finally discovered the coupons, he mailed them over a week late and did not tell Ms. Ramones. When the holiday weekend arrived and only a few people used the pizza coupons, Ms. Ramones had too many supplies on hand and the fresh ingredients spoiled.

3. Cassie works for an agency that provides services to people with disabilities. Most of the agency's funding comes from private donations. Cassie discovered that several large donations are being spent in ways that the donors did not specify. For example, a donation for counseling is being spent for building repairs. A grant for training is being spent for salaries.

   When Cassie talked to Ms. Koehler, her supervisor, Ms. Koehler's reply was, "Forget it. The donors do not really care about how we spend their money. We have to meet our needs. We have to help our clients. If people found out about this, we could lose our donors and other funding. Our clients would suffer."

Adjusting to the Workplace

Goals

- Describe how to adjust to a workplace's corporate culture.
- Identify positive workplace etiquette behavior.
- Describe the areas of concern for ethics and values in the workplace.

Terms

- corporate culture, p. 311
- business casual, p. 312
- workplace etiquette, p. 314

Real Life Focus

In what type of workplace will you feel most comfortable? Why?

- Youthful?
- Conservative?
- Creative?
- Traditional?
- Team-oriented?
- Individual-oriented?

When you begin working, you have to understand the workplace environment and culture. Just as you learn different situations and rules when you start a new school year, you must learn different situations and rules when you begin working full-time. Every career and workplace has different characteristics.

Corporate Culture

To make sure you are successful in your workplace, you will need to learn the company culture of your new workplace, including its dress code.

You have characteristics that make you unique, that make you different from every other person. In the same way, each organization has qualities that make it different from every other organization. The values and customs that give each organization a unique personality is the organization's **corporate culture**.

The corporate culture of an organization defines its communication, rules of behavior, company ethics, and style of dress. Formal policies, unspoken rules, and expected behaviors create a company's corporate culture. As a new employee, you will need to learn the corporate culture of your workplace quickly—both the written and the unwritten customs.

Some ways to learn about a company's corporate culture are as follows:

- **Study how people interact with each other.** Do they appear serious and formal? Are they thoughtful about their work, but relaxed with each other? Do they speak to one another quietly and professionally?

■ *Ask questions.* Everyone has had a first day of work and probably had the same questions you have on your first day. Keep a written list of questions. When you have a break, ask coworkers several questions at a time to avoid interrupting them while they work. If necessary, ask follow-up questions until you understand the answers.

■ *Listen.* If someone offers a suggestion, take it seriously. You may think that the advice is not important, but be open to suggestions. Ask the speaker questions to make sure the advice you heard was accurate. Watch body language for hidden messages.

■ *Try to learn who has the power to make decisions.* The individuals with the most important titles may not be the actual decision makers. Assistants often are very powerful because they have access to the decision makers and may influence them.

As you learn the written policies and unwritten rules of the company, you will see where you and your job fit into the company's plans and structure. After working for a while, you will be able to choose whether you want to advance to a higher position. You may see that your current position is just a job that will not be your career. Discover what you must do to succeed.

Appropriate Dress

One part of a company's corporate culture is the way employees dress at work. Some companies have a written dress code. Many companies have employee uniforms. Some companies require their employees to dress formally. Other companies allow casual dress. Many companies have one day a week, usually Friday, when employees can wear casual dress. A Society of Human Resource Management poll states that 95 percent of U.S. companies have some type of casual dress day.

Employers may classify workplace dress as formal, business casual, or casual. Formal dress requires a shirt, jacket, and tie for men and a dress or a suit for women. **Business casual** clothing includes slacks with a belt, a collared shirt tucked in, and possibly a jacket or sweater. Women have the option of wearing a skirt or dress. For formal or business casual dress, athletic shoes are inappropriate. Work sites with a casual dress code have few rules for dress, though casual dress

Why is knowing your clients' dress code important?

Scott Cornell/Shutterstock.com

codes do not permit clothes that are too sloppy or show too much of your body. Dress for work, not for the weekend.

Alejandro's company has a casual dress code. He can wear jeans, a collared shirt, and running shoes for a typical workday. However, after arriving at work one day, he remembers that a client is visiting for an important meeting. Alejandro does not have enough time to return home and change clothes. He quickly looks in the mirror and thinks, "Oh, no! These clothes won't impress the customer."

The appropriate workplace clothes help your workplace success. Jeans and sneakers may be all right for Alejandro on a typical workday, but he should wear a jacket and possibly a tie the day he has an important meeting. A simple solution would have been for Alejandro to keep a change of more formal clothes at work.

The rules of hygiene and neatness apply to every workplace, no matter the particular dress code style of your workplace. Make sure you are well groomed and have clean hair and nails.

Different work situations require different forms of dress. For example, dress that is all right for your workplace may not be appropriate at a client's workplace. Remember the precautions discussed in Chapter 12 about dressing for the interview? The same advice pertains to a client's workplace. When attending a meeting at a client's workplace, you should investigate the client's dress code before the meeting so you can dress appropriately. You might ask the person who scheduled your appointment about the company's dress code. People may judge you by the way you dress and will remember anything inappropriate. You should dress for the situation.

Web Connections

Some web sites offer good advice about projecting a positive image at work. This helpful information includes workplace etiquette, appropriate dress, and workplace adjustment.

Access the Web Connections link for Chapter 13. Review some of the sites. Make a list of strategies and tips that will help you in the workplace and in school. What careers would use each item listed?

www.cengage.com/school/iyc

During the summer, Loren works for his Aunt Ana Paula, an attorney with a well-known tax law firm. Loren learns about legal processes and procedures. He attends court proceedings several times a summer.

Loren enjoys everything about his legal experiences except the workplace. He dislikes having to wear a jacket and tie to work every day. Also, he is uncomfortable with having to speak so quietly in the law offices.

Loren knows he cannot be happy working in such a formal workplace. Instead of working with tax law, he wants to do legal work for people with disabilities. Loren decides to research other legal careers where the workplace would fit his goals and lifestyle.

Science labs, blue-collar workplaces, food service, and outdoor sites often have stricter dress codes because of safety issues. They may require closed-toed or even steel-toed shoes, long pants, hair tied back, and no jewelry.

Because of the popularity of body art, company dress codes may have specific rules mentioning body art specifically. Some employers think that tattoos and body piercings are a distraction. Those employers believe that in the workplace, tattoos should be hidden and body piercings removed. That code is true often in the healthcare industry and sometimes in the food service industry. A company can enforce a dress code if it is in writing and does not discriminate between males and females.

Attendance

Every workplace has an attendance policy. It is necessary to keep the organization and work teams efficient and the customers happy. Sometimes as an employee, you will have to use a time clock or sign in and out to document your work hours.

The attendance policy has many uses. Of course, one is recordkeeping—to keep track of days off and shortened work days. Another reason is for safety. If there is a fire, weather incident, or other concern, the employer can account for those present.

Attendance also includes arriving to work on time. Being ready to work when the day begins may mean coming in a few minutes early to put on your uniform or work equipment. Time your day appropriately. Being at the workplace every day and on time indicates that you are part of the team.

Workplace Etiquette

Blaj Gabriel/Shutterstock.com

Each workplace has a unique corporate culture. However, many professional manners are common. These standards are called **workplace etiquette**. The work environment treats men and women equally. However, employees with higher positions in a company are usually treated more respectfully.

You can show professionalism on the job by:

■ Showing a positive attitude.

■ Showing up for work every day on time.

■ Being dependable, honest, and trustworthy.

■ Adopting good manners.

■ Doing what you say you will do.

■ Treating others with respect and courtesy.

■ Listening without interrupting.

■ Being energetic and enthusiastic.

■ Speaking clearly using good grammar.

■ Avoiding gossip.

You must use workplace etiquette not only in your actions, but also in your electronic communications, such as emails and IMs. Before sending a message or an email, read it twice. Ask yourself, "Would I say this in front of a customer?" Whatever you send on a company computer is the property of the company.

*Raquelle received an email joke about an ethnic group from her friend,
TJ. Using her work computer, Raquelle sent the joke to several people
in the office. One person reported the email to Raquelle's supervisor,
Ms. Studebaker. She called Raquelle into her office and warned her
about sending offensive material. She also cautioned Raquelle not to
spend company time on personal matters. A second offense will result in
Raquelle's email being monitored.*

Etiquette is especially important in today's diverse workplace. You work
with other people and must respect each other's differences. Put a smile in
your voice and display your social skills.

Consider

What are some of the effects of negative workplace behavior? How does
that behavior transfer to negative customer service?

Ethics and Values

Certain traits and skills will help you become an outstanding employee
in any employment situation. Many key work skills are the same as the
skills you need for success in school. In addition, having a positive attitude, accepting responsibility for your actions, communicating effectively,
and working competently in a team are necessary skills for a successful
career.

Attitude

Every employer expects you to come to work with a positive attitude and
to keep that attitude throughout the day. A good attitude increases your
energy and helps boost your coworkers' attitudes. Happy people feel
more energetic and confident. Their feelings of happiness make them like-
able and cooperative on the job. As a result, happy people are often more
successful at work.

On the other hand, a bad attitude acts like a virus. It spreads through
the workplace and affects others negatively. A poor attitude often turns
productive workers into negative, incompetent workers. Those workers
may start trouble and blame others for problems.

Employers expect you to prevent personal problems from interfering
with your work activities. However, they realize your private life will
not always be perfect. Sometimes you may want to be anywhere else
but at work. On those days, you need to control your negative mood.
While hiding sad or angry feelings may be difficult, you should do
your best to handle them privately. If you are overwhelmed by
personal problems, talk to your supervisor about taking time off to
work them out.

*When Kyler's mother woke him early Saturday morning for his
landscaping job, he knew that he should not have stayed out so late the
night before. Grumpy from the lack of sleep, he yelled at his mother.*

Kyler missed meeting the company truck that traveled to the day's jobs, so he was late for work. He had to drive himself, which cost him gas money. Because of his tardiness, Kyler missed the choice job of using the lawnmower. Instead, he was left running the weed trimmer and the leaf blower.

Kyler nicked Ms. Bowman's new sapling because he was thinking about how long the morning seemed. The cut was so deep that he had to replace the young tree. Not concentrating again, Kyler blew grass into the swimming pool. That mistake cost him a half hour to skim out the grass clippings. Plus, his supervisor would not let Kyler put the extra cleanup time on his timesheet. If Kyler had gotten more sleep and had gone to work with a better attitude, he would have enjoyed his job as much as he usually did.

Here are some things you can do to help you overcome a bad attitude:

- Smile—if you act as though you are in a good mood, you soon will be.

- Practice positive thinking.

- Change negative thoughts to positive ones. Instead of thinking that you cannot do something, think, "That will be tough, but I will do the best I can."

- Surround yourself with positive people as much as possible.

Attitude spills over into customer service. Anytime you work with the public, you need to keep a positive attitude. After all, according to the editor-in-chief of *Marie Claire* magazine, it takes the average customer three seconds to decide which item to buy.

Accepting Responsibility

Everyone makes mistakes. However, not everyone accepts responsibility for a mistake by saying, "I'm wrong" or "It was my fault." An employer or a teacher wants you to take the responsibility for any mistakes that you make and not shift the blame to someone or something else. Employers will expect you to be responsible for your mistakes and to correct them quickly and smoothly.

Being accountable and responsible does not involve just facing your mistakes. You also are responsible for keeping your supervisor informed of the progress of your work. You are responsible for the quality of your own work and for finishing it on time.

The average U.S. worker wastes over an hour every workday, according to *Business Insider*. How? They surf the Web, check email and Facebook, make phone calls, or talk to their coworkers. How do some employers solve the problem? They watch their employees more closely. They may be walking around the workplace and checking to see what is on employees' computer screens. Do not waste time. Be responsible and do your work.

If your supervisor or teacher criticizes your work, do not take the criticism as a personal attack. Receiving feedback is to your advantage. If your supervisor takes time to explain a situation to you, he or she is taking an interest in your growth on the job. Critical feedback allows you to learn from your mistakes. You can avoid making the same mistake again, and you will impress your supervisor with your positive attitude.

Accepting responsibility shows your honesty, willingness to learn, and concern for the needs of the business—all characteristics employers value and reward.

Technology

As mentioned previously, email can be a problem if an employee checks it constantly. Social media, especially Facebook, Twitter, and texting, can become even more of a problem than email.

"Hello—you've got a job to do." That is the primary reason employers dislike social media. Some workplaces now block Facebook and Twitter. If employees use their cell phone too much, especially with texting, some workplaces block cell use as well. For example, many libraries, hospitals, and some schools block Internet access except on computers provided on-site. In fact, over 54 percent of companies interviewed by Robert Half Technology banned employee access to social media sites unless the employee shows a legitimate work reason for using the sites.

Many workplaces now have technology policies, which often include use of Facebook and Twitter. Employees often must sign the policy when they are hired.

Electronic devices such as smart phones and MP3 players annoy both supervisors and coworkers. The use of MP3 players is more acceptable in creative industries, such as web and graphic design. They act as a do-not-disturb sign for the individual.

Employees often justify the use of electronic devices by saying that they are "multitasking." However, people are not multitasking as well as they think they are. You cannot acknowledge people while you are using an electronic device. Your mind cannot concentrate on two or more tasks as well as it can on one task at a time. The campaign for banning texting while driving is a major example. So is the ban of texting while on the job for many companies.

The negative side of social media worries many employers, as well as schools. Complaining about an employer, making inappropriate comments, or posting rude photos can cost you your job. Also, be careful about blogging about your job. Someone at work may see your blog. Even though you may think your blog is free speech, if the company thinks you have said something against its image, you may be fired. Especially dangerous to your job is blogging on a company computer. When negative comments become public on social media, the employer suffers. Keep your comments private.

Cyber-bullying through social media is a problem in many schools and some workplaces. Conflict resolution is a way for the "teaser" or "bully" and the victim to try to settle their differences. Work with an adult, such as a guidance counselor, as a mediator. Meet privately so both parties can talk in an effort to come to some kind of agreement. You may already be volunteering as a peer mediator to help students in your elementary school avoid bullying situations. If so, good work!

ACTIVITY 13.2

Your Company/Your School

Answer the following questions about your workplace. Then answer the same questions about your school. Your school is your workplace also.

1. Corporate culture

   a. What ten words would you use to describe your company/school?

   b. What is most important to your company/school?

2. Workplace etiquette

   a. What behaviors are rewarded in your company/school? Why?

   b. How common is gossip in your company/school? Who starts rumors?

   c. What are the rules for using electronic devices, such as an MP3 player and a cell phone, in your company/school? What are the rules for using the Internet and personal email?

3. Perceived barriers, actual barriers

   a. Who fits into the company/school culture, and who does not?

   b. Who is promoted or rewarded? Why?

buzbuzzer/iStockphoto.com

Growth in the Workplace

Goals

- Describe overcoming roadblocks to effective workplace communication.
- Identify ways for a good relationship with your supervisor.
- Explain the next steps for career success.

Terms

- actual barrier, p. 320
- perceived barrier, p. 321
- cross training, p. 323

Portfolio

Real Life Focus

Describe why each statement is not good school behavior.

1. If I stay up late, I can sleep in class.
2. If I am hungry, I should be able to eat in class.
3. The best time to go to the restroom is during class.
4. If someone is in my seat, I should demand that person move.
5. If I am having trouble with another student during class, I should immediately tell that person how I feel.
6. I should interrupt my teacher without raising my hand.
7. My family should be able to call me on my cell phone whenever they want during the school day.
8. Feeling lazy is a good excuse for not doing my homework.
9. The teacher should give me the supplies I need to do my classwork.
10. Texting is quiet, so it is okay to do it in class.

How would these questions apply to workplace expectations?

Workplace Communication

Good communication happens when everyone in a conversation or meeting ends up having the same knowledge.

Rosangela knew she had to change the design of the student section of the web page. She had some creative ideas she tested with students who use the web page frequently. Rosangela presented the ideas to Fiona, the web page editor. However, Fiona could not understand the concept behind Rosangela's design.

To help Fiona understand her ideas better, Rosangela created a sample opening page and several of the links. When Fiona saw the ideas on the screen, she understood Rosangela's design. What Rosangela could not communicate in words, she expressed using a visual model.

Communication is one of the most important reasons a business succeeds or fails. Employers, employees, and customers must communicate with each other. A breakdown in communication can be costly for everyone involved.

Effective Communication

When you communicate with supervisors and coworkers in the workplace, you want them to understand the meaning of your message. Otherwise, misunderstandings are likely to occur. The following guidelines will help you communicate effectively:

■ Plan what you want to say so you do not have to create it as you speak.

■ State why you are communicating so your listener or reader understands.

■ Use words the listener or reader understands.

■ Do not preach, ramble, or talk down to your listener or reader.

■ Keep your message clear and to the point.

Roadblocks to Career Growth

Regardless of your career goal, you may run into barriers that you will have to overcome. Barriers can slow your career growth. They also can prevent you from achieving career success. Being aware of barriers will help you find ways to avoid them.

How can you avoid barriers to your career?

Brand X Pictures/Jupiter Images

Dario was the strongest starting forward on the Eagles soccer team. The players expected him to be captain. However, Coach Breem chose James as co-captain. James, an outstanding goalie, had been on the team for only a year. He did not have the team history that a captain usually has. At a recent team meeting, some team members asked that Dario be the only team captain. The players said that they could not support a team that had an inexperienced captain. Some of the boys even wanted Coach Breem fired. How might the coach have avoided this barrier to success?

An **actual barrier** is an obstacle that prevents you from being allowed, or even hired, to perform a job. An example is a law enforcement officer not meeting the height requirement or a jockey not having enough riding experience. You have read information on hiring barriers in previous chapters. Actual barriers may also prevent you from achieving your career goals.

Jill was excited and honored. Abdul, the team captain, had asked her to be on Snyder Park's Quiz Bowl team. It was one of the best teams in the region, having gone to state the past two years.

The team knew that Jill was hearing-impaired and held a meeting with Abdul and the team adviser, Mrs. Gale. They thought that she would not be able to react quickly enough to quiz questions because she used an interpreter. Jill was hurt when she heard that they had asked that she be an assistant to Mrs. Gale, not a team member. When Jill discovered the team members' comments, she knew she had to find a way to overcome this barrier of prejudice.

Jill and her interpreter set up a rehearsal schedule. They practiced quiz questions daily with a buzzer for the week before team practice started. When the team began practice, Jill, with her interpreter, asked to be part of the first practice round. She ended up answering 75 percent of the questions first. Jill's team members apologized and invited Jill to join the team.

A **perceived barrier** is an obstacle that is not a true barrier, but is assumed, as with Jill's experience with the Quiz Bowl team. The barrier exists in people's minds—your mind, an employer's mind, or a customer's mind. Perceived barriers to career growth, such as age, experience level, gender, or cultural background, can slow your progress to career success.

Your Relationship with Your Supervisor

Developing a positive relationship with your supervisor is critical. Your supervisor is the one person who can recommend you for a promotion— or deny you one. Here are a few helpful tips for developing a good relationship with your supervisor.

Do:

■ Begin work on time.

■ Respect your supervisor's time. Organize your thoughts so you do not waste his or her time.

■ Be honest in your contact with your supervisor.

■ Finish projects. Be someone who is dependable as a team member.

■ Turn in accurate work.

■ Respect your supervisor's authority.

■ Have solutions in mind when you bring up a problem.

Do not:

■ Disturb your supervisor with problems you can resolve yourself.

■ Complain about your supervisor to others.

■ Bring personal problems to work.

■ Waste time.

■ Take every harsh reply or unfriendly action personally.

At some point during your working years, you may have a supervisor who is not supportive. Although the situation may not be your fault, you still are responsible for creating a positive working relationship with that person.

Anya is an LPN at a large hospital. Her supervisor, Mrs. Collins, a head nurse, is bad-tempered and critical. Anya has worked at the hospital for several months. She knows Mrs. Collins and tries to avoid her bad moods as much as possible. Anya has earned Mrs. Collins's respect by paying careful attention to the details of the job and staying after hours to complete her work. Although they are not friends, Anya manages the relationship well.

Today employers seem to expect more from their employees. At work, as well as at school, your workload may be increasing. Your supervisor and your teachers may be expecting more from you in less time. Sometimes, technology adds to the workload, rather than making it easier. The result is often an increase in stress. Be aware of stress in your life. If you react to stress with rude remarks, your job or school situation can suffer.

Real People / Real Careers

Ashley Niehoff / *Zookeeper / Primate Keeper*

Ashley Niehoff cannot remember a time when she did not love animals. She loved having animal stories read to her. She had so many stuffed animals that they took over the top bunk of her bed. But her favorite was a stuffed gorilla named Coco. And now gorillas, and other primates, have become the main subjects of Ashley's career. She works for the Cincinnati Zoo as a primate keeper.

Because her family kept nearly 100 animals—both farm animals and pets—Ashley had the encouragement to pursue her career. She chose a local college not only for its excellent biology program, but also because the college had a program that helped Ashley with her learning disability. Once Ashley interned at the Zoo her junior year, she continued working there while in school her senior year. The day after she received her bachelor's degree, she began working as a zookeeper.

Ashley's coworkers include lemurs, gorillas, and colobuses. Besides feeding and cleaning them, Ashley trains the lemurs and talks to the public. The zoo wants the animals to remain as wild as possible, so she teaches them natural behaviors as jumping, climbing, and watching for other animals.

And where does Ashley see herself 10 years from now? "Really, I see myself where I am now. I may be a little more involved with the zoo's training program. This is what I always wanted to do—work with exotic animals. It's a lot of hard physical work, but at least for the next decade, I'll be happy where I am."

For more information about:

* animal care and service workers

* veterinarian-related careers

Access **www.cengage.com/school/iyc** and click on the appropriate links in Chapter 13.

Source: *Personal Interview,* September 2011

Photo by Matthew C. Jordan

What's Next?

The person who knows *how* will always have a job. The person who knows *why* will always be his or her boss. As a good employee, you will begin with *how* and end with *why* as you grow in your career.

Teams—Again

You learned that managers of companies are placing more emphasis on teamwork. Teamwork is necessary in today's highly technical, fast-changing, global world. Many of the problems and challenges that companies face are too complex for one person to handle. Instead, employers combine workers' talent, experience, and creativity. Teams are effective in finding solutions to complex problems. The ability to work effectively on a team is an important skill that employers expect from their employees.

Daisy was the assistant editor of the school yearbook. As a member of the yearbook team, Daisy discovered she had effective team skills. She was able to organize and assign tasks easily with the right team members. The yearbook adviser commented several times that Daisy's yearbook team worked more smoothly than other teams had in recent years.

After college, Daisy's effective team skills helped her get a job with a well-known publishing company that used teams for most of its work. Daisy loves her job and enjoys bouncing ideas off her coworkers. The managers of the publishing company noticed her exceptional team skills and increased her work responsibilities and her pay. Daisy is on the path to a successful career.

Building an effective team sometimes can be difficult. For example, misunderstandings among team members can prevent group harmony. As a team member, you can help prevent confusion by asking questions and making sure all team members understand each detail of the project.

Because team members rely on each other, they should be cross-trained to know each other's job skills. **Cross training** allows each team member to learn multiple tasks. When one person is absent, the rest of the team members still can work effectively.

consider

What are some situations when you were a leader? What leadership skills did you use?

Leadership

Effective teams have an effective leader. Though leaders have different styles, most have common traits. Companies that have teams usually choose team leaders based on the following basic characteristics:

- *Ability to gain respect and trust.* Effective leaders inspire others to value and believe in them. They find ways to help team members feel good about themselves. These leaders recognize the contributions of others.

- **Dependability.** Effective leaders do what they say they will do. They take responsibility for their actions and decisions.

- **Ability to communicate effectively.** Effective leaders encourage all team members to participate in discussions and listen without prejudging. They keep members informed and give honest feedback.

- **Flexibility.** Effective leaders adapt to change and consider new ideas.

- **Good judgment.** Effective leaders gather and analyze appropriate information. They base their decision on the information they found. They identify and consider the consequences of risks. Leaders use their experience to make sound decisions in a timely manner.

- **Courage.** Effective leaders are willing to stand up for unpopular ideas. They resist pressure and manage stressful conflicts. Leaders are willing to take reasonable risks to reach team goals.

- **Honesty.** Effective leaders are truthful in their work with others.

Choices

Remember that the career choices you make do not lock you into a career track. A person will change careers an average of eight times between age 18 and 42. Failure can be a step in the right direction—the way you should have gone all along.

ACTIVITY 13.3

Learning from Others

The work habits you learn in school often will help you be successful on the job. Employers often have similar expectations, despite the difference in workplaces.

1. Interview a family member about his or her employer's expectations. What are the expectations at work concerning each of the following?
   - Attendance
   - Punctuality
   - Cooperation
   - Completing assignments
   - Respect for authority
   - Dependability
   - Honesty
   - Teamwork

2. What are your school's expectations for each of the above points?

3. What are the rewards for completing your school responsibilities?

4. How are work expectations and school expectations similar?

Compare your interview results and your answers with the class.

Chapter Summary

13.1 What Employers Want

- Identifying the skills employers want in their employees is critical for work success.

- The function of an effective team is to find solutions to specific problems using the problem-solving steps.

- Conflict resolution techniques can help settle disagreements and prevent them from interfering with working effectively.

13.2 Adjusting to the Workplace

- Knowing the corporate culture—the personality—of the workplace helps employees adjust within their career.

- Practicing workplace etiquette helps career success.

- Understanding workplace ethics and values is critical for adjusting to a workplace environment.

13.3 Growth in the Workplace

- Analyzing roadblocks, including actual and perceived barriers, can help career growth.

- One must develop a good relationship with his or her supervisor to prevent a roadblock to career success.

- Communicating effectively, working well as a team, and developing leadership skills will promote career growth.

Chapter Assessment

Vocabulary Builder

Match each statement with the term that best defines it.

1. Team members learn multiple tasks
2. Professional manners
3. Way to settle problems productively
4. Work with others to complete assignments
5. Ability to manage and control one's own work and feel satisfied
6. An obstacle that is not a true barrier, but is assumed
7. An obstacle that prevents one from being allowed to perform a job
8. Values and customs that give an organization a unique personality
9. A neutral person who helps resolve a disagreement
10. Skills and personal qualities needed to have a fulfilling career
11. Clothing that is not formal, but is not sloppy or weekend wear

a. actual barrier
b. business casual
c. collaborate
d. competencies
e. conflict resolution
f. corporate culture
g. cross training
h. empowerment
i. mediator
j. perceived barrier
k. workplace etiquette

Review What You Have Learned

12. Name two basic qualities all employees should have. Why are they important?
13. Why are teams so important in today's workplace?
14. What are the six steps of problem solving?
15. Why is conflict resolution important to a team?
16. Why is fitting into the corporate culture of a company so important?
17. What are some of the basic rules of workplace etiquette?
18. Describe two ways to overcome a negative attitude.
19. Why is clear communication necessary on the job?
20. What can one do to develop a good relationship with a supervisor?

Case Challenges

Each of the following cases presents a workplace situation. In each case, an employee's actions are questionable. Consider the following questions for each case:

- What is the problem with the employee's action?
- How should the employer resolve the problem?
- How do you think a good employee would act?

21. Keith seems to challenge Dustin at work every chance he gets. The situation is difficult because Keith and Dustin are the only cooks scheduled weekday evenings. Dustin knows he will start an argument eventually when Keith's behavior becomes too much.

22. When Arba picked up her dry cleaning, she noticed that the dress, which had been one piece, was now separated into two pieces. Arba took the dress back to the dry cleaner and told him she wanted the dress sewn back into one piece. The cleaner yelled at Arba in front of other customers, saying he was not at fault.

Make Academic Connections

23. LANGUAGE ARTS   Email is quick and often less formal than letters or memos. However, informality may be a disadvantage. People are sometimes less careful in sending emails with mistakes. Rewrite the following email.

> You haven't been in you're office, so I'll try an email instead.
>
> I have attached a copy of the employee compensation report for your review. There is some confidential information in the report, so dont share it with just anyone. The Human resources Department did a terrible job on it, but I think I was able to save the situation.
>
> I have proofread the report carfully, so you shouldn't find much wrong with it. Get it back to me by Tuesday, or I'll be after you!

24. MATH   More workplaces are using teams to accomplish workplace tasks. Form a team with several other students. Work together to calculate the average height of the team members in feet and inches.

Afterward, discuss what behaviors promote teamwork. Based on your team's behavior, how do you think your team would perform in a workplace?

Workplace Connection

25. Agree or disagree with the following statements.
- People should be able to talk on cell phones in restaurants.
- People should be able to talk on cell phones at school.
- People should be able to talk on cell phones in theaters.
- People should be able to talk on cell phones on airplanes in flight.
- Talking on a cell phone in the car is no more distracting than eating or tuning the radio.
- Cell phones should be used in cars only for emergencies.
- Cell phones can save lives.

In groups, create a list of guidelines for responsible cell phone use.

Blogging: My Personal Ethics

Your workplace behavior begins with your personal moral code or ethics. List and explain your personal ethics, including your feelings about bullying. Refer to sections in this chapter for your starting points.

Blog

Understanding the Workplace

Lesson 14.1 Employment Laws

Lesson 14.2 Employment Forms

Lesson 14.3 Employment Types and Employer Expectations

Rainer-Plendl/iStockphoto.com

What Do You Know

1. What types of discrimination might there be in the workplace?

2. Who should you contact if you are being discriminated against at work?

Ellen is a trainer for an educational consulting firm that provides professional development training for educational institutions, corporations, and nonprofit organizations. Ellen was recently laid off from her job. She was told that her firm was forced to eliminate positions to save money because of the poor economy. Ellen is 61 years old; however, she enjoys working and has no desire to retire. She is also single and cannot afford to retire at this time.

After being back in the job market for over six months, Ellen has had no luck finding a new job. She has interviewed for several positions, but has had no job offers. After her last interview, Ellen was very discouraged. She wasn't sure what to do or why her job search had been unsuccessful. She decided she was going to have to look for jobs outside the education and training field. She decided to talk with her friend Trinidad, a local business woman, to see if she might be able to provide any job leads.

Trinidad's husband works at the same educational training firm where Ellen used to work. He told Trinidad that another person had been hired to replace Ellen as a trainer. When Ellen told Trinidad she had been laid off so the firm could "save money," Trinidad said the rumor was that Ellen had decided to retire. Ellen learned that the person who had been hired to replace her was much younger and was being paid a much lower salary than she had received. Ellen was beginning to understand what had really happened—she had been laid off because she was older and making too much money. She started to wonder if her age may have been the reason she had not been offered other jobs recently.

Ellen knew there were laws against age discrimination and decided to contact an attorney. Ellen's attorney explained the laws to her. They are investigating the situation further to determine if age discrimination actually took place. If so, Ellen may have a good case for a lawsuit against her former employer.

Planning a Career in . . . Education and Training

Take your passion for learning and helping others and use it in a career in Education and Training, which is one of the 16 career clusters. If you enjoy working with people and helping others to learn and grow, you might enjoy a career in education and training.

This profession is in the professional and technical job category. Professions within this career cluster include teachers, college and university professors, school administrators, corporate training specialists, and private educational consultants.

Within this career cluster are a variety of certifications and degrees. To enter this profession will require a minimum of a four-year college degree. There may be some exceptions to this in the private sector and within technical colleges.

Employment Outlook

- Job opportunities for elementary school teachers are expected to grow about as fast as average.
- Job openings for all public teachers depend on the needs of the specific geographic area.

Career Possibilities

- Teacher
- School Administrator
- Corporate Trainer

Needed Skills

- Oral and written communication.
- Problem solving and critical thinking.
- Leadership and teamwork.
- Technology.

What's It Like to Work in Education and Training?

Education and Training can be a very rewarding field as you help students learn, grow, and become vital members of society. Public teachers sometimes deal with students who cause disruptions in class. However, there are many personal rewards to the profession.

The pay varies based on the person's education, state or region in the U.S., and years of experience. Teachers who are just starting off in the profession usually receive lower salaries compared to those who have years of experience.

Most teachers are paid to work approximately 35–40 hours per week. However, there are many duties outside the regular school day that greatly increase the number of hours worked on their own time. These include grading papers, planning classes, and attending school events.

Every day will be different since you are dealing with students and parents. No matter how much planning a teacher does, there is always something that can change the focus of the day. Since teachers deal with so many people, good communication skills and patience are necessary for this career.

What about You?

Do you like helping others to learn? Do you have good communication skills? Are you a critical thinker and problem solver? Do you have patience with others? If so, Education and Training may be the field for you.

AVAVA/Shutterstock.com

Employment Laws

Goals

- Describe basic labor standards.
- Explain different legislation for safe and fair working conditions.

Terms

- minimum wage, p. 332
- overtime, p. 332

Real Life Focus

Jeff is 15 years old and works 30 hours per week in a manufacturing plant in addition to going to school. He works nights and on weekends to get as many hours as he can. He gives some money to his mom for household bills, but is also saving for a car. His grades have slipped as he doesn't have much time to study.

The other day Jeff's boss, Harold, came to him and said there would be some safety people who worked for OSHA coming to the plant. Harold told Jeff to try and avoid the safety people so they could do their job. He also told Jeff that if they asked him how old he was that he should say he is 18 years old. He told Jeff that if he did not lie about his age, he would lose his job.

Is what Harold asked Jeff to do ethical? Investigate labor laws to determine how many hours Jeff should be working and whether or not he should be working in a manufacturing plant.

Basic Labor Standards

Employers must follow local, state, and federal laws that pertain to employment regulations. Being familiar with the laws yourself will help you be better prepared for the work world. For example, do you know at what age you can legally work and how many hours you can work? Do you know the minimum wage you can earn? Have you ever been paid for overtime? Do you know how that is calculated or how much overtime you can work? Do you know about the laws that pertain to working in a safe environment?

The information in this chapter will help you learn about employment laws that are the employers' legal responsibilities. Therefore, when you are employed, you will be able to determine if these laws are being enforced and feel confident asking questions if they are not being followed. These laws were passed to help employees. Many were passed decades ago. One such example is the Fair Labor Standards Act (FLSA).

The Fair Labor Standards Act

Prior to the FLSA, individual employers set their own wages for employees and developed their own rules for the work environment. Many employers paid very low wages to their employees. This was prevalent during the Great Depression, when many people were looking for employment. Due to the low pay, many employees could literally not afford basic needs such as food and shelter.

The most well-known case that impacted labor reform and demonstrates how little employers were paying their employees is the 1936 case of Joseph Tipaldo. He was a manager of a laundry in Brooklyn, New York and paid his female employees only $10.00 per week. This was in violation of the New York state wage law. The minimum wage law in New York at this time was $14.88 per week. Tipaldo was told to pay the employees $14.88 each week. However, he forced his employees to give him the difference ($4.88) back each week.

He was sent to jail for violating the law, but his lawyers took his case to the U.S. Supreme Court with the defense that this law was unconstitutional. The U.S. Supreme Court agreed, and voided the New York law. Tipaldo was free to continue his practices until federal law changed in 1938.

Employers also exploited children in the labor market. Since the mid-1800s, many children worked instead of going to school. Many of those jobs were dangerous. Employers would pay children less than adults because they could not do all of the jobs the adults did, but many children worked up to 16 hours per day and 6 days each week. These brutal working conditions resulted in many children being injured or killed.

As you can imagine, there were many situations besides the Tipaldo laundry case that affected adults and children involved in labor injustices. Therefore, the FLSA was signed into law in 1938. This was a landmark law for the United States' social and economic development. As with any law, there are specific guidelines on who must follow it. The FLSA applies to employers who do business in more than one state and who meet certain annual sales requirements. Practically all employers and businesses must follow the regulations set by the FLSA, although a few, including small farms, are not required. The federal agency that enforces the FLSA is the Department of Labor. The original version of the FLSA has changed over time with various amendments passed through the years. The FLSA now regulates three areas: (1) workers younger than 18 years of age; (2) wages and hours; and (3) equal pay. It is also important to know that all states have child labor standards and employers must follow those standards as well.

Lewis W. Hine/George Eastman House/Getty Images

Workers Younger Than 18 Years of Age One aspect of the FLSA is designed to protect working youth. An employer may hire a worker who is 18 years of age or older for any job. The FLSA does not limit the number of hours in a day or days in a week an employee may be scheduled to work, if the employee is 16 years old or older. Those who are 16 or 17 years of age may be hired for any nonhazardous job; however, some states have specific laws noting specific lengths of breaks or meal times that must be taken. If the employee will do job-related driving on public roads, he or she must be at least 17 years old and have no driving violations. There are some restrictions on those under the age of 16, including the number of hours they can work and which jobs they can and cannot do based on hazardous conditions.

The following are a few examples of hazardous jobs working youth under the age of 18 may never perform. Exceptions may be made if the person is in a type of apprenticeship position or working in an agricultural environment.

- Manufacturing or storing explosives
- Coal or other mining
- Meat packing or processing
- Wrecking and demolition
- Anything involving exposure to radioactive substances
- Anything involving power-driven equipment

If an employer hires a worker who is 14 or 15 years old, they may work outside school hours in certain occupations related to retail and food service, but some restrictions will apply. For example, these students may not work more than 3 hours on a school day, 18 hours in a school week, 8 hours on Saturday or Sunday, or 40 hours in a week when school is not in session. Work may not begin before 7:00 a.m. or end after 7:00 p.m. except during the summer months when 7:00 p.m. is extended to 9:00 p.m.

Wages and Hours Employees covered by the FLSA are entitled to the minimum wage and overtime pay of at least one and one-half times the normal rate of pay. **Minimum wage** is the lowest hourly wage an employer can pay in the United States. The minimum wage is changed periodically by Congress. **Overtime** is considered any time worked more than 40 hours of work in one seven-day workweek. Wage exceptions include circumstances related to workers with disabilities, full-time students, those under age 20 in their first 90 days of employment, and tipped employees. Employers are required to keep records on employees' wages and hours.

Equal Pay One amendment to the FLSA, the Equal Pay Act of 1963, forbids pay discrimination because of gender. Employers must pay equal wages to men and women who perform equal work. Pay rates may be different based on other things, such as seniority, skill level, or shifts.

Labor Unions

The unfair working conditions that existed in the United States before the 1930s caused workers in some occupations to form labor unions. The labor unions were established to improve workers' wages, benefits, and working conditions. Employees would join the labor unions and support their efforts by picketing and striking. Many employers resisted labor unions and fired workers who joined unions. Violence often broke out among employers, union members, and nonunion workers.

To clarify the rights and obligations of unions and employers, Congress passed the National Labor Relations Act (NLRA) in 1935. Because of the NLRA, the unions became strong. In response to union strength, in 1947 Congress passed the Taft-Hartley amendments, which added a "right-to-work" provision to the NLRA. Therefore, individual states could pass laws that prohibited a union and an employer from a union-shop contract. Under a union-shop contract, all qualified employees, whether they chose to join the union or not, were required to pay union dues as a condition of employment. Today about half of the states have passed right-to-work laws; the other states uphold the practice of union-shop contracts.

Employment Discrimination Laws

As you apply for jobs, you will see information about federal Equal Employment Opportunity (EEO) laws, which are enforced by the U.S. Equal Employment Opportunity Commission (EEOC). These are laws prohibiting job discrimination for various reasons. The Equal Pay Act is just one type of EEO law that prohibits employment discrimination. Others include the following.

- The Civil Rights Act of 1964 (Title VII) prohibits discrimination based on race, color, religion, gender, or national origin.

- The Age Discrimination in Employment Act of 1967 protects individuals who are 40 years of age or older.

- The Americans with Disability Act of 1992 (ADA) prohibits discrimination against qualified individuals with disabilities.

- Title II of the Genetic Information Nondiscrimination Act of 2008 (GINA) prohibits employment discrimination based on genetic information.

- The Civil Rights Act of 1991 provides monetary damages in the case of intentional employment discrimination.

Career FACT Today 22 states are "right-to-work" states that ban union-shop contracts: AL, AR, AZ, FL, GA, ID, IA, KS, LA, MS, NC, ND, NE, NV, OK, SC, SD, TN, TX, UT, VA, and WY. You may choose a job in a state in which you may be required to join a union.

Due to employment discrimination laws, employers must have a reason why they are not hiring a job applicant other than factors listed above, as long as it does not interfere with the applicant's ability to do the work.

Consider

How would employment in the U.S. be different if FLSA was not enforced? What if there was not an EEOC?

Safe and Fair Working Conditions

Congress has also enacted other laws to protect employees' health, safety and working conditions. Employers have developed company policies based on those laws and all employees are expected to follow such policies. Several such laws are discussed on the following pages.

Drug Free Workplace Act (DFWA)

Companies that contract business with the federal government for more than $25,000 are required by the Drug Free Workplace Act of 1988 to have policies on drug awareness. These companies must certify that they are maintaining a drug-free workplace. The law does not mandate or authorize drug testing. However, many companies have begun drug testing for employees due to the DFWA. Companies are required to implement the following:

- Publish a policy statement prohibiting unlawful manufacture, distribution, possession, or use of controlled substances in the workplace and specify the action that will be taken if a violation of the policy occurs.

- Provide a copy of the policy statement to each employee.

- Establish an ongoing drug-free awareness program to inform employees of drug abuse dangers.

Family and Medical Leave Act (FMLA)

This act provides all public agencies with 50 or more employees with regulations for unpaid leave. Qualified employees may receive up to 12 weeks of unpaid, job-protected leave per year. Most importantly, their group health benefits must be maintained during the leave time. The FMLA was designed to help employees balance family and work and, if need be, medical situations. It also promotes equal employment opportunities for men and women as they both deal with family matters. Leave may be taken for any of the following reasons:

- Birth and care of a newborn child of an employee.

- Placement of an adopted or foster care child to the employee.

- Care for an immediate family member (spouse, child, or parent) with a serious health condition.

- Medical leave in which the employee is unable to work due to a serious health condition.

Of course, stipulations apply. Employees are eligible for such leave if they have worked at least one year and have worked at least 1,250 hours during that time. In 2009, FMLA regulations were updated to implement new military family leave entitlements as well.

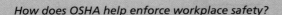

How does OSHA help enforce workplace safety?

lisafx/iStockphoto.com

Occupational Safety and Health Act (OSHA)

OSHA was established in 1970 to enforce health and safety standards in the workplace. OSHA's goal is to help employers and employees reduce on-the-job injuries, illnesses, and deaths. Manufacturers and other types of companies must follow strict standards for the safety and health of their employees. For example, certain construction site workers must wear hard hats and healthcare personnel must wear sterile, disposable gloves when handling blood. Following OSHA regulations is serious business. Companies are fined and employers can be jailed if they violate such regulations.

OSHA is serious about enforcing the laws to protect workers. One example is the 2001 case in which a federal appeals court upheld the 17-year prison sentence of an Idaho employer who had ordered an employee to clean out a storage tank filled with hydrogen cyanide gas. The employee suffered severe brain damage and will need extensive care for the rest of his life. This is just one example of an OSHA violation in which a worker was put at risk.

As OSHA strives to keep workers safe and healthy, companies can reduce workers' compensation insurance costs, medical costs, and other related costs the employer must bear. To do this, OSHA enforces that regulations are followed, assists with training programs, and cooperates with companies to make sure a safe and healthy environment is being provided to employees.

> During the summer months, Vanessa worked at her hometown library. She enjoyed the working environment as she could work independently shelving books, helping at the research desk, and various other tasks. The people she worked with were all very helpful and nice, but her supervisor, Jack Norman, told her she had to quit wearing sandals. It was a library policy and all employees must wear closed-toe shoes.
>
> Vanessa did not understand the policy and talked to her mom about the issue. She felt that Mr. Norman was being too rigid and she wanted to wear sandals. Her mom suggested that she ask Mr. Norman to explain why it was a policy. The next day Vanessa asked Mr. Norman to explain the policy.
>
> Mr. Norman explained that the library required employees to wear closed-toe shoes as a safety precaution. Carts filled with books were heavy, the carts have large wheels, and such carts could easily cause injuries to an unprotected foot. Even books themselves could be dangerous if they fell from high library shelves. This explanation helps Vanessa understand the policy, which she followed for the rest of the time she was employed at the library.

Whistleblower and Retaliation Protections

Sometimes employees witness wrongdoing on the job that endangers the health, safety, or lives of others. For example, managers may not follow safety codes, workers may dump hazardous waste unlawfully, or equipment may not be maintained and may pose danger to employees and those around them. However, many employees will feel hesitant to report these wrongdoings because they believe their employer will fire them or punish them in some way if they do so. This is why there are Whistleblower and Retaliation Protections.

OSHA administers the employee protection or whistleblower provisions. These provisions apply to several acts such as OSHA regulations, consumer product safety, corporate fraud, asbestos hazards, and many more. The whistleblower protections prohibit employers from firing or discriminating against employees who have expressed safety or quality assurance concerns to their employer. This provides a safe environment in which employees can choose to report possible violations. Deciding when to speak out and when to remain silent is a personal choice based on personal values, but employees have the opportunity if they so desire.

ACTIVITY 14.1

Investigating Employment Laws

Choose one employment law discussed in this lesson. Using the Internet, media center, or other resources, create a flyer advertising the law as if it were brand new.

Goodluz/Shutterstock.com

Employment Forms

Goals
- Describe different employment forms.
- Explain various withholdings from gross pay.

Terms
- Employment Eligibility Verification Form, p. 337
- W-4 Form, p. 339
- gross pay, p. 340
- net pay, p. 340
- Social Security, p. 341
- Medicare, p. 341
- fringe benefits, p. 341

Real Life Focus

Grayson worked hard in school and finished his associate's degree with a GPA of 3.5. He was excited that he just accepted his first full-time employment job at Capstone Heating and Air. The administrative assistant at Capstone told Grayson to go to the main location in the next town, complete the paperwork at the Human Resources (HR) office, and report to work by noon.

Grayson's car was in the shop and his friend, Curtis, dropped him off at the HR office and then left to run errands. Curtis told Grayson he would pick him up in 30 minutes. Grayson went up to the HR office and completed some paperwork. Then the HR employee told Grayson that she needed to make a copy of his driver's license and Social Security card. Unfortunately, Grayson did not have his Social Security card with him; therefore, he could not complete the HR process.

When Curtis came back to pick up Grayson, Grayson asked him to drive him home so he could get his Social Security card. But Curtis had to go to work and didn't have time to take Grayson back to HR. Curtis told Grayson he would just have to wait until tomorrow to go back to HR to complete the process.

What should Grayson do? Investigate necessary employment forms and what is needed to secure employment.

Employment Eligibility

Companies in the United States must lawfully pay you a wage. To do so, you must be registered with the federal government as a legal employee. This section will give you information about specific forms you must complete and identification you must have in order to be employed.

The first form your employer must complete is the Employment Eligibility Verification Form (Form I-9). The **Employment Eligibility Verification Form** verifies your legal ability to work in the United States. The Department of Homeland Security is a division of the U.S. Citizenship and Immigration Services. This division distributed the Form I-9. An example is provided on the next page (Illustration 14-1).

Illustration 14-1: Completed Employment Eligibility Verification Form

OMB No. 1615-0047; Expires 08/31/12

Department of Homeland Security
U.S. Citizenship and Immigration Services

**Form I-9, Employment
Eligibility Verification**

Read instructions carefully before completing this form. The instructions must be available during completion of this form.

ANTI-DISCRIMINATION NOTICE: It is illegal to discriminate against work-authorized individuals. Employers CANNOT specify which document(s) they will accept from an employee. The refusal to hire an individual because the documents have a future expiration date may also constitute illegal discrimination.

Section 1. Employee Information and Verification *(To be completed and signed by employee at the time employment begins.)*

Print Name: Last	First	Middle Initial	Maiden Name
Stendhal	Robert	R	NA

Address *(Street Name and Number)*	Apt. #	Date of Birth *(month/day/year)*
2700 Pierpoint Way	100	11/14/1997

City	State	Zip Code	Social Security #
Hamilton	Ohio	45011	555-00-5000

I am aware that federal law provides for imprisonment and/or fines for false statements or use of false documents in connection with the completion of this form.

I attest, under penalty of perjury, that I am (check one of the following):

[X] A citizen of the United States

[ ] A noncitizen national of the United States (see instructions)

[ ] A lawful permanent resident (Alien #) _____

[ ] An alien authorized to work (Alien # or Admission #) _____
until (expiration date, if applicable - *month/day/year*) _____

Employee's Signature *Robert J. Stendhal*	Date *(month/day/year)* 09/20/2013

Preparer and/or Translator Certification *(To be completed and signed if Section 1 is prepared by a person other than the employee.)* I attest, under penalty of perjury, that I have assisted in the completion of this form and that to the best of my knowledge the information is true and correct.

Preparer's/Translator's Signature	Print Name

Address *(Street Name and Number, City, State, Zip Code)*	Date *(month/day/year)*

Section 2. Employer Review and Verification *(To be completed and signed by employer. Examine one document from List A OR examine one document from List B and one from List C, as listed on the reverse of this form, and record the title, number, and expiration date, if any, of the document(s).)*

	List A	OR	List B	AND	List C
Document title:	_____		_____		_____
Issuing authority:	_____		_____		_____
Document #:	_____		_____		_____
Expiration Date *(if any)*:	_____		_____		
Document #:	_____				
Expiration Date *(if any)*:	_____				

CERTIFICATION: I attest, under penalty of perjury, that I have examined the document(s) presented by the above-named employee, that the above-listed document(s) appear to be genuine and to relate to the employee named, that the employee began employment on *(month/day/year)* _____ and that to the best of my knowledge the employee is authorized to work in the United States. (State employment agencies may omit the date the employee began employment.)

Signature of Employer or Authorized Representative	Print Name	Title

Business or Organization Name and Address *(Street Name and Number, City, State, Zip Code)*	Date *(month/day/year)*

Section 3. Updating and Reverification *(To be completed and signed by employer.)*

A. New Name *(if applicable)*	B. Date of Rehire *(month/day/year)* *(if applicable)*

C. If employee's previous grant of work authorization has expired, provide the information below for the document that establishes current employment authorization.

Document Title:	Document #:	Expiration Date *(if any)*:

I attest, under penalty of perjury, that to the best of my knowledge, this employee is authorized to work in the United States, and if the employee presented document(s), the document(s) I have examined appear to be genuine and to relate to the individual.

Signature of Employer or Authorized Representative	Date *(month/day/year)*

Form I-9 (Rev. 08/07/09) Y Page 4

Illustration 14-2: Completed W-4 Form

------------------------------ Cut here and give Form W-4 to your employer. Keep the top part for your records. ------------------------------

Form **W-4** Department of the Treasury Internal Revenue Service	**Employee's Withholding Allowance Certificate** ▶ Whether you are entitled to claim a certain number of allowances or exemption from withholding is subject to review by the IRS. Your employer may be required to send a copy of this form to the IRS.	OMB No. 1545-0074 20**11**

1 Type or print your first name and middle initial.	Last name	2 Your social security number
Robert R.	Stendhal	555-00-5000

Home address (number and street or rural route)	3 ☑ Single ☐ Married ☐ Married, but withhold at higher Single rate.
2700 Pierpoint Way #100	**Note.** If married, but legally separated, or spouse is a nonresident alien, check the "Single" box.
City or town, state, and ZIP code	4 If your last name differs from that shown on your social security card,
Hamilton, Ohio 45011	check here. You must call 1-800-772-1213 for a replacement card. ▶ ☐

5	Total number of allowances you are claiming (from line **H** above **or** from the applicable worksheet on page 2)	5	1
6	Additional amount, if any, you want withheld from each paycheck	6	$
7	I claim exemption from withholding for 2011, and I certify that I meet **both** of the following conditions for exemption.		

• Last year I had a right to a refund of **all** federal income tax withheld because I had **no** tax liability **and**
• This year I expect a refund of **all** federal income tax withheld because I expect to have **no** tax liability.
If you meet both conditions, write "Exempt" here . . . . ▶ | 7 |

Under penalties of perjury, I declare that I have examined this certificate and to the best of my knowledge and belief, it is true, correct, and complete.

Employee's signature
(This form is not valid unless you sign it.) ▶ *Robert J. Stendhal*   **Date** ▶ *09/20/2013*

8 Employer's name and address (Employer: Complete lines 8 and 10 only if sending to the IRS.)	9 Office code (optional)	10 Employer identification number (EIN)

For Privacy Act and Paperwork Reduction Act Notice, see page 2.   Cat. No. 10220Q   Form **W-4** (2011)

When the I-9 Form is completed, your employer will ask for one or more pieces of photo identification. You may use your driver's license or passport for identification. To follow the law and provide proof that you are who you say you are, employers may make a copy of your photo identification and keep it on file.

A form you will need to complete when you accept a position with a company is the W-4 Form. The **W-4 Form** is your way of telling your employer how much money to withhold from your paycheck for federal income tax. U.S. tax law allows you to claim at least one "personal allowance." This personal allowance keeps a certain amount of your income from being taxed. Therefore, your employer will subtract the amount of income protected by your personal allowance from your paycheck before figuring the amount to withhold. There will be various amounts withheld from your paycheck due to federal and state taxes.

Before you complete the W-4 Form, you will be provided with a Personal Allowance Worksheet to help you determine the number of personal allowances you may claim. It is always good to keep a copy of your W-4 Form in a safe place.

Employers are also required to keep a copy of your Social Security card. A Social Security card is necessary not only to get a job, but also to collect Social Security benefits and other government services. Your parents probably applied to get your Social Security number when you were born. If you do not have a Social Security number, take your birth certificate to the Social Security office in your area and apply for your card.

Consider

What does the Form I-9 tell your employer? What does the W-4 Form tell your employer?

Withholdings

As mentioned in the previous section, various amounts will be withheld from your salary due to federal and state laws. Money may also be withheld from your salary to help you purchase health insurance or save for retirement. Once you begin your job, you will be paid a specific rate. The pay rate may be paid based on an hourly, monthly, or yearly salary. Payroll periods will be determined by the company. Payroll periods may be once per week, twice per month, or once per month.

Know that the total amount you make will not be paid to you because part of what you earn goes to taxes. For example, if you make $10.00 per hour and you work 10 hours per week, you will not bring home $100.00 at the end of the week. By law, taxes are withheld from your **gross pay**, the amount you earn based on your pay rate. You may also authorize an employer to withhold other amounts to pay for various programs. The amount you bring home after all withholdings is your **net pay**.

It is your employer's responsibility to send the withheld tax money to the appropriate federal, state, and local governments. The money you pay in taxes is used to pay for services that benefit the entire population, such as court systems, highways, parks, schools, sanitation services, police and fire protection, emergency medical services, and more. The total of all of your taxes is often one-fourth or more of your yearly income. When you receive your paycheck stub, your gross pay will be listed along with all of your withholdings and your net pay. If you do not understand any withholdings, ask your employer immediately.

Federal taxes that are typically withheld from your gross pay include income tax and Social Security tax. The amount of the withholdings depends on your gross income. These two types of taxes, along with other common withholdings, are explained below.

Income Tax The Internal Revenue Service (IRS) requires all employees to submit a completed tax form by April 15 each year. The IRS is a division of the U. S. Department of Treasury, which collects federal income taxes and enforces federal tax laws. Those who are self-employed and others who may be exempt from tax withholding from their earnings for other reasons pay an estimated tax to the IRS each quarter, four times per year.

If not enough taxes were withheld or paid and you owe more taxes, you must send the IRS the additional amount you owe with your tax return. If too much was withheld or paid, the IRS will send you a refund after you file your taxes. If you do not want to owe money each year, you can adjust your choices on your W-4 form. The IRS prefers your withholding to be close to the amount of tax you owe. However, due to varying income and personal circumstances, this may not be possible every year.

Web Connections

Many web sites can help you understand the types of withholdings that can be deducted from your gross pay. Click on the Web Connections link for Chapter 14. Search at least two of the sites listed. As you are reviewing sites, write down brief descriptions of three to five deductions that you are not familiar with. Share your results with the class.

www.cengage.com/school/iyc

Social Security Tax The Social Security Act is a federal social insurance program that is also referred to as the Federal Insurance Contributions Act (FICA). The Social Security tax withheld from your paycheck may be labeled FICA. **Social Security** provides income and health benefits for retirees, for underage survivors of employees who contributed to Social Security, and for employees who are disabled and cannot work. The funds for these people come from taxes paid on employees' wages. Both the employer and the employee contribute to pay a Social Security tax, which varies based on your salary and whether you are employed by a company or self-employed.

The typical contribution for both the employee and employer is 7.65 percent; however, by law numbers change each year to keep the program up to date with price and wage levels. For example, in 2011 the law reduced the employee's share of the Social Security payroll tax by 2 percent. You may see the Social Security payroll tax withholding separated into Social Security and Medicare. **Medicare** is the health benefits part of Social Security.

There are exceptions to employees having Social Security tax withheld from their paychecks. Government and school employees often do not pay Social Security tax because they have their own programs that provide similar benefits. Those who are self-employed may pay more than 15 percent self-employment tax.

State and Local Withholdings State and local governments may also have tax regulations that will result in additional withholdings from your paycheck. For example, if you live in a state or community with state or local income tax, additional taxes will be withheld from your paycheck. Those who live in large cities typically pay more taxes than residents in small towns. This is because large cities incur higher costs for the services they provide.

Additional Withholdings You may choose to have additional money withheld from your paycheck for a variety of purposes. For example, you may have the opportunity to purchase health insurance or deposit money into a retirement account. Other withholdings include fringe benefits, work-related deductions, and garnishments.

Fringe benefits are forms of compensation provided to you by your employer other than wages. Fringe benefits may include health insurance through the employers' group health insurance plan, life insurance, and pension plans. You may be required to pay a portion of the cost of the fringe benefits by having funds withheld from your paycheck. However, the cost of these benefits will be less than if you had to pay for them on your own.

Work-related deductions include union shop dues and payments to other organizations such as a health club. Another common work-related deduction is the cost of cleaning uniforms required for the job. Employers will provide the uniforms, but the cost of professional maintenance may be your responsibility.

Federal and state laws also uphold wage garnishment. Earnings may be garnished to protect the rights of your creditors, the people to whom you owe money. Employers are required to withhold the earnings of employees for the payment of a debt as directed by the court. However, the Consumer Credit Protection Act (CCPA) also prohibits employers from firing employees whose wages are being garnished. Employees are also protected as to the maximum amount of earnings that may be garnished. Wage garnishment may also be required by a court for child support, bankruptcy, or federal or state tax payments.

ACTIVITY 14.2

Leadership

Calculating Net Pay

Work in teams to calculate the net pay for the following people. Within the team, determine who would bring home the most net pay in one week.

- Ethan is a salaried employee who makes $40,000 per year. He is paid twice per month and is paid year round. Seventeen percent of his salary is withheld for federal taxes, 4% is withheld for state taxes, and an additional 15% is withheld for fringe benefits. What is Ethan's net pay each pay period?

- Galena is an hourly employee who makes $18.50 per hour. She works 40 hours per week, is paid weekly, and is paid only for the weeks she works. She works 48 weeks per year. Fifteen percent of her salary is withheld for federal taxes, 4% is withheld for state taxes, and an additional 10% is withheld for fringe benefits. What is Galena's weekly net pay?

Portfolio

mrloz/iStockphoto.com

Employment Types and Employer Expectations

Goals

- Discuss types of employment.
- Explain various employer expectations.
- Explain components of performance evaluations.
- Describe how to resign from a job.

Terms

- hourly employees, p. 343
- salaried employees, p. 343
- independent contractor/ freelance workers, p. 343
- ethics, p. 345
- discretion, p. 346
- performance evaluation, p. 347

Real Life Focus

Leona is new in her supervisory role. She must do an annual performance evaluation on each of her four subordinates. She knows that she wants to assess whether they have been on time to work and their absences. She also knows it is important to determine whether they do their work or goof off too much.

She tries to recall what was on her employee performance evaluations at previous jobs, but cannot remember all of the components.

What are other things Leona should think about evaluating? How can she find out what she should be evaluating?

Types of Employment

Hourly employees are paid a set wage for each hour worked. Most hourly jobs are based on a 40-hour week, which means if you work more than 40 hours per week, you would be eligible for overtime pay. If you miss work, your pay will usually be reduced by the number of hours missed. Two exceptions are sick days and vacation days. Your employer may pay for a specific amount of time off when you are sick and may provide paid vacation days as well. The number of paid vacation days you will receive is usually based on the time you have worked for the company and the length of your regular workweek.

Salaried employees are paid a set annual salary. That annual salary is divided into pay periods, such as monthly or weekly. The work week will usually be 37 ½ to 40 hours per week. However, with salaried positions there is usually no overtime pay for additional hours worked. Salaried employees in supervisory or management positions understand that it is their responsibility to get the job done—even if doing so exceeds the 37 ½- to 40-hour work week. As a salaried employee, you will have a certain amount of paid time off for illness and will have paid vacation time. The length of your paid vacation is usually determined by how long you have worked for the company.

Independent contractors/freelance workers are in business for themselves. They are not considered employees of any specific company or organization. Instead, the business that hires them is their client. Independent contractors may have several clients and may be working on several jobs simultaneously. Because clients do not provide employee benefits such as insurance, pensions, or paid vacations, using independent contractors saves the client money. Independent contractors are responsible for providing these benefits for themselves, which adds to the cost of running their business. An independent contractor is also responsible for paying his or her state and federal income taxes on a quarterly basis.

In general, independent contractors make their own decisions about how, where, when, and by whom the contracted work will be done. Clients, however, have the right to say when the work must be completed and to set the quality level of the finished work, provided that quality level meets the minimum requirements of the state and local government building codes and regulations. In addition, independent contractors usually provide their

Real People / Real Careers

Kim Freeman / Social Studies Teacher

Kim Freeman started a trend in her family. She was the first one to earn her bachelor's degree. Her family encouraged her to go to college and choose a degree that interested her.

Because her family believed that a degree in business would benefit Kim, her college major was Marketing. Combining her love of people with human relations, she enjoyed doing marketing research to understand why consumers liked certain products but hated others. In addition, Kim took courses such as sociology and psychology, which focused on human relations and how to understand the human mind. She also enrolled in as many history courses as her schedule permitted—from Black Studies and Women's Studies to European, Asian, and African History.

Rather than directly using her marketing degree, Kim became a youth leader for several religious organizations, as well as a business partner with Junior Achievement. As she explains, "Those positive experiences were the gateway that led me to a career in education. Social studies encompasses a wide range of topics that relate historical events to events that impact our society and individual lives on a daily basis."

Why did Kim choose teaching high school students, particularly career and technical students? She offers reasons for her choice: "During my senior year in high school, I was enrolled in a career and technical program that offered me the opportunity to work in a government agency one semester. I realized that college is not for everyone. Career and technical education provides students with options that they may not have if they stay in a traditional high school setting. And high school students are great! They have formed opinions about very important issues in life. The students can be challenged to think critically and defend their positions. The overall goal is to be accepting and appreciate others with diverse beliefs and experiences."

For more information about:

* teaching careers

* careers in education and training

Access **www.cengage.com/school/iyc** and click on the appropriate links in Chapter 14.

Source: *Personal Interview*, September 2011

own tools and equipment. Hourly or salaried employees know how much money they are going to make during any particular pay period, but this is not true for independent contractors. Independent contractors may make a profit on a job, or they may lose money—there are no guarantees.

Employer Expectations

Fulfilling your employer's expectations will help you advance along your *P*A*T*H to Success*. Your employer will expect you to perform your job tasks skillfully, to have a positive attitude, to communicate effectively, and to cooperate with your coworkers. Meeting employer expectations requires you to provide good customer service, act ethically and use discretion, and overall do a good job for your employer. Part of doing a good job means using employer resources properly and responsibly, avoiding excessive absences, and being at work on time. Good communication skills are also expected of every employee. Employers will evaluate how well you perform your job and how well you satisfy their expectations and needs. Finally, your employers will expect you to follow traditional standards if you decide to resign your position.

Customer Service

Possibly the most important component of a successful business is customer service. Customer service simply means doing the best job possible for the customer, treating that customer with respect, and doing everything you can to make the customer happy. Without good customer service, the business will not survive. Regardless of which company you work for, if you have any dealings with customers, your employer will expect you to follow the old adage "The customer is always right." These customers, who may also be referred to as clients, patients, or patrons, are the reason your job and your company exist. If customers are dissatisfied with your service or product, they will not be your customers very long. However, if you provide service that exceeds a customer's expectations, the customer will not only remain loyal to your company, but may possibly recommend your company to others, which in turn will help your company to grow.

Ethical Behavior and Discretion

Ethics is defined as rules of behavior based on ideas about what is morally good and bad. Most professions have a written code of ethics that all members of that profession are expected to follow. For example, the American Medical Association has a code of ethics that binds all of its physician members. In addition, many employers will have a code of ethics that all employees are expected to follow. This code of ethics may or may not be in written form. Make certain you understand and follow the code of ethics for your profession as well as your employer's ethical code.

How does a written code of ethics benefit an employer? How does it benefit employees?

auremar/Shutterstock.com

When you think about ethics, what does this mean? It may be as simple as understanding that you don't steal from your employer—or from anyone else, for that matter. However, being ethical at work may be more complicated.

What about using your work email as your personal email account? Would you consider this ethical? Before you answer, think about who pays for the email service. You're right—the employer does. So, since it is unethical to use company resources for personal reasons, it would be unethical to use your company email as your personal email. Some employers have definite rules about using email for anything other than work-related communication.

> Alice and Lamar are taking computer applications from Mr. Matthews. Yesterday's lesson pertained to the ethical use of computers in the workplace. This topic was discussed at great length and the students enjoyed learning about using the computer for work-related projects and internal communication. They began to understand how using a computer for personal purposes at work is detrimental to the workplace as it wastes work time, reflects poorly on the employer, and costs the employer money.
>
> The discussion led to learning more about company policies and how to help employees make better decisions when thinking about using the computer for personal purposes. Mr. Matthews asked the class to take the word ETHICS and write a statement about the ethical use of computers in the workplace for each letter. Alice and Lamar developed the following:
>
> **E**xamine your options.
> **T**hink about the alternatives.
> **H**old back if your action could embarrass you or get you in trouble.
> **I**nvestigate the company policy carefully and know the consequences for breaking the policy regulations.
> **C**heck your conscience.
> **S**eek advice if you are unsure.

Discretion is defined as the quality of having or showing good judgment and the ability to make responsible decisions. Most employers consider their employees to be representatives of the company or organization even when they are not at work. This means that what you do on your own time may reflect positively or negatively on your employer. For example, information about your company's customers and your fellow employees should not be discussed because it is confidential. Discussing customer information with others could possibly cause your company to lose that person as a customer and thus lose the company money. Breaking this confidence could cause you to lose your job.

Some companies require employees to sign a confidentiality, or non-disclosure, agreement. By signing this document, you agree to keep everything you do and everything you learn at the company a secret— even after you no longer work for that employer. You could face legal consequences if you break this agreement.

Good Attendance

As discussed in Chapter 13, whether you work for a small or large company, good attendance is extremely important. Your employer will expect you to avoid excessive absences, avoid being tardy, and not leave work early. If you're not at work when you should be, who would do your job? Employee absences cost the employer money. Therefore, employees with a history of excessive absences and tardies may be fired. Do not let this happen to you! Be responsible and report to work on a timely basis.

Communication Skills

Communication skills are those skills, both written and oral, that allow individuals to convey information to one another. Good communication skills provide for better understanding between two or more people. Employers expect their employees to communicate well with one another, with customers, and with managers. Good communication within an organization results in high productivity, which in turn leads to overall growth and success for the organization itself.

Consider

The text explained how using company email might be considered an ethical issue. What are some other behaviors that might be considered unethical on the job?

Performance Evaluation

Almost every employer conducts periodic performance evaluations of employees. A **performance evaluation** assesses how well an employee is meeting an employer's expectations. Some of the criteria an employer might use for evaluating an employee's performance on the job include (1) overall job skills, (2) attitude, and (3) work habits. The employer is looking generally at whether or not you are meeting his or her expectations as an employee. A performance evaluation provides you with feedback about work areas in which you are especially strong, as well as those areas where you need to improve.

The evaluation process may vary depending on the size of the company. In a small business, the evaluation is usually informal. This evaluation may be written or verbal. It may also be done at any time. In a large company, the evaluation will probably be more formal and will almost always include a written evaluation form. It will also probably involve a face-to-face meeting with your supervisor.

Responding positively to your performance evaluation, even if it is a poor evaluation, is an important component of job success. Learn to see these evaluations as opportunities to improve and to advance your career rather than as a personal attack by your supervisor. Accepting responsibility for your actions and your inactions is a sign of maturity and growth. If the evaluation is negative, accept responsibility for those things that are your fault and ask for suggestions on how you might improve.

If you believe the negative evaluation is not fair, ask for an explanation of how the employer came to these conclusions about your work. Just remember to keep your responses positive and professional.

Courteous Resignation

Resigning from a current job carries with it certain generally accepted rules. Always remember that you may want your current employer to serve as a reference for you in the future. For this reason, always do your very best to do a good job while you are employed and always leave the current job in good standing. One way of doing this is by giving the employer plenty of notice that you will be leaving. Most employers expect at least a two-week notice. This gives the employer time to find and hire someone to take your place or make other arrangements. Not giving proper notice will damage your reputation as an employee and may possibly endanger your ability to gain future employment. Your resignation should be in writing. The letter of resignation should be short and positive and should include the date you will be leaving.

ACTIVITY 14.3

Leadership

Learn from Others

Search the newspaper, library, Internet and other sources for ten job advertisements. Write down employer expectations and type of employment. Employer expectations may include communication skills, working at night, etc. Type of employment may include any discussed in this chapter or others. As a class, write the employer expectations on the board and keep a tally of those that occur most often. Then ask family members, friends' parents, or other employed adults if these are expectations of their employers. Also ask if there are additional employer expectations where they work. Ask how you can improve overall so that when employed you can be prepared to meet your employer's expectations. Share your results with the class.

Blend Images/Jupiter Images

Chapter Summary

14.1 Employment Laws

- Employers must follow local, state, and federal laws that pertain to employment regulations. Employees should become familiar with various laws such as the FLSA, Equal Pay Act, Equal Employment Act, and the National Labor Relations Act to better understand their rights.

- Several laws have been enacted to protect employee's health, safety, and working conditions. Examples include the DFWA, Family and Medical Leave Act, OSHA, and Whistleblower and Retaliation Protections.

14.2 Employment Forms

- Certain forms must be completed by employees so they may be eligible for employment and have appropriate taxes withheld from their pay. These forms include the Form I-9 and W-4 Form.

- Various withholdings will be deducted from an employee's gross pay to calculate net pay. Withholdings may include federal, state, and local taxes as well as fringe benefits, work-related deductions, and garnishments.

14.3 Employment Types and Employer Expectations

- There are different types of employees. These include hourly, salaried, and independent contractors/freelance workers. There are advantages and disadvantages to each type of employee.

- Employers have certain expectations of all employees. Some of these expectations include employees providing courteous customer service, following all of the company's ethical codes, and using discretion and good judgment.

- All employees receive periodic performance evaluations. Some evaluations are written and some are not. An employee's reaction to the performance evaluation can greatly impact that employee's future. A positive reaction will usually result in positive results. By contrast, a negative response can damage the employee's future opportunities with the company or even result in dismissal.

- Employees are expected to follow certain generally accepted rules when they resign from a job. Failing to do so may damage the employee's reputation.

Chapter Assessment

Vocabulary Builder

Match each statement with the term that best defines it.

a. discretion

b. Employment Eligibility Verification Form

c. ethics

d. fringe benefits

e. gross pay

f. hourly employees

g. independent contractor/freelance worker

h. Medicare

i. minimum wage

j. net pay

k. overtime

l. performance evaluation

m. salaried employees

n. Social Security

o. W-4 Form

1. Provides income and health benefits for retirees and disabled employees who cannot work

2. The lowest hourly wage an employer can legally pay

3. The amount of pay you bring home

4. The quality of having or showing good judgment and making responsible decisions

5. Used to tell your employer how much money to withhold from your paycheck for federal income tax

6. Any time worked more than 40 hours per week in one seven-day workweek

7. Employees who are paid a set wage for each hour worked

8. The amount you earn based on your pay rate

9. The health benefits part of Social Security

10. Rules of behavior based on ideas about what is morally good and bad

11. Those who are in business for themselves

12. Forms of compensation provided to you by your employer other than wages

13. Employees who are paid with a set annual salary

14. Verifies your legal ability to work in the United States

15. Assesses how well an employee is meeting an employer's expectations

Review What You Have Learned

16. Why are there local, state, and federal laws that pertain to employment regulations?

17. Why are there laws pertaining to safe and fair working conditions?

18. Describe the forms employees must complete during the hiring process.

19. Why are there so many different kinds of withholdings that may be deducted from your paycheck?

20. Describe the differences between hourly employees, salaried employees, and independent contractors/freelance workers.

21. What do employers expect from their employees?

Case Challenges

After reading both case studies, analyze each situation. Determine if the people are being ethical. Explain the ethical issues involved. What would you do if you were the employee?

22. Scotty is an employee of Jackson Electric and was injured last month on the job. He was working to help establish electricity to customers who had lost their power after a tornado. A tree fell close to the area he was working and hit a power pole; Scotty received a high voltage electrical charge. He has currently lost the use of one arm, but with rehabilitation he should regain its full use. He cannot do his job at this time and is on disability. His employer has told Scotty that if he does not recuperate within one month, she will be forced to fire him.

23. Anessa has worked for the Ostering Processing Center for seven years. There have never been any problems with drug use at this employer; however, the employer has required drug testing for employees each month. Anessa never had a problem with the testing, but other employees do think it is against their constitutional rights to be tested for drug use each month. A new manager was hired six months ago and Anessa was told by other employees that this manager is not requiring the drug testing. However, the new manager is turning in false paperwork indicating that she is following the drug testing rules.

Make Academic Connections

24. MATH   Interview three people who will share with you their pay stubs so that you can see their gross pay, withholdings, and net pay. Calculate the percentage of withholdings for federal taxes, state taxes, and fringe benefits separately. Be prepared to share your percentages with the class.

25. BUSINESS   Visit a temporary staffing agency and ask questions about their employee performance evaluations. What are the components of the evaluation? How often are employees evaluated? What are the implications of a negative evaluation? Write a summary of your findings. Be prepared to share your findings with the class.

Workplace Connection

26. Review the employment laws discussed in this chapter. If you could draft new employment legislation that could become law, what new employment law would you write? If you cannot think of a new employment law, what would you change about existing employment laws? Why are these changes or new law necessary? What could you do to get others interested in these changes or the new law? Be prepared to share your changes or new law with the class.

Portfolio

27. Assume you are now in charge of doing job performance evaluations for employees at your company. Create a job performance criteria worksheet. Be realistic and include all pertinent components to be assessed.

Blogging: Employer Expectations

As you continue to blog or journal, consider the employer expectations discussed in this book and through the various activities. Reflect upon one employer expectation you believe is most important. Discuss why it is important and how it impacts the workplace. Access www.cengage.com/school/iyc and click on the appropriate links for Chapter 14.

juan carlos tinjaca/Shutterstock.com

Capstone Project: Part 5

You have reached the final part of the Capstone Project. You will give a presentation using your research paper from Part 3 and your visual from Part 4. Your teacher will give you the specific guidelines for your presentation, as well as the grading criteria.

You should organize your presentation by including:

1. Introduction

2. Research highlights

3. Primary sources

4. Understanding of the topic

5. Visual

6. Conclusion/Results

Here are some tips for your presentation:

- Remember that your audience is your family and your class.
- Speak naturally at a medium pace. Use your visual's information as a focus instead of reading the words or narrating the video's action.
- Project your voice, speaking clearly and distinctly.
- Repeat critical information. Use natural gestures for emphasis.
- If you use slides, pause briefly after each one to give the audience time to understand each slide's information. If you use a video, you may wish to pause within the film.
- Make eye contact with the audience as much as possible.
- Avoid reading your notes. Use them as points to keep you on track.

Prior to the formal presentation, you will perform a practice presentation for a group of your classmates.

The steps in the presentation process are:

_____ *Finalize Presentation*

_____ *Finalize Visual*

_____ *Peer Review*

_____ *Edit*

_____ *Presentation*

_____ *Bring saved paper and visual on a flash drive to your teacher*

Good luck!

Glossary

401(k) retirement savings investment with deferred taxes until the money is withdrawn later

529 plan an educational investment account designed to help you prepay tuition or save for education

A

accreditation measurement process to ensure schools have basic quality

Action Plan a list of steps to a goal

actual barrier an obstacle that prevents one from being allowed to perform a job

adult workforce development post-secondary career and technical education programs

advanced placement studying college-level material in high school

apprenticeship learning a trade while working as a skilled employee

apps software shortcuts to assist with business or entertainment

articulation agreements contracts between a high school and a college for coursework completed

assessment way of collecting and evaluating data for measurement purposes

associate degree a degree usually completed in two or more fulltime years

attitude refers to the way you feel about something

B

bachelor's degree college or university degree that takes an average of six years to complete

backup plan an alternative plan

behavioral interview an interview designed to determine how the applicant has behaved in situations in the past

blog an online journal written for others to read and regularly updated

blue-collar career a type of career that usually has manual labor and an hourly wage

body language mannerisms, gestures, and facial expressions

budget a spending and saving plan

Bureau of Labor Statistics the U.S. Department of Labor agency that compiles career information statistics

business casual clothing that is not formal, but is not sloppy or weekend wear

C

campus culture characteristics that give each school or training program its unique personality

career a long-term work history in a particular field

career and technical high school specialized career training in high school

career cluster a group of all of the possible careers in an entire subject area

career day an event that allows you to talk with many businesses at one time

career fair an organized time that allows you to listen to and interact with people in careers that interest you

career maturity using one's career path to make an informed career decision

career plan the schedule for the career journey

Career Portfolio collection place for documents that help with career decisions

career preparation education and training options

career preparation provider any program, school, or business that offers education/training

career satisfaction the pleasure that comes from working in a career that allows one to use his or her passions

CareerBuilder an employment web site that lists new jobs daily and provides email alerts

certificate document that is proof of completion of necessary career skills

certificate of deposit short- or long-term, interest-bearing investments offered by banking institutions

check a written order to the bank to take money from your account to pay a person or business

checkbook register space to track your checking account deposits and withdrawals

checking account a service provided by banking institutions to allow you to deposit and withdraw money

chronological resume a resume that presents your information by date in reverse order

collaborate work with others to complete assignments

college prep courses high school courses that help with post-secondary education

combination resume   a resume that combines functional and chronological formats

Common Application   college submission web site used by hundreds of colleges

communication style   how one says or writes something, when one says or writes it, and why one says or writes it

community college   government-supported local college that offers associate degrees

competencies   skills and personal qualities needed to have a fulfilling career

compounding interest   interest that is calculated on the balance, additional deposits, and interest earned

conflict resolution   way to settle problems productively

co-op program   combines high school courses with paid work experience

corporate culture   values and customs that give an organization a unique personality

co-signer   person responsible for paying back a loan if you do not

cover letter   a letter that introduces you to employers

credit card debt   the amount you owe on credit cards that you cannot pay

cross training   each team member learns multiple tasks

culture   your social, ethnic, and religious background influences that have certain beliefs and behaviors

D

debit card   cards that allow for immediate deductions from a checking account

decision-making process   offers a way to plan carefully, based on the steps for problem solving

demographics   information about a population

dining interview   an interview that takes place over a meal

disability   physical or mental impairment that greatly limits major activities

discretion   the quality of having or showing good judgment and making responsible decisions

discrimination   occurs when people act on their prejudices negatively

diversify   to become more varied or vary your range of skills

dual credit   advancing credit taken for both high school and college credits

dual enrollment   PSEO courses taken on college campuses

E

early action   an early college application method that is not binding

early decision   an early college application method that is binding

e-commerce   buying and selling goods over the Internet

EFC (Expected Family Contribution)   the amount FAFSA says you and your family should contribute towards your education/training

electives   optional courses not needed for graduation

electronic resume   a resume designed to be transmitted over the Internet and stored and accessed on a computer

Employment Eligibility Verification Form   verifies your legal ability to work in the United States

employment professionals   recruiters, headhunters, search consultants, and employment agencies

empowerment   ability to manage and control one's own work and feel satisfied

entrepreneur   person who creates a business

equity   equal pay and freedom from employment discrimination

ethics   rules of behavior based on ideas about what is morally good and bad

evaluate   to assess yourself to determine the quality of your performance

extrinsic rewards   external rewards

F

Facebook   a social networking site that many businesses use as a marketing tool and a method for finding employees

FAFSA   forms required for education/training financial aid

FDIC   federal insurance designed to protect your money

financial plan   a blueprint containing your personal goals, timeline for reaching your goals, and an understanding of how to save to reach your goals

fixed expenses   expenses that are the same amount each month

formal assessment   written by psychologists and career counselors who research careers and career skills to create the tests

fringe benefits   forms of compensation provided to you by your employer other than wages

functional resume   a resume that matches your capabilities to the job

futurecasting   making predictions based on trends

G

gap year   a year between high school graduation and the start of post-secondary education

GPA   grade point average

grant   money provided by government, schools, or private donors that you do not need to repay

gross pay   the amount you earn based on your pay rate

group interview   an interview with more than one interviewer

H

heart   what you believe is important to your choices in life

hidden job market   jobs that are not advertised through traditional means or posted online

hourly employees   employees paid a set wage for each hour worked

I

income   the amount of money you earn

Indeed   a search engine that allows you to search several sites, newspapers, professional associations, and company career pages

independent contractor/freelance worker   those who are in business for themselves

influence   the power of someone or something that affects you directly or indirectly

informal assessment   activities in which you talk to someone working in a career, work in a specific career, or observe someone working in a career

informational interview   talking to people about careers to gather facts and gain an understanding about a career area you are considering

insurance   coverage you can purchase to provide reimbursement or replacement in case of loss

interest inventories   surveys designed to help you relate your interests to career clusters

Internal Career Design   unique to you, matching your interests, abilities, personality, and work values to an ideal career field for you

internship   program that provides practical experience working in a career

intrinsic rewards   rewards with incentives built in

investment   putting money into something with an expectation of a financial gain

IRA   overall term for a retirement plan with tax advantages

J

job   a paid position involving a specific time and specific tasks set by an employer

job interview   a conversation between a job applicant and one or more people in a company or organization to discuss the applicant's qualifications for a specific job

job market   the total number of vacant jobs available to people looking for employment

job shadowing   an informal assessment activity where you spend several hours observing a worker at his or her workplace

job sharing   two employees split a full-time position and pay

L

labor force   all people aged 16 and older who are working or actively seeking employment

lifelong learning   constantly improving education and training throughout life

LinkedIn   a business-related, professional social networking site

long-term goals   goals a person could expect to achieve in five or more years

M

mediator   a neutral person who helps resolve a disagreement

Medicare   the health benefits part of Social Security

medium-term goals   goals a person could expect to achieve in one to two years

mentor   a person who supports you through listening and advising

microblog   a blog limited to a certain number of characters

minimum wage   the lowest hourly wage an employer can legally pay

monitor   to keep track of the success of the career decision

Monster.com   one of the largest employment web sites and search engines to search by job title, skills, keywords, and/or location

motivation   influences that may have a greater effect on your behavior and decisions

N

need-based   financial aid that depends solely on your family's income

needs   something that is necessary for you to live your life

net pay   the amount of pay you bring home

networking building relationships as you spread the news of your job search among the people you know—and people they know—and asking for their help

nontraditional careers careers with one gender of 25 percent or fewer workers

O

O*Net OnLine a tool containing information on hundreds of standardized and occupation-specific descriptions to assist with career exploration and job analysis

occupation type of work with specific skills

Occupational Outlook Handbook provided by the Bureau of Labor Statistics, this gives information such as projections for the job market, employment change, and the labor force

offshoring relocating a business from one country to another

online banking option for paying your bills over the Internet

online learning learning conducted through a web site

on-the-job training learning career skills under an experienced worker's supervision

outsourcing a company hires workers outside the company

overtime any time worked more than 40 hours per week in one seven-day workweek

P

passion strong, positive feelings you experience while enjoying something

perceived barrier an obstacle that is not a true barrier, but is assumed

performance evaluation assesses how well an employee is meeting an employer's expectations

performance interview an interview in which the applicant must demonstrate a specific skill

personal fact sheet a written document that summarizes basic information about you and your education, experience, skills, and other pertinent data

personality assessment the results reveal the behavior style that makes you unique

Plan B career backup plan

post-secondary education any education beyond high school

pre-employment tests screening tools that help employers determine if applicants have the knowledge and skills to perform job duties successfully

priorities the items of greatest importance on one's schedule

procrastinate delaying planning

professional career a type of career that usually requires a college degree and specialized training

Q

QR/quick response code a square bar code that automatically gives you information and/or links you to a web site's URL

R

reasonable accommodations changes needed to the job or the work environment to provide assistance to do the job properly

references people you know who are not related to you who will give you a positive recommendation

resume a record of your experience and qualifications related to a specific job or career

roadblocks barriers that may slow or stop the progress of planning and time management

S

salaried employees employees paid with a set annual salary

SAR (Student Aid Report) results of the FAFSA process

savings account a bank account on which you earn compounding interest

scholarship financial aid money you do not have to repay, usually awarded on achievement

screening interview a preliminary interview which the employer uses to determine if the applicant has the basic skills and personality for the job

search engine a web site that gathers and lists information available on the Internet

search routine a regular, unvarying procedure you use to search for jobs

self-assessment the results of these tests are based on what you think of yourself

self-awareness knowing yourself at the present time

self-motivation the determination to stay on track and avoid distractions

self-understanding the true knowledge about oneself

service learning volunteering your time to help an organization or the community

short-term goals goals a person could expect to achieve in less than one year

skill sets a unique set of skills for specific occupations

skills assessment measures how well you perform specific tasks now and whether you can master certain skills in the future

smartphone a type of mobile phone that has capabilities beyond communication, photos, and video

social environment the community where you live and work, along with your lifestyle choices

social media a type of web site that offers interaction through electronic comments and discussions

social networking sites that allow users to build a profile and connect with others

Social Security provides income and health benefits for retirees and disabled employees who cannot work

STEM courses related to Science, Technology, Engineering, or Math careers

stocks shares in a company

structured interview a more formal interview

student loan money that a student borrows and must repay

T

talents natural strengths and abilities

task timeline chart a personalized schedule of job search tasks that need to be completed, when they need to be completed, and how long they will take to complete

tax shelter investments designed to reduce the amount of your taxable income

telecommuting a company links its offices to employees at another location

telephone interview an interview conducted over the phone

time wasters the distractions that cause a person to lose track of time

traditional resume a printed resume you provide to the employer through the mail or in person

transferable skills work tasks that are used in various types of careers

trends general direction or change over a period of time

Twitter a microblog that many people use to post personal information, but it can be used as a job-search tool as well

U

unstructured interview an interview that has little structure and is more informal

URL the web site address

V

values principles and qualities important to you

variable expenses expenses that may be different amounts each month

virtual interview a type of interview that is often conducted online via the Internet

virtual learning educational materials and courses available on the Internet

W-4 Form used to tell your employer how much money to withhold from your paycheck for federal income tax

W

wants something you desire, demand, or would like to have

wiki a web site that is created by a person or group that users can edit

Wikipedia a web site that is a free encyclopedia created by its users

work environment the surroundings and conditions of your workplace

work values aspects about a career and the workplace that are important to you

workforce trends changes employees make to allow them to meet their personal and professional goals and responsibilities

workplace diversity a workplace includes a variety of workers with different backgrounds, viewpoints, experiences, and ideas

workplace etiquette professional manners

workplace trends changes employers make to be more competitive

work-study program provides money, paying students for qualified campus jobs

Index